Parental guidance
recommended

Parental guidance recommended

How to raise emotionally healthy children

Dr Louise Porter

PhD, MA(Hons), MGiftedEd, DipEd, BA, BIntStuds

with cartoons by Peter MacMullin

First published 2015
by Small Poppies International
P.O. Box 2254
Milton
Queensland
Australia 4064

www.louiseporter.com.au

Cover design by Encompass Design and Publishing

Cartoons by Peter MacMullin

National Library of Australia Cataloguing-in-Publication data:

Porter, Louise
    Parental guidance recommended: How to raise emotionally healthy children

    Bibliography and index
    ISBN 9780980469578 (pbk)

    1. Parenting 2. Child rearing 3 Child development 4. Child psychology
    5. Discipline of children

649.1

Contents

Figures

Boxes

For Hannah

who taught me about love,

and worry... and tenacity.

Have patience with everything unresolved in your heart and... try to love the questions themselves as if they were locked rooms or books written in a very foreign language. Don't search for the answers, which could not be given to you now, because you would not be able to live them. And the point is, to live everything. Live the questions now. Perhaps then, someday far in the future, you will gradually, without even noticing it, live your way into the answer.

Rainer Maria Rilke
Letters to a young poet

16 July 1903

An introduction to guidance 1

Given that you've picked up this book, I'm guessing that you might want to get clear about parenting while your children are still young. Or perhaps you're not happy with how your children are behaving, or maybe you feel badly about yourself as a parent. Perhaps when in the evening you finally get a chance to reflect back on your day, it seems that all you've done is be the rule police: 'Don't touch... Get down from there... Don't talk with your mouth full... Eat your vegies... Leave your sister alone!'. This wasn't what you signed up for when you became a parent. You thought it would be about having someone to love – and yet here you are: angrier than you've ever been in your life, fed up, stressed, and perhaps even worried about how your children will turn out if their behaviour doesn't improve.

The pregnancy books never warned you about this toxic cocktail of feelings. They might have told you the secret that you did not know *love* until you became a parent... but they did not warn you that neither did you know *anger* until you became a parent.

In this book, I hope to convince you that the problem is not you... and it is not your children. Instead, you have been set up for failure. You have been handed down a set of beliefs about children which tell you to use rewards and punishments. However, these do not work. But when they do not, rather than questioning the model, we blame either our children or ourselves.

Instead, this book gives you a different model, known as guidance. An enormous body of research over 50 years shows that, compared to a rewards-and-punishment system, guidance produces better adjusted and considerate children who have warmer relationships with their parents. As the title of this book indicates, parental guidance is indeed recommended.

But as I describe the guidance approach, I am aware that every choice we make about our parenting and on behalf of our children can bring on guilt. As parents, we are bombarded about messages (often contradictory) about what we 'should' do on every issue imaginable, ranging from staying at home full-time versus working outside of home, using child care, sleeping arrangements for babies, feeding our infants, to name but a few.

I want this book to be your guilt-free zone. Just as my mother used to slave over a manual washing machine because automatic machines had not been invented yet, so too we can only use the parenting methods that we have been exposed to. Therefore, as you read through the ideas in this book, *please* (I implore you) do not let yourself get sucked into feeling guilty about the parenting methods you've been using so far. You might feel sadness or regret but you can't do what you don't know and, therefore, guilt is not called for. Everything that has happened up to this point in your life has brought you here now – and that's way better than never.

TWO STYLES OF PARENTING

Fifty years ago, a researcher named Diana Baumrind identified four main parenting styles.[1] We can reject two of them out of hand – permissiveness and neglect – because of their negative outcomes for children and parents. That leaves just two styles.

The first of these is a method that I call *controlling* because it puts parents in control of children's behaviour. It uses rewards (such as praise, treats, stickers or pocket money) to get children to do more of what we want, and punishments (reprimands and time out, for example) to discourage behaviours that we do not like. This style was given the formal title of *Behaviourism* in 1914,[2] although of course it was part of folk lore long before that.

Around a decade later, the *guidance* approach emerged, labelled at the time as humanism. It uses no rewards or punishments, but instead *teaches* children to manage their emotions and impulses so that they can act considerately. It teaches thoughtful behaviour (such as sharing or remembering not to hurt someone) in the same way that we teach children to ride a bicycle or to write their names. When children make mistakes with these developmental tasks, we don't punish them, but just teach them again and give them extra chances to practise.

BELIEFS

Progress is often held up not by ignorance, but by a fixed belief in something that is not so. Two beliefs are the basis for everything we do in our parenting. These are a belief about human nature itself; and where we locate our personal control (either in external events, or within ourselves). The place to start, then, is to understand these two beliefs. This will help, because being clear about the ideas behind the two parenting styles will help you to avoid using a little of both, which will fail you.

Beliefs about children

Most of the books written about parenting and most of the advice you'll have received so far comes from the controlling school. At its core is the belief that children (in fact, human beings in general) cannot be trusted. We can see this distrust in many everyday statements made about children:

- Children are 'attention seeking'.
- They are 'manipulative' (especially if they are three-and-a-half and female!).
- They do things deliberately to 'get at you'.
- We are told that we have to 'come down hard' on disruptive behaviours; otherwise they will keep happening (given children's evil natures).
- If you give children an inch, they'll take a mile. Therefore, we have to be firm, have rules and limits and set boundaries.
- We must not give in to children because if we do, they will have won and we will have lost.
- If we spare the rod, we will spoil the child.

It's almost as if we believe that children are on the march and out to get us. Yet if someone said those kinds of statements about different racial groups – as in, 'Asians are attention seeking' or 'Whites are manipulative' – I hope that we would find them offensive and would both dismiss the message and discredit the messenger. But we forget to question these stereotypes when they refer to children.

We might dismiss these claims from lay people as being the result of ignorance, but here is a sample of statements made by education 'experts':

- Kids, when they are little, are – in a way – kind of nuts. They are not born reasonable and unselfish, they are born unreasonable and selfish'.[3]

- Children are not born good; they have to be disciplined; otherwise they are a threat to the rest of society.[4]

- Children are not born human, they are made so.[5]

- Today's youth is rotten to the core, it is evil, godless and lazy... It will never be able to preserve our culture.[6]

The fact that the last quote was written on clay tablets 3000 years ago tells us just how long-standing is our cultures' distrust of children.[7] In contrast to this sour view of human beings, guidance trusts human nature. It trusts the extensive research evidence that cooperativeness is the natural stance of our species, with infants reliably cooperating with and assisting others from as young as one year of age.[8] This disposition is not just the ability to hunt in packs that some other primates display, but our willingness to share goods (to be generous), to be helpful (altruistic), and to share information that assists others to solve their problems.[9] We rely on this cooperation: telling others about our needs would never occur unless we trusted that they will be moved to meet these; communication itself could not happen unless the tribe cooperated to call an object by the same label; and, given our lack of natural weapons (such as claws or fast ground speed) for defending ourselves against predators, our survival as a species has depended on the group's willingness to defend and protect the vulnerable.[10] And children's adherence to rituals (such as where to put their bag in their child care centre or classroom) and insistence that others play games by the rules tell us that they are aware (from as young as three years of age) that in addition to 'I' and 'you', there is a 'we' with joint goals – that is, we are all in this together.[11]

Given that cooperativeness is inbuilt, then, the question for parents isn't, 'How do I get my child to cooperate with me?' but, 'How do I make sure that I don't damage my child's natural desire to cooperate?'. The bulk of the answer lies in the fact that children cooperate with people who have cooperated with them.[12]

Second, guidance trusts the research evidence that humans are inherently empathic. From a very young age, infants who have received empathy from their parents become roused by another's distress, will endeavour to interpret it, express concern, and attempt to comfort others.[13] It is the human spirit to care for others.

Third, guidance trusts that children are rational – that is, that every one of their actions is an attempt to meet their needs. This is true for adults too: we constantly strive to meet our needs. No one wakes up in the morning complaining that they are bored with always being happy and therefore they plan to mess up all day so that, tonight, they can be miserable – just to mix things up a little. No: all day, every day we try to meet our needs.

As it happens, sometimes children's efforts to meet their needs are unskilled. For example, when a playmate takes a toddler's toy, the owner might try to get it back by using her fists instead of her words. Although this is not an ideal way to solve a problem, her outrage at the injustice is righteous. Therefore, we would not punish her for being outraged, but we will teach the child a less hurtful way to act on that feeling.

Fourth, guidance trusts that children want to become competent: they *want* to learn, to be able to do the things we can do, to make sense of, to understand, to master and to have an effect on their world;[14] and they want us to be proud for them. This is why they call out when on the top of a jungle gym, 'Look how high I am!' and why no three-year-old ever complains about having to learn to run. Guidance trusts that, like us, children are innately driven to grow and to become the best version of themselves.[15] This innate propensity for growth is seen in intrinsic motivation, in young children's tendency to explore spontaneously, in curiosity, and in our drive to pursue activities that give us satisfaction.[16]

> Trust children. Nothing could be more simple – or more difficult. Difficult, because to trust children we must trust ourselves – and most of us were taught as children that *we could not be trusted.*[17]

External versus internal motivation

The second differing belief between the two styles is where we locate our motivation. The controlling style believes that we are motivated by the consequences (rewards or punishments) that our behaviour earns for us. In other words, we are motivated from the outside.

Guidance believes this is not so. It believes that we are all motivated *internally*: to meet our needs. This means that the controlling style's faith that threatening children with consequences will prevent disruptive behaviour, is misplaced. True, ahead of time children might weigh up the chances of being caught and will estimate how unpleasant any punishment might be. But, if their need is compelling enough, they will choose to perform the behaviour despite the risks. If parents didn't mind the ethics of it, we could use cattle prods or tasers to punish children – but there would still be a child somewhere someday who would declare, 'Don't care! Didn't hurt!'. In short, there is nothing we can do to *make* children conform – but there is a lot we can do to nurture them so that they want to cooperate with us.

Even everyday life tells us that people are not controlled by consequences. If they were, our prisons would be empty. If behaviour were controlled by its consequences, no one would enter low-paying professions, when they know that they could be paid more elsewhere – and no one would ever change jobs to a lesser-paid position in search of more job satisfaction. If behaviour were controlled by its consequences, no one would ever do voluntary work in the community, because there is no external reward (pay) for voluntary work, only the internal satisfaction that comes from knowing we are making a contribution to others. And if behaviour were controlled by its consequences, no one would ever have rebuked a young child: 'What did you do that for? Didn't you know you were going to get into trouble?' to which the child has replied, 'Yes, I knew that. But, gee, it was worth it!'.

The official term for the distinction between external and internal control is our locus of causality. This term refers to where we *locate* the *cause* of our actions and wellbeing. Despite the clumsy language, this personal characteristic is more vital for our emotional wellbeing than any other quality. And in terms of our parenting, all of our practices pivot on this belief.

If we think that outside events 'make' us miserable, we are said to have an external locus of causality (that is, the cause of our feelings is located externally). People who blame outsiders for their feelings might complain, for example, that they can't feel happier until someone they love loves them back, or until their boss stops being a pain, or until their children behave better.

In contrast, guidance recognises that, although life events can happen that are beyond our control, we are still responsible for how we experience these. We are in command of what we think about outside events. And our thoughts, in turn, bring about our feelings. Therefore, if we want to change how we feel, we will focus on changing our thinking. We are accountable for the thoughts we invite in and entertain. This stance is known as an internal locus of causality.

This concept has two implications for us as parents. The first is that no one else can 'make' us feel anything. Our children, for example, cannot 'make' us angry. When we believe that other people can cause our feelings, we give them power over us. We develop a victim mentality in which we feel at the mercy of others, oppressed by them and helpless to do anything about it. Then we blame them for our misery – and, when our attempts to make them do things our way fail, we become angry. In contrast, being willing to take responsibility for our own lives frees us from blaming other people (including our children) for how we react to their actions, and instead gives us power over ourselves to do what will meet our own needs.

The second implication for parents of an internal locus of causality is that we cannot make our children do anything. They did not come equipped with a remote control (much as we might fantasise about that!).

> You can't make people do anything. You can only make them wish they had – through punishment. Then eventually they will make you wish that you hadn't.[18]

In summary, guidance believes that external consequences (rewards and punishments) do not *make* children behave. Instead, *every behaviour is an attempt to meet a need.* We are motivated from the inside, not from the outside. This idea is as simple as it is revolutionary. It changes everything about how we parent. It shifts the focus from who has the power, to who has the need. And *that* spells the end of consequences.

VALUES

When it comes down to it, our values are an ethical stance that provides us with a guide on how to live a meaningful or well-lived life that has a positive effect on ourselves and others.[19]

In light of the differences in their foundational beliefs, the two parenting styles have opposing values. These are less testable by research than are their beliefs or practices. This means that we are free to choose our values. Therefore, we have a responsibility to choose them wisely[20] – because, if we don't stand for something, we will fall for anything.

Respect

The controlling style often calls on children to 'respect' their parents. But what we're really talking about here is enforcing blind obedience, largely out of fear. Calling this 'respect' just makes it sound more reasonable.

In contrast, guidance respects children and asks them to respect their parents in the dual senses of treating each other with civility and appreciating each other's qualities.[21] This type of respect in families is reciprocal, not a one-way deference towards parents.

Equal rights

Controlling discipline believes that adults have more rights than children. I've never understood the reasoning behind this, but it seems to be simply that we have more rights because we got here first or that little people don't matter as much as grown-ups. This stance sees children as less worthy than adults and as only *becoming* human.[22] (This is seen when we refer to babies as objects (*It*) when even the family dog gets called *he* or *she*.)

This belief that children are not really people yet is behind common statements from the likes of politicians, who justify expenditure on education on the grounds that 'children are our future'. We see it in 'tiger' parents who push their children to 'meet their potential'. Behind these expressions is a belief that children don't matter except for how they turn out later.

Instead, based on its respect for children, guidance believes that adults and children have equal rights to get their needs met. Placing equal value on all people means that the right to meet our needs is not diminished by our gender, race, religion – or *age*. In short, children are people already, whose needs matter *now*. Meeting their needs is important because it will help children to be safe, fulfilled and happy at the time and, when we meet their needs over and over again throughout their childhood, they will have a solid foundation of emotional wellbeing that will help them to withstand life's setbacks.

The statement that adults and children have equal rights does not mean that they are the same, but simply that their *humanity* is the same. Within democracies, we understand this concept of equality without sameness: on election day, both mine and the Prime Minister's (or President's) vote each get counted only once. And, throughout the election cycle, we both enjoy equal protection under the law. However, we clearly have different roles within our society.

So it is in our families. Both parents and children have the same right to have our needs met, but we have different roles. As adults, we will know some things that children do not – for example, that it's unsafe to run onto busy roads, or to pour water into electrical sockets, or to develop a negative reputation for being a bully. Therefore, we will take action to protect children from outcomes that they can't know about in advance.

Unconditionality

If we give our child a hug for doing well in an exam, that is a reward. It is conditional. The controlling style believes that anything desirable (such as a parent's love or a healthy sense of worth) should be earned.[23] You might note the use of the word *should* here, which signals that this is a value statement, not a belief. This explains why people continue to believe it even in the face of evidence that giving children conditional love and approval harms children and leads to outcomes that are the opposite of what we want, such as less helpfulness (altruism) and escalating aggression.[24]

But if we give our child a hug because we feel like it, that is love. There are no strings attached. It is unconditional. Guidance believes that, like every human being, our children want and need this unconditional love, to know that nothing they do will change our love for them.[25] Guidance believes that our approval and affections should not be given conditionally to children as a reward for being nice, obedient and docile. That is, we love them on our terms. If children have to earn our love, it does not count because it forces them to choose between seeking our approval and maintaining their own self-respect.[26]

Individuation

The controlling style sees children as subordinate to their parents and subject to parental expectations, not being free to choose for themselves. In contrast, guidance respects that children are their own people and gives them the freedom to be themselves (– see Box 1.1). It accepts that our children are not instruments for meeting our needs, either now or in the future. It values and welcomes that they are separate and unique individuals who have their own life, needs, thoughts, opinions, values and interests.

It is not our job to dictate our children's life scripts because children cannot be fulfilled by doing their duty and sacrificing themselves to live out our version of who they should be: postponing being true to our own goals in this way is joyless.[27] This stance is reflected in Tom Gordon's advice to parents: 'You gave them life. Let them live it'.[28]

> **BOX 1.1 FREEDOM TO BE ONESELF**[29]
>
> - The freedom to see and hear what is here
>   instead of what should be, was, or will be.
>
> - The freedom to say what one feels and thinks
>   instead of what one should.
>
> - The freedom to feel what one feels
>   instead of what one ought.
>
> - The freedom to ask for what one wants
>   instead of always waiting for permission.
>
> - The freedom to take risks on one's own behalf
>   instead of choosing only to be 'secure' and not rocking the boat.

Considerateness

The controlling style wants children to do as they are told, because it does not trust them to make moral decisions on their own (given their evil nature). However, obedience does not guarantee that children will act morally, unless adults are policing them.

Guidance does not value obedience. The fact that someone commands us to do something is not a good enough reason to do it.[30] Instead, guidance values considerate behaviour. It asks children to consider others: to think about how their actions affect other people. This is our ethical responsibility as humans.

In my presentations around the world, I have discovered that considerateness is a universal human value. Parents everywhere want their children to be considerate. However, many parents assume that compliance will teach thoughtful behaviour, but it does not. Obedience does not involve any moral reasoning on the child's part. This is the ability to balance the interests of all those involved, rather than focusing solely on self-interest.[31]

Indeed, teaching compliance is positively dangerous, in four ways. First, research has shown that pedophiles molest children between 150 and 560 times before they get caught, with an average of 380 victims.[32] When researchers asked convicted pedophiles how they got away with this high rate of abuse, each and every perpetrator reported that it was because children are trained to do what adults tell them.[33] *Children are unsafe if they do not know that they are allowed to say 'No' to grown-ups.*

A second sense in which teaching children to comply makes them unsafe is that compulsive compliance is unhealthy. An excessive need to please and obey adults has serious emotional outcomes for children.[34] *Children's emotional wellbeing suffers when they deny their own needs in an effort to please others.* And, as I will be discussing in chapter 3, demanding compliance also violates children's need to be in command of their own decisions (which is known as the need for autonomy).

Third, one-half of all school bullying could more rightly be termed 'mobbing'. The typical scenario is when the leader of a clique suggests to a couple of wannabes that they pick on a weaker peer. If the followers had the courage to stand up to their powerful leader by refusing to be mean, the ringleader wouldn't be brave enough to bully the target alone. That, after all, is why he or she is trying to rope in the supporters in the first place. *If young people feel compelled to do as they are told by a powerful peer, the children around them become unsafe.*

Fourth, even those defendants at war crimes trials who admit to their atrocities nevertheless deny that it was their fault, on the grounds that they were only following orders. *Whole communities become unsafe when people do as they are told by immoral leaders.*

For these four reasons, guidance does not want children to do as they are told. Instead, as I said, it wants them to act considerately. To be able to do this, children need:

- awareness of their own feelings and how their actions affect others
- the capacity to regulate their emotions and impulses, as appropriate
- empathy for others
- a willingness to cooperate with others
- a sense of potency (or self-efficacy), which is a belief that they can make a difference to their lives and to how they feel and behave, by staying in command of what they think.

Children develop these skills themselves and the willingness to use them when they have a warm relationship with parents who empathise with them and honour their need to be the authors of their own lives. In short, children consider adults who consider them.

Guidance believes that we cannot teach children to be considerate by using rewards and punishments, because these cause children to focus on what happens *to them* when they perform a behaviour: 'Will I get caught?... Will I be told off?... Will I lose computer time?... Will I be told I'm a good girl/boy?... Will I get a sticker, some ice-cream, extra pocket money?'. All these questions contain the words *me* and *I*: 'What happens to *me* when *I* do this?'. Instead, the essence of considerateness is to ask, 'What happens to *other people* when I do this?'.

Compassion

Under a controlling style, when children's behaviour violates our needs, we are likely to judge the children negatively, referring to their actions as *inappropriate, misbehaviour, naughty, bad,* or *unacceptable.* These judgments try to convince them that they are responsible for how we react. This opens the door to punishing them, on the grounds that they 'deserve' it for making us feel badly.

Yet adults who use this language about children's behaviours don't apply these same judgments when children mis-spell a word, fall over when learning to walk, or fall off when learning to ride a bicycle. Instead, they understand that these are natural mistakes for children of that age.

In contrast, whatever the type of mistake (behavioural or developmental), guidance adopts the same compassionate understanding.[35] It accepts that everyone does the best they can and that, like us, children are just trying to meet their needs. Instead of judging them for using a strategy that happens to bother us, we use compassion and listen for the need behind the behaviour.

Leadership

The final values difference between the two styles is that the controlling style assumes that parents have the right – in fact, duty – to discipline children. Under this style, the parent is the *boss*. This form of power is negative.

In contrast, the guidance approach locates our power *within* ourselves. It is a positive power to choose how we react to situations, what we do to achieve growth, and how to fulfill our own needs. As Susan Jeffers states, this kind of power has nothing to do with anyone else.[36] It means that there is more than enough power to go around, because everyone has power over themselves. This distinction is so vital that I devote chapter 2 to detailing it further.

FIGURE 1.1 THE CONTROLLING STYLE

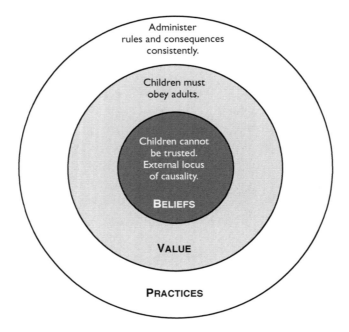

CONTROLLING PRACTICES

Based on its negative assumptions about children, a controlling style of parenting believes that children have to be civilised, trained and disciplined. According to this model, to achieve compliance, parents must impose rules on children, and then reward behaviour that we want our children to repeat, and punish behaviour that we want to discourage. Figure 1.1 illustrates these layers.

Rules

The controlling style believes that rules are necessary, both to prevent disruptive behaviour and to give children the security of knowing what we expect of them.[37] This idea is a hangover from the Victorian era, when parents imposed rigid schedules on infants for their own convenience but justified these on the grounds of children's supposed 'need' for routine.

Consequences

Controlling parenting uses two types of controls to enforce compliance.

- Behavioural controls comprise:
  - ○ *Rewards* for achievements and behaviours that we want children to repeat: praise; stickers, stamps or stars; extra time doing a favourite activity; pocket money; food; and, in school, grades and awards.
  - ○ *Punishments* to discourage behaviours we do not like: reprimands; time out; fines such as the loss of pocket money (or allowance); loss of privileges such as taking away their computer; and physical punishment (spanking or smacking).
- Psychological controls are attempts to make children suffer emotionally if they do not meet our expectations. These include the withdrawal of our love or affection, and inducing guilt and shame in children.

Consistency

The controlling approach emphasises that parents have to be consistent. This is necessary because consequences are so ineffective that they have to be used each and every time a behaviour occurs.

GUIDANCE PRACTICES

Guidance does not need rules. There is no evidence that children behave well because there are rules: they behave well because they *can*.[38] If you hide behind a technocratic system of rules, the children will not be able to find you and will try out particular behaviours to discover what you stand for and what you won't stand. Instead, guidance communicates to solve problems as they arise.

Given that there are no rules, there is no need for consequences. Guidance believes that there is no way to coerce children without making them afraid.[39] They end up scarred and scared.

Given that there are no consequences, there is no need to be consistent. This is realistic because life is inconsistent. *People* are inconsistent.⁴⁰ On some days you are more tired than others, some days more easy-going than others, some days you're full of energy and some days you're not. Children are perfectly able to adjust to the emotional landscape of their lives, particularly when you tell them about your needs.

Nevertheless, it is true that the more practice you get, the more quickly you will learn something. For example, if we wanted our son to learn to swim, we could take him to swimming lessons every day for two weeks and he would swim at age level by the end of those two weeks. But if we didn't have that kind of time and instead took our daughter for swimming lessons once a month, she would still learn to swim, but it would take longer. Similarly, the more practice children get at regulating themselves, the more quickly they will learn it. Guidance therefore believes that consistency is unnecessary – but repeated practice helps.

Under the guidance style, then, we can respond in any way to a given behaviour, depending on what is possible or makes sense at the time. Having said that, we will *steadfastly* insist that our children consider other people. But how we choose to resolve a conflict can depend on the circumstances at the time. Being flexible and wise in this way is likely to work better than trying to be more stubborn and insistent than a child.

Prevention

In place of consequences, the first practice of the guidance approach is (as far as possible) to respond to and meet children's needs. This is valuable in itself, but will also avoid meltdowns that arise when children are protesting about an unmet need.

We can also prevent children's meltdowns by understanding normal development, so that we do not ask children to achieve the impossible. This understanding, however, is not the same as patience. *Patience* implies that we are tolerating something that is inconsiderate, which is never appropriate. In contrast, *understanding* accepts children's natural limitations.

The other main preventive measure is not to use controlling discipline. This is because one of our three emotional needs is for autonomy, or to be in command of ourselves (– see chapter 3). When parents violate this need in children, the children resist, rebel and retaliate, triggering a 'dance' of escalating adult coercion and child defiance (– see chapter 6).

Acknowledge achievements

One of the beliefs that I mentioned earlier is that children want to be competent. Therefore, they don't need rewards to motivate them to achieve, because they are already motivated. And they certainly don't need to be judged to be a 'good' girl or boy for pleasing us, as if they were not worthy beforehand.

But everyone *does* need informative feedback or affirmation that they have made a difference in their world or have achieved something spectacular. Therefore, guidance gives information (which is termed acknowledgment) in place of praise and the other rewards, both to celebrate with children when they are excited about something they have achieved, and to thank them when they have behaved thoughtfully. I describe this distinction and its implications for children's self-esteem and motivation in chapter 4.

Communicate compassionately

The third practice of the guidance approach is that it uses compassionate communication to solve problems. In this way, it works *with* children, rather than doing things *to* them.

The first communication skill is to *listen* – even when children's behaviour bothers us. In the knowledge that children are trying to meet a need, we will look for the need that is driving the behaviour. The second communication skill is to be assertive so that children learn about our needs. Third, when their behaviour generates a problem for both for us and for themselves, we will collaborate with children to solve the problem.

The use of these three communication skills avoids the need for rules. Children don't need regimentation, limits, boundaries, or rules. They simply need to learn who you are, so that they can consider your needs. Having a rule in place would not make solving the conflict any easier. We would still have to communicate to solve the problem. Meanwhile, children who are having difficulty regulating their emotions and impulses will not learn to do so by being punished for breaking the rules. Instead, they need to develop the skills for considering others by solving real problems as they arise, through listening to others, being assertive and collaborating with us to find a solution.

FIGURE 1.2 THE GUIDANCE APPROACH

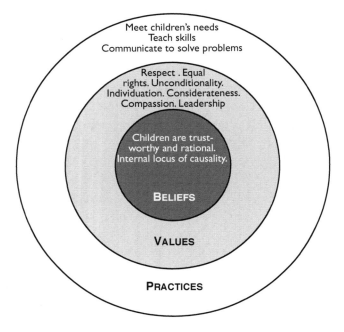

Teach skills

Given its compassionate understanding that children are still learning, rather than punishing them for not knowing a certain skill, guidance teaches it. If children are having difficulty sharing play equipment with a companion, for example, on the first few occasions we will explain the reasons for sharing – such as that it shows other people that you want to consider and include them. Second, we teach them to manage their feelings (in this case perhaps their sadness at having to share), and their impulses, such as their temptation just to snatch an item from their playmate.

Support children's self-regulation

The main error that I see when parents are first using the guidance approach is that they believe that everything can be solved by talking.

However, when children are in meltdown mode, we have to stop talking and help them get back in control. For this purpose, guidance uses the only two strategies documented to work for our species. These are to get some help from someone who cares about us (*time in*), or do something relaxing and soothing until we have calmed down (*time away*).[41] I describe these methods in chapter 8.

Whereas the controlling style sees these two methods as rewards for 'bad' behaviour, guidance believes that children need our compassion the most when they appear to 'deserve' it the least. That is, they need our support when they are distressed, even if their distress produces behaviour that bothers us.

Protective force

On rare occasions, distressed children may behave in ways that endanger themselves (such as running onto a road) or which hurt others. In that case, talking will not do the work we need it to do. (A lecture that 'Force equals mass times speed' will not dissuade children from running onto a busy road.) Instead, we may have to use force to protect them from harm, perhaps grabbing them by whatever body part we can reach to stop them at the kerb. Similarly, we can use force when children who are in meltdown have become frightened by the intensity of their feelings. At this time, they need us to be their safety net.

Another time when we can use protective force is when children are being aggressive. In that case, obviously we will take action to protect their targets from being hurt. But we also need to protect the perpetrators from developing an antisocial habit or becoming disliked by their peers. Their limited life experience means that they will not know that this is the cost of hurting others repeatedly. Therefore, we will protect them from paying the price.

The aim of protective force is literally to protect children from injury or injustice. This is in contrast to coercive force whose aim is simply to enforce compliance ('Do it because I said so').[42] The second difference is that coercive force is used often, whereas protective force is a rare event, reserved only for crises, which will usually involve issues of safety.

Box 1.2 Differences between the controlling and guidance styles

Controlling style	Guidance approach
Beliefs	
Distrusts human nature. Believes that children are: ■ selfish ■ uncooperative, manipulative, attention seeking ■ competitive.	Trusts that children: ■ are naturally cooperative ■ are empathic ■ are rational ■ want to become competent ■ want to grow into the best version of themselves.
Behaviour is governed by its consequences.	Every behaviour is an attempt to meet a need.
Mistakes happen when children are wilful and defiant.	Mistakes are an unskilled attempt to meet a need.
External locus of causality.	Internal locus of causality.
Children need taming, socialising, limits and discipline.	Children need guidance.
Children need incentives to behave well.	Children need skills to behave well.
Children need limits and boundaries.	Children need to hear about our needs so that they can consider us.
Children need consequences.	Children need teaching.
Values	
Children should defer to adults.	Respect is reciprocal.
Adults have more rights than children.	Adults and children have equal rights to get their needs met.
Children are subordinate to adults.	Children are separate individuals with their own life, opinions, interests, needs and values.
Children must earn love and self-esteem.	Children need unconditional love and self-worth.
Values compliance.	Values considerate behaviour.
Judgmental about children's emotions and behaviours.	Compassionate about children's errors and limitations.
The parent is the boss, who has power *over* children.	The parent is the leader, who uses power *with* children.

BOX 1.2 DIFFERENCES BETWEEN THE CONTROLLING AND GUIDANCE STYLES (cont'd)

Controlling style	Guidance approach
Practices	
Impose rules.	Prevent conflict by meeting children's needs, understanding their limitations and not imposing controls.
Reward good behaviour.	Acknowledge children's achievements.
Punish 'inappropriate' behaviour.	Communicate to solve problems. Teach children skills. Support children to self-regulate. Look for solutions.
Administer consequences consistently.	Is steadfast in its insistence that children must behave thoughtfully, but parents' responses differ according to the circumstances.
Use coercive force.	Rarely, will use protective force.
Parents' feelings	
Parents feel out of control because a controlling style provokes escalating behavioural difficulties in children.	Parents feel in control, without having to exercise coercive power.
Parents have low self-efficacy and therefore can be emotionally reactive (explosive).	Parents have high self-efficacy. They are emotionally balanced.
Expressions	
Do this right now, or else!	I'd like us to find a solution that works for everyone.
Don't make me ask you again!	I'd like to hear how this sounds to you.
Just do as you're told!	I'm wondering what you need right now.
Don't talk back to *me*!	Would you be willing to…?
How many *times* do I have to tell you?	Can you explain why doing it is a problem for you?
I don't care what you think.	Please help me understand what you have in mind.

> **BOX 1.3 OCCASIONS TO USE PROTECTIVE FORCE**
>
> - protect children from injury
> - protect children from injustice
> - provide a safety net for children whose feelings are scaring them
> - protect children with antisocial behaviour from developing a negative reputation
> - protect children from being rejected by their peers as a result of their antisocial behaviour.

Look for existing solutions

Instead of focusing on what is going wrong and trying to fix it, guidance accepts that no problem occurs all the time. Therefore, we can look out for what is already working at those times when the problem is less severe than usual, so that we can do more of that.[43]

EVIDENCE ABOUT GUIDANCE

The controlling style sounds simple: just reward behaviour that you approve and punish behaviour that you disapprove. But the method doesn't work. (The evidence for this bold statement is summarised in Box 1.4 and is available in full on my website.) The controlling style does not reliably achieve even the limited goal of making children comply and, in the service of that goal, it has negative side-effects for the children who are its targets, for the parents who have to administer it, and for children's relationships with their parents.

The reference list for Box 1.4 is testament to the sheer amount of research evidence in support of this conclusion. What you can't tell from this list, though, is how unanimous the findings are. In over 50 years of research, *not a single study* has shown a controlling style to produce superior outcomes to guidance. And the findings are consistent across cultures,[44] the age range from babies to young adults, and across settings from homes, early childhood centres, schools and universities. This research has demonstrated that, of all influences on children's outcomes, the quality of children's relationship with their parents is the most powerful.[45]

OBJECTIONS TO GUIDANCE

This evidence will be enough to convince many. Nevertheless, as I said earlier, our values are not as open to proof as are our beliefs or practices. And our distrust of children is so ingrained that it can be difficult at first to take guidance on board. Accordingly, at first exposure, parents have a range of objections to guidance.

New fad

The first objection to guidance arises from an impression that it must be just a new-fangled fad. Instead, as I described earlier, it emerged under the title of humanism in the late 1920s and has been written about continuously ever since.[46] The surprising thing to me about guidance is not that it is new but that, despite this 80-year history, so few people are familiar with it. The controlling style is so deeply embedded in our history and cultures that most adults simply don't know anything else.

Distrust of children

One protest based on negative beliefs about children is the claim that *surely* a given behaviour is in fact attention-seeking or manipulative. *Surely* children just want to get their own way. My answer is that this is true of everyone: we all want our own way. But if children are producing unskilled behaviours to achieve that, this means they do not have the skills to behave more thoughtfully.[47]

Another claim that reflects our sour beliefs about human nature is that a given child is just being disruptive deliberately and has a 'bad' attitude. However, children are not born with bad attitudes: they learn these from years of being misunderstood, having their needs discounted, and being punished.[48]

Sometimes, a whole generation is said to have a bad attitude: to be all about me, narcissistic, self-aggrandising, entitled, obnoxiously self-confident... and so on. However, every generation is about Me until they grow up.[49] And their accusers were themselves criticised for having the same flaws and are the very same individuals who wanted to live in a yellow submarine!

BOX 1.4 OUTCOMES OF THE TWO PARENTING STYLES

Controlling

Guidance

Behavioural outcomes

Children fail to learn self-regulation and prosocial means of solving problems and therefore require constant adult supervision.[51]

Are better able to regulate their own behaviour and have fewer behavioural problems as a result.[50]

Increasing uncooperativeness, defiance conflict and hostility over time.[52]

Children are increasingly cooperative and decreasingly anti-social over time.[53]

More likely to become delinquent.[54]

Low rates of delinquency.[55]

Display appropriate self-assertion, without escalating into defiance or oppositionality.[56]

Morality

Low levels of moral reasoning.[57]

Develop principled moral reasoning.[58]

Focus on self-interest, rather than on the effects of their behaviours on other people.[60]

Have more empathy for and compassion towards others.[59]

Behave morally only when they anticipate receiving rewards or punishment for their actions.[62]

Children are more likely to internalise their parents' values.[61]

Will help others only when a reward is offered.[63]

Increased altruism.

Increased dishonesty.[64]

Learning style

Low motivation.[65]

Motivation is intrinsic rather than being a quest to outdo others.[66]

Greater negativity towards and less enjoyment of school.[67]

Increased interest and engagement in schoolwork.[68]

Children are focused on grades rather than on gaining new competencies.[69]

Feel better about themselves as learners.[70]

Lack initiative and persistence.[71]

Show a preference for challenge.[72]

Socially prescribed perfectionism.[73]

Self-referenced perfectionism.[74]

Anxiety about doing well sabotages their performance.[75]

BOX 1.4 OUTCOMES OF THE TWO PARENTING STYLES *(cont'd)*

Controlling	Guidance
Educational outcomes	
Declining academic achievement and reduced creativity.[76]	Improved academic performance (particularly of disadvantaged students).[77]
Poor language comprehension skills.[78]	Improved language and literacy skills.[79]
Less enjoyment of and proficiency at extracurricular activities and increased likelihood of ceasing participation.[80]	Stronger working memory and executive functioning skills that contribute to improved self-regulated learning.[81]
Emotional outcomes	
Emotional and somatic problems increase significantly over time.[82]	Healthy emotional adjustment overall, with greater social and emotional maturity.[83]
More angry, negative, withdrawn, depressed, anxious, unhappy, lonely hostile when frustrated, and suicidal.[84]	Less vulnerable to depression, with declining emotional difficulties over time.[85]
Stressed by adversity.[86]	More resilient in adversity.[87]
Inability to regulate negative emotion leads to escalating outbursts, both in frequency and intensity.[88]	Better able to regulate emotion and, in turn, regulate their own behaviour.[89]
Poorer emotional knowledge, with emotional constriction and suppression of emotions such as sadness, anger and fear.[91]	Able to integrate their emotions and exercise choice over their expression.[90]
Anxious about parental rejection.[92]	Self-confident, with minimal anxiety about failing.[93]
External locus of causality and less well-formulated sense of identity.[94]	Internal locus of causality and high self-efficacy.[95]
Low or achievement-driven self-esteem and reduced sense of their own worth.[97]	Authentic high self-esteem.[96]

Box 1.4 Outcomes of the two parenting styles *(cont'd)*

Controlling	Guidance
Social outcomes	
Negative expectations of peers lead to antisocial interactions, including relational and physical aggression.[98]	Develop a disposition of social trust that is the basis of all their interactions with others.[99]
Use fewer constructive strategies for problem resolution in conflict with peers.[100]	Children are socially competent: they share power, can reason with others, make suggestions, negotiate, compromise, collaborate, and share intimacy.[101]
Are less well liked by their peers.[102]	Increased peer acceptance.[103]
Higher rates of peer victimisation.[104]	Socially outgoing, generous, less competitive and less aggressive towards others.[105]
Higher rates of bullying.[106]	Reduced bullying.[107]
Victims of bullying are less willing to report it to adults, because they do not trust adults to protect them.[109]	Young females are more assertive within their relationships.[108]
Are more likely to be withdrawn.[110]	
Are more likely to choose deviant peers as friends.[111]	
More susceptible to peer pressure.[112]	
Have a more competitive social hierarchy.[113]	
Relationships with parents	
Are less connected to and have a less secure relationship with their parents.[115]	Improved connectedness to and engagement with parents.[114]
Are resentful of and hostile towards their parents, rejecting both them and their values.[117]	Feel close to their parents and respect their wishes.[116]
Decreased desire to relate to their parents or care how they feel.[118]	Willing to take their parents' needs into account.[119]
Are prematurely and excessively independent of their parents.[120]	Are more willing to cooperate and interact with their parents and are less negative towards them.[121]
	Voluntarily disclose their whereabouts and activities to parents.[122]

And even if the new generation were riddled with young people with these flaws, it is not being responsive to children and meeting their needs that leads to obnoxious behaviour in children, but being controlling – because control teaches children to act out of self-interest instead of having regard for others.[123]

Fear of a loss of power

Some parents think that if they abandoned rewards and punishment, they would lose control. This is another instance of *either-or* thinking: that *either* I control my children, *or* they will run riot. Although it is more likely that children will be micromanaged and unnecessarily constrained than that they will be allowed to run wild, still our societies fear being permissive.[124]

After all, we believe that we must control children to suppress their evil tendencies. The Victorian era expression of this was a fear of 'spoiling' children; the modern equivalent is the unfounded accusation of an epidemic of 'helicopter' parents who hover over their children, fussing and indulging unnecessarily, or of 'bulldozer' parents who mow down all obstacles from their children's paths so that the children never need to experience failure.[125] But our scorn for parents who 'over-parent' entirely misses the point that in fact they are not overly nurturing, but overly controlling.

Faith in consequences

Behind our fear of permissiveness are poisonous beliefs about human nature... and too much faith in consequences. After all, doesn't everyone *know* that children need consequences to learn to behave? This is plain common sense, right?

But even our own life experience tells us that this isn't so. Every one of us has learned almost everything we know without experiencing consequences. For example, as an Australian, I have learned not to swim with sharks – not because I once did it and lost a limb as a consequence so will never do it again, but because I have *learned* that sharks can be dangerous. We have all learned all sorts of information – by reading, watching TV, searching the internet, or by listening to our parents and teachers. Humans are clever like that.

The belief that children *need* consequences to learn to behave is so powerful that it is not just an idea that the mind possesses... but an idea that *possesses the mind*.[126] We fail to question it, to notice that it is *only an idea*. At various times in our history, ideas – such as that the earth is flat – have been unanimous, and yet they still proved to be wrong. Just because a lot (even a majority) of people believe something, that does not make it true.

Desire for justice

Some parents value punishment as a form of justice for victims of hurtful behaviour. They assert that the targets of children's aggression want (and deserve) to see the perpetrator punished. That is not my experience. During my research, I observed that children want (and deserve) to have the aggression stop. However, we have taught them that the only way to achieve that is to punish the perpetrator. Instead, whereas punishment seeks retribution for past mistakes, guidance teaches children skills in order to prevent future misdeeds.

Focus on the future

Some parents are willing to sacrifice their children's current needs to assure their children's future and secure their own social status from having successful children. In an effort to guarantee their children's success, these 'tiger' parents relentlessly pressure their children to excel, and they use psychological controls to shame children for not meeting their expectations. However, supportive parenting produces far better outcomes, with the children of tiger parents having lower educational attainment, a disabling form of perfectionism, more anxiety and depression, and greater feelings of alienation from their parents.[127]

Get tough approach

One of the more strident claims that I hear in my courses is that we are not doing children any favours by refusing to impose consequences on them when they harm others. The rebuttal from guidance is that as a result of their actions, children are already suffering (and need protection from) natural consequences such as peer rejection. By using guidance, we are simply refusing to impose contrived or artificial consequences, because these do not teach children the skills they need for solving problems.

A similar query is, 'But aren't consequences the way of the 'real' world? How will children adjust if we don't teach them this now?' (I have always wondered where the 'real' world is, but I now suspect it's where pizza delivery guys live.) Yes, we adults work for wages or a salary because an income secures our basic needs for food and shelter and some choice in life, but a lot of what we do is completely without pay – and yet we still do it: we have hobbies, we volunteer in the community, we tend our gardens, we do housework, we look after our family members. If people needed artificial consequences in order to do things, very little would get done.

The desire to prepare children for the 'real' world of rewards and punishments is another case of considering that what children need now is irrelevant. It believes that only deprivation, struggle and sacrifice will prepare them for life's hardships.[128] (Alfie Kohn calls this militaristic reasoning the *Better Get Used To It* syndrome.)[129]

Instead, guidance believes that now *is* important and that children will suffer many things throughout their lives (perhaps even cancer, for example) but that does not mean we should expose them to adversity now. Although adolescents will need to learn to drive a car, we don't give them driving lessons in early childhood. This is because guidance accepts the copious research evidence that the best preparation for withstanding life's setbacks and disappointments is for children to have been supported by responsive parenting.

Second, children should not be subjected to the injustices inherent in rewards-and-punishments systems while their personality is still forming. By the time they are older, they might be able to withstand the judgments inherent in controls, but not during their tender years.

Third, whereas adults can escape noxious working environments (at least to some extent), children cannot escape but instead are at the mercy of the settings in which we place them.[130] Therefore, those environments must meet their needs, not subject them to hardship out of some misguided desire to toughen them up.

A little of both

Another question that parents often ask me is whether they can still use controlling discipline some of the time. This question comes about because they mistakenly think that guidance will work for everyday hassles, but will not handle the big issues. Others think that guidance might be fine for one child, but not powerful enough for another. My first answer to both questions is that you cannot be a little bit authentic. Every time you manipulate children through rewards or punishments into doing as they are told, you will damage your relationship with your children, and this will take time to heal.

Second, the assumption that guidance is lame is false: it is *steadfast* in its insistence on considerate behaviour while, for the children's part, expecting them to think about their actions is a much more demanding task than asking them simply to do as they are told.

The argument is sealed, in my view, by my own observations that the very children with the most disruptive behaviour – who most appear to 'need' controls – are the very children who are showing by their dogged refusal to be cowed by punishment that controls are not working and never will. These children have received more punishments than children who behave considerately, and still their problems persist. These are the children who would rather risk our condemnation than sacrifice their free spirit. For the remainder – those who conform – consequences (rewards and punishments) are unnecessary, because these children cooperate with us anyway.

LEARNING THE GUIDANCE APPROACH

Learning any new skill can be daunting. Learners go through the stages illustrated in Figure 1.3, beginning from our comfort zone but then moving through discomfort until we emerge skilled and confident again.

Stage 1: Unconsciously unskilled. Before we have been exposed to new ideas, we don't know what we don't know. This first step on the staircase is a comfortable place to be because we don't have to reflect on or question our practices. We are unaware of alternatives.

Stage 2: Consciously unskilled. In this second phase of learning, we start to question some of our previous beliefs and practices in light of new information. We now know what we don't know. But, at the same time, we worry that we don't know the new methods. During this stage, you might find that you agree with the ideas and values of guidance, but are asking, 'Yes, but what do you want me to *do*?'.

FIGURE 1.3 STAIRCASE OF LEARNING[131]

This second stage of the learning process is the most difficult because we experience it early on, before we have confidence in ourselves and in our new methods. We might also feel sad that we did not know about guidance earlier, or guilty about the parenting style we have been using so far. However, as I mentioned earlier, the fact that we did not know something sooner may cause us regret, but that our life path did not expose us to ideas earlier is not a cause for guilt.

Stage 3: Consciously skilled. In this stage, we are trying some new practices, but they seem awkward and false. We think other people will notice that we don't know what we are doing, or that we are frauds. (We felt like this when we first learned to drive a car, when we had to think about every specific skill and were sure that we would never be able to do it.) Nevertheless, our confidence grows once our new methods begin to work.

Meanwhile, it is useful to remind ourselves that we are making progress with each new skill that we try out. We won't learn it all instantly. But this is true when we learn any new skill: we don't think that one tennis lesson will qualify us to play at Wimbledon. Your job in this stage is to have faith that, when it comes to using guidance practices, you will get there – even if you don't yet know what 'there' will look like. To paraphrase Martin Luther King, we can still take the first step even though we cannot see the top of the staircase.

Stage 4: Unconsciously skilled. In this final stage, our new learning has become automatic and is integrated into our personal style. In most circumstances, we can do it without thinking (just like being an experienced driver). It doesn't feel awkward anymore but instead is natural, and we are confident about what we are doing.

Although as you work through these phases, learning the guidance style can seem challenging, in fact you already know most of its practices. You use most of its skills in your other walks of life: you listen to your friends, are assertive in your close relationships, and use problem solving. But the idea that children need consequences is so influential that we forget to use these same skills with our children. And the belief that children can't be trusted causes us to doubt whether using them would work.

CONCLUSION

If your beliefs, values and practices are all aligned in the left-hand column of Box 1.3 your stance will be a controlling one, in which case this book is not for you. More commonly, however, parents' beliefs and values are in the right-hand column, but their practices are from the left (from the controlling style). If this sounds like you, the promise of this book is that you can come to live your values by using guidance practices. For most of us, although we endorsed guidance values before we became parents, we have been trapped by not knowing any alternatives to rewards and punishments. By default, therefore, we end up using the controlling style, even though it violates our values and causes us to feel badly about ourselves as parents.

Meanwhile, the controlling style makes parenting harder than it needs to be, because it escalates conflict between us and our children and leaves us having to figure out how to make them behave as we'd like. Our anger and attempts to control our children squanders their goodwill, and now it is harder again to get them to cooperate.

Guidance liberates us from the belief that we have to be in charge of our children and must design and implement consequences. By acting as the leaders rather than the boss, we will be able to teach our children, without manipulating them into conformity. This does not mean treating children as if they were adults: we simply treat them as people. After all, *children are people too*. We will trust our children to know their own minds. And, by guiding, we will be teaching them the skills they need to run their own lives. This will give them the freedom to live thoughtfully and with purpose.

SUMMARY OF PRINCIPLES

- Guidance trusts human nature.
- Adults and children have the same right to get their needs met.
- Every behaviour is an attempt to meet a need.
- If you don't stand for something, you will fall for anything.
- Children need unconditional love.
- Children need us to accept them as separate and unique individuals who have their own life, values, needs, interests and opinions.
- Although you may not be in control of *what* you experience in your life, you are in charge of *how* you experience your life.
- Guidance teaches skills, instead of punishing children for not knowing them.
- Punishment seeks retribution for past misdeeds. Guidance teaches in order to prevent future ones.
- You gave your children life. Let them live it.
- Individual children, surrounding children, and whole communities become unsafe when people are trained to do as they are told.
- Children do not behave well because of rules: they behave well because they can.
- Children are people too.

2   Leadership styles

When I first introduce the distinction between the controlling style and guidance, people at my courses often think of the two styles as opposites. However, the opposite of the controlling style (in which adults control children) is submissiveness (in which adults exercise little control). As illustrated in Figure 2.1, guidance occupies the middle ground, with both parents and children having power over themselves. Sometimes, as Alfie Kohn says, the alternative to black and white isn't necessarily grey: it might be orange.[1]

THE RANGE OF LEADERSHIP STYLES

Behind the misperception that the two styles are opposites is the assumption that the only alternative to control is to do nothing.[2] Instead, parents tend to adopt one of three leadership styles. The first is submissiveness. Some might call this being a doormat. When conflict arises, those who are submissive fail to stand up for their needs, commonly trying to ignore the issue and hoping it will go away.

A second (opposite) style is being the boss. This style is all about who has the power. Bosses decide that they are right and therefore are justified to impose their will on children, no matter what. Bosses can cause them to feel miserable by withholding rewards, delivering punishments or inducing shame in an effort to enforce compliance. Parents using controls occupy this role.

The third style – leadership – is the stance taken by the guidance approach. Parents who adopt the role of leaders use power *with* their children, taking account of both their own and the children's needs. The issue, then, becomes not who is in charge or has the power, but who has a need.

FIGURE 2.1 RELATIVE POWER OF PARENTS AND CHILDREN

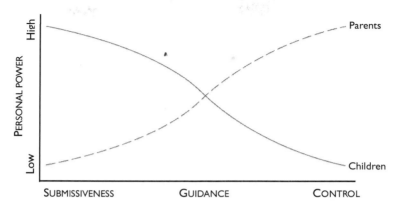

SUBMISSIVENESS (THE DOORMAT)

Submissive people do not realise that they are permitted to ask for what they want. They are often referred to as 'nice', because they think and behave in the ways listed in Box 2.1. All of the words for being assertive are within their vocabulary, but pain holds them back from uttering them. The source of this pain is when children are wounded by others' reactions to their expression of needs, and so they shut down all awareness of their own needs.[3]

Next, they fear what it would mean for them if others did not give them what they ask for.[4] It would tell them that other people don't think they are even worth considering.

Third, punitive reactions to their expression of need as children has caused them to be driven by a fear of losing the approval of others. As a result, nice people either give *up* or give *in*. This is in contrast to people who have permission to be real, who are governed by a desire to contribute to the wellbeing of everyone, and therefore give *to* others willingly.[5]

Being nice has its price. Most submissive people are emotionally inhibited in general; they criticise themselves for not honouring their own needs; they resent giving to others; and they experience low self-esteem, anxiety, and depression. And their relationships lack intimacy and trust because people don't respect superficial niceness: they suspect it.[6] Being nice might appease others but it leaves a 'hole in the soul' in response to a life that is not genuinely lived.[7]

When we habitually submerge our own needs and place a higher priority on others' needs, we are indulging demanding thinking. I describe this in chapter 5 but for now we can identify it in language such as 'I *should... I have to... I can't* consider myself...'. Rather than being 'responsible', submissiveness is not taking responsibility for ourselves and for meeting our own needs. Neither is it noble because, although it is admirable to care for others, we must also take care of ourselves. Like draining water from an electric kettle, if we progressively drain ourselves of energy, we will burn out and not be able to meet anyone's needs – our own *or* others'.

No one recommends that parents submerge their needs for the sake of their children. Nevertheless, I have seen three types of submissive parents. The first group are those who are meek with everyone, being too scared to assert their needs or resolve conflict within any of their relationships. When parenting, they use such a pleading or meek tone that their children accurately read that they have no intention of insisting that the children consider them.

BOX 2.1 SUBMISSIVE PATTERNS[8]

Thoughts and emotions	Resulting actions
Nice	
Fear disapproval from others.	Try to earn worth by acting worthily and meeting others' expectations.
Fear disapproving of ourselves (known as guilt).	Let others determine our actions so that we gain approval.
Defer to authority, even when it is not legitimate.	Attempt to gain approval by courting the favour of those in authority.
Martyrs	
Have a sense of duty or obligation.	Devote ourselves to those in similar pain, which distracts us from attending to our own needs.
Believe that martyrdom is 'good for the soul'.	Are driven to endless activity, striving for perfection rather than for excellence, and striving not only to be acceptable to others, but to be indispensable to them.
Believe that our devotion will oblige others to return the favour in future.	Don't stop till we drop.

A second group of parents are submissive only with their children. This can come about when the children are especially precious because of being difficult to conceive or carry to full term, having a chronic illness or disability, or having been adopted, for example. Alternatively, parents who have gentle natures can simply be shocked and intimidated by their spirited children's temper or ferocious outbursts. Even when these meltdowns are normal for the child's age, these parents can't believe their eyes when the children lose it. They might not want to boss their children but don't know what else to do.

With both these types of parents, the children don't know where they stand with their parents. They can't grow up until they can grow down – that is, until they are relieved of the burden of being the ones shaping their family life. Therefore, if your children have been intimidating you, it can help just to say to yourself, or even to tell them firmly with a clear gaze and calm voice, 'You know, you don't scare me'. This can be a huge relief for these children, who have more power than they can cope with. Now that you're back in charge of yourself and functioning again as leader of the family, they can relax.

A third group of duty-bound parents are the martyrs who, like the first, operate from a sense of duty but impose guilt on their children for their sacrifice, demanding appreciation from their children. They adopt the martyrdom patterns listed in Box 2.1. Although seeing themselves as self-sacrificing, these parents are giving to their children in the hopes of getting something back. This arouses fears that they might not get enough back in return,[9] which sets up a need to use controls so that they won't be short-changed. It also causes them to feel angry and resentful because, when we are so needy, nothing can ever be enough.[10]

Self-sacrificing parents *believe* that their relationships could be represented as shown in Figure 2.2. However, children of martyrs are subtly manipulated into feeling guilty for having needs and for receiving care. As a result, they come to resent having to be grateful for being given something they did not ask for, or for being looked after when, as children, that is their birthright. They lose respect for their parents and resent having to be 'nice' in return. They feel helpless and often have to engage in 'parent watching' to decipher what their parents need, because their parents won't tell them directly. This burden is exhausting. In short, instead of the picture in Figure

2.2, resentment flows in both directions, as illustrated in Figure 2.3. Both parents and children feel hurt and, while the children might know why, the parents often go to their deathbed still thinking they have been wronged by their children's lack of gratitude.

FIGURE 2.2 THE APPARENT SHAPE OF SUBMISSIVE PARENTING

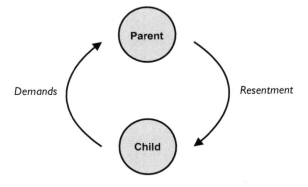

FIGURE 2.3 THE ACTUAL SHAPE OF SUBMISSIVE PARENTING

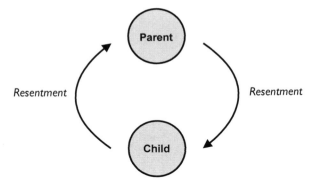

AGGRESSION (THE BOSS)

Whereas people who are submissive roll over in response to others' needs, people who are the boss bowl over anyone who blocks their goals.[11] When parenting, the exercise of control is aggressive in that it forces children to do our bidding, it is confrontational, and it overrides children's needs and rights on the justification that adults have priority. Parents have power because they can make children suffer for their mistakes by limiting their access to goodies and humiliating them with punishment.

The religious justification of this style is that parents have a divine right to control children,[12] while the secular assumption seems to be that we're the boss because we got here first.

This style emphasises power and involves negative judgments about children and their behaviour that try to convince them that they are responsible for upsetting us. As a result, controlling parents see disruptive behaviour as a threat to their authority and impose punishments in an effort to regain control.[13]

Judgments entail *you-messages* that tell other people about themselves, in contrast with *I-messages* (which I discuss in chapter 7) that tell them about us and our needs. These *you-messages* contain hidden blame and criticism:

- You are too insensitive to figure out how to help me.
- You're bad/thoughtless/selfish to have caused me a problem.

When we think in these judgmental ways, we believe that children deserve to be punished.

> Parenting that focuses on what's wrong with children or what's wrong with their actions relies on a belief that scolding them, making them feel bad, and punishing them will motivate them to act differently.[14]

FIGURE 2.4 THE SHAPE OF AGGRESSIVE (CONTROLLING) PARENTING

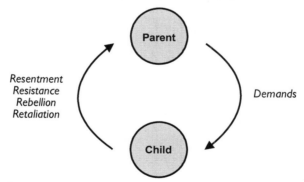

Aggression *works*: it often gains aggressors what they want and gives them the illusion of control over their lives. However, when we try to control our children, we feel overwhelmed and (paradoxically) powerless because we can't in fact make them do anything; we don't like ourselves as parents; and we regret that our children avoid us.

At the time, aggressive parenting denies children the chance to change their behaviour out of consideration for our needs, causes them to lose face, increases their resentment and resistance, and reduces their willingness to consider us. These negative effects of consequences (both rewards and punishments) come about because they place us in control of children. This triggers a 'dance' of coercion and defiance that I describe in chapter 6.

In the longer term, controls have all the negative outcomes for children that I listed in Box 1.4, including escalating behavioural problems; reduced moral reasoning; ineffective learning styles; poorer academic attainment; emotional problems such as low self-esteem; social difficulties such as increased bullying; and a hostile relationship with their parents.

Reasons not to reward

Even when controlling methods appear to be benign or 'nice', rewards and punishments are 'two sides of the same coin':[15] they both impose on children a certain way of being and they both communicate to children that our approval of them is conditional. This will translate into conditional self-approval [16] (that is, a low or an achievement-driven self-esteem). Therefore, Alfie Kohn refers to rewards as 'sugar-coated control'.

They might appear benign but all reward systems involve punishment. To illustrate this, let's say that you give your son a dollar every day that he makes his bed but, today, he did not make it to your standards, and therefore you do not give him the dollar. Because loss of a hoped-for reward feels like a punishment,[17] your son feels punished: he is poorer than he hoped to be. (If you doubt this effect, imagine how you would feel and react if you were the only person in your workplace not to receive an end-of-year bonus.) Alternatively, if your son is spirited, he will declare that he doesn't care and didn't want the dollar anyway. And now you are left with nothing that will motivate him.

In chapter 4, I describe the negative effects of praise on children's self-esteem, motivation and style of perfectionism. Two other rewards that parents commonly use are star charts and pocket money. These each have their own specific complications.

Star charts. The problem with star charts and other reward systems is that, once you put one behaviour on a reward system, the children will often refuse to do anything else unless these too are rewarded, with the result that the program is contagious. At the same time as spreading to more and more of their behaviours, a star system also spreads to other children in the family. Brothers and sisters see the child with the poorest behaviour getting the most rewards, so they get in on the act too. Soon, you have star charts going for every conceivable behaviour for all your children, when the problem started out as one issue for just one child.

Within a very short time, you end up doing more work to control your children's behaviour than they are doing, and therefore the star chart appears to be even more necessary than it was at the outset. In the meantime, the children can sit back and watch it all happening, taking very little responsibility for themselves.

Eventually, in sheer exhaustion, you give up on the whole system – and then feel guilty and incompetent, wondering what went wrong, You blame yourself when, in fact, controlling others will never work, no matter how expertly you do it.

Pocket money (allowances) as a reward. You and I do not get paid for vacuuming our floors or mowing the lawns. We do these tasks to keep our households functioning. So it is with our children. They should not expect to be paid for contributing to the household, because that is a natural part of cooperation. If you gave pocket money as a reward for doing chores, you would find that in the long run, the children won't do anything for you unless you pay them for it. Your need for consideration and help will be disrespected, and the children will not have learned about their social obligations to the family unit.

Instead, children need pocket money so they can have some hope that they will be able to buy something their heart desires. This right should not be contingent on their behaviour: if you believe they are not contributing enough to the family, you need to communicate to solve that issue, rather than withhold pocket money.

Reasons not to punish

Naturally, punishments are inherently unpleasant and therefore have some particular disadvantages over and above those of rewards. They can escalate into abuse; they teach children to ignore us when we threaten to punish them and don't follow through (because we never intended to in the first place, because we're not that mean); and they can intimidate onlookers who worry about what would happen to them if they too were to make a mistake.[18]

It's also very difficult to get right. The colloquial use of the term *punishment* disguises the fact that surprisingly little is known about its effective use in everyday settings.[19] Most research has focused in laboratories on rats, pigeons and monkeys being exposed to electric shocks, sprays of water, blasts of air, squirts of lemon juice, ammonia odour and physical restraint, none of which parents can use.

Research with humans has shown that punishment can sometimes (unreliably) secure children's compliance. But to achieve this, we have to be able to deliver punishment immediately (within seconds), frequently (consistently) and intensely, which is impractical. And, because it is impossible for you to see everything that happened and to know all the circumstances surrounding a misdeed, it is very difficult to be fair. Therefore, you run a high risk of misinterpreting the circumstances and punishing the wrong person; not realising that the children did not intend the results of their actions; failing to appreciate that the outcome has already frightened (punished) the children; and not understanding their perception of events. As a result of your unjust responses, your relationship with your children suffers because the children learn that they cannot call on your support and cannot trust you to be fair.

A practical shortcoming of all forms of punishment is that you can use them only *after* a child's behaviour has inconvenienced or hurt someone. And because we put off punishing children, someone is typically inconvenienced over and over again before we do anything about it. This means that the target has been hurt unnecessarily, the perpetrator has been allowed to develop an antisocial habit, and your tolerance has been pushed beyond its limits. Instead, guidance can offer children support as their feelings start to escalate, before they have become distressed or have hurt someone else.

Moreover, it is self-evident that people are not punished for committing misdeeds – but for being caught. In that case, punishing children is not likely to discourage the misdeed (given that it seems not to deter criminals), but instead will just teach children how to avoid being caught the next time and to be dishonest by denying that they were the culprit when they are accused of doing something 'wrong'.[20]

Finally, punishment on its own cannot teach a desirable behaviour, but only suppress an undesired one.[21] It fails to teach moral reasoning, as it focuses children's minds on self-interest instead of the effects of their actions on others. And it fails to teach them skills for resolving problems, such as the ability to self-regulate, be flexible and adaptable, solve problems, listen, or empathise with others.[22] Spitefully seeking retribution or revenge against children, it only teaches that 'Might makes right'.[23]

Other than signalling who is in charge, punishment fails to produce any lasting behavioural improvements.[24] In other words, punishment doesn't work very well. Its ineffectiveness is shown in the fact that children who behave most disruptively receive the most punishment – and yet they continue to be disruptive. This causes Alfie Kohn to ask: 'If punishment is so effective, how come I have to keep doing it?'.[25] And if controls did happen to make children comply in the short term, this paradoxically demonstrates that the children are manageable and therefore do not need punishment.[26] In other words, it is unnecessary.

Meanwhile, its disadvantages far outweigh its advantages, producing all of the negative outcomes listed in Box 1.4. These outcomes lead to a clear conclusion: there is no right way to do the wrong thing. This conclusion applies both to punishment in general, and to the use of time out and physical punishment.

Time out is a punishment which says to children that it is wrong to feel as they do and they must sort themselves out – alone. Although some will contend that, of the various forms of punishment, time out is reasonably mild, what is really being withdrawn from children during time out is not our attention, but our care and protection.[27] This can cause children to comply, but only because the loss of your love is so devastating. At the time, it can lead to expressions of distress and protest that attract more punishment[28] and, in the longer term, has all the disadvantages of the other forms of punishment, including conveying to children that they are unworthy.[29]

Spanking is the use of physical force to cause pain (but not injury) to a child as a tool of discipline.[30] In the U.S., it is used by 93 percent of parents of two- to four-year-olds; 58 percent of parents whose children are aged five to nine years; and 40 percent of parents of 13-year-olds.[31] Parents who use corporal punishment with young children do so 3.6 times a week, which amounts to a total of *187 times a year!*[32] In a recent study, early childhood teachers administered corporal punishment from 15 to 65 times *per day*.[33] Whereas hitting an adult would be an illegal assault, in only a few countries is it illegal when children are the victims, with (at the time of writing) the most recent country to make it so being my homeland of New Zealand. It joins a group of minor nations, with the major Western powers conspicuous in their continued endorsement of this practice.[34]

Many episodes of child abuse (that is, injury to a child) are the result of an escalation of physical punishment.[35] This risk alone implies that hitting children is unacceptable. Moreover, even without physical injury, there is considerable, consistent and robust evidence of the detrimental effects of spanking or smacking children.[36]

- *Socially*, spanking makes children more aggressive, particularly past the age of eight years. As a result of being spanked, children are more likely to use violence against both adults and peers,[37] and to be the victims of violence.[38]

- *Emotionally*, when practised by parents and when accompanied by anger, physical punishment (as distinct from child abuse) is associated with lowered self-esteem that, in turn, contributes to increased rates of depression and other psychiatric disorders in adulthood. At the time, children suffer emotional distress, perceive that they have been rejected, fear the loss of adult approval, and experience sadness, guilt, shame, anger, and humiliation at their loss of dignity.[39]

- *Behaviourally*, physical punishment does not reduce antisocial behaviour.[40] Indeed, it increases the severity of children's behavioural problems across time, raising the risk of behavioural problems at school entry by over 400 percent.[41] These problems include reduced cooperation, escalating oppositional behaviour, and increased antisocial acts during childhood and adolescence and into adulthood.[42] Part of the mechanism is the link between physical punishment and reduced moral reasoning.[43]

- In terms of its *cognitive* effects, regardless of other parenting qualities, physical punishment reduces two- to four-year olds' IQ by an average of 5.5 points, with a 2-point loss at older ages.[44]

- Physical punishment damages *relationships* between parents and children.[45]

The conclusion is clear: smacking (or spanking) children is a training ground for violence, differing from child abuse in its effects only by degree.[46] We know this because those of us who were smacked as children (who remember very little else of our childhood) even a quarter of a century later have clear memories of the humiliation and indignity of being hit. For these reasons, guidance believes that we cannot teach children to be humane by using inhumane methods.[47]

ASSERTIVENESS (THE LEADER)

In place of either submitting or becoming aggressive when children's behaviour interferes with our capacity to meet our needs, guidance advises that we hold on to our intention to connect and cooperate with others, and assert our own needs. Another term for assertion is 'levelling'.[48] It means giving other people information about ourselves, our thoughts, feelings and needs.

Unlike submission, assertion respects ourselves, because not expressing what we need is just as inconsiderate as not listening to what others need.[49] And, unlike aggression, assertion respects that other people have rights and needs too.

Assertiveness is based on some core principles. First, it assumes that, regardless of age or other distinguishing characteristics, we each have the same rights to have our needs fulfilled and are happier when we can do so.[50] In other words, the right to be assertive is reciprocal.

Second, we are each responsible for our own feelings and actions: the only behaviour we can change is our own.[51] It is our responsibility to check in with our emotions and use these as a signal about whether our needs are being met.

Third, assertiveness looks after children because they cannot know that their actions are having a negative effect on us now, when the same behaviour might not have bothered us in the past. Because children are not mind readers, if we do not tell them what we need, chances are they will not know.[52]

Therefore, the key benefits of assertiveness are that it maintains our accountability to ourselves and others. By looking after our own rights, it gives others permission to do the same for themselves. It respects children's right to know where they stand with us and gives them predictability and, with it, control. For our part, we feel better about ourselves, are physically and emotionally healthier than when we suppress emotions, and can relate to others more honestly and effectively, with our feelings remaining in control. It protects our relationships because it avoids resentment. Accordingly, an assertive relationship with our children resembles Figure 2.5.

FIGURE **2.5** THE SHAPE OF ASSERTIVE PARENTING

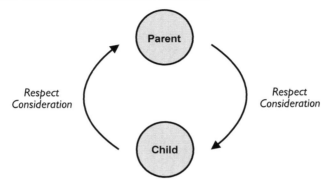

Respect Consideration   *Respect Consideration*

BOX 2.2 CHARTER OF PERSONAL RIGHTS[53]

- I have a right to my own behaviour thoughts and feelings, and I am responsible for their outcomes.
- I have a right to offer no justifications for my behaviour.
- I have the right to make mistakes.
- I have a right to have my thoughts and feelings listened to without judgment.
- I have a right to ask for what I want. I do not have to wait for permission.
- I have a right to reject other people's opinions of me.
- I have the right to set my own priorities.
- I have the right to choose whether to offer assistance to others. I am not obliged to help everyone every time. I can say 'No' without feeling guilty.
- I have the right to change my mind.
- I have the right to say 'I don't know' or 'I don't understand'. I do not have to have all the answers.

BOX 2.3 ASSERTIVE VERSUS AGGRESSIVE MESSAGES

When you have just sat down for a quiet spell, young children often think that this is an invitation to climb all over you. You could say, 'Get off. Leave me alone' which is a 'you' message: '(You) get off'. Without meaning to, you might have given your children the idea that they are a nuisance.

When you say instead, 'I'm really tired at the moment and need some time to rest', children are less likely to think that they are a nuisance, because you have told them about your needs, not about themselves. This is usually closer to what you meant to say.

BOX 2.4 A COMPARISON OF SUBMISSIVENESS, AGGRESSION AND ASSERTION[54]

Submissiveness	Aggression	Assertion
Your behaviour		
Do not express wants and feelings directly, or express them in a self-deprecating way.	Express wants, ideas and feelings at the expense of others.	Express wants, ideas ideas and feelings in direct and appropriate ways.
Your intent		
To please, avoid conflict or rejection.	To dominate, humiliate or punish others.	To communicate.
Your feelings		
Anxious, disappointed with self, often angry, resentful, hurt and powerless.	Self-righteous, superior, sometimes embarrassed later.	Confident, feel good about self, both at the time and later.
Your response to feeling angry		
Deny, repress, bottle up anger or express it indirectly.	Explosive, blame others for our feelings, deny self-responsibility.	Take responsibility for identifying the unmet need behind our feelings.
Others' feelings about themselves		
Guilty or superior.	Humiliated, hurt.	Respected, valued.
Others' feelings about us		
Irritation, pity, disgust, confusion about our needs.	Angry, vengeful, feel justified at the prospect of 'getting even'.	Usually respect (although sometimes annoyance).
Outcomes		
Do not get what we want; anger builds up.	Often get what we want at the expense of others.	Often get what we need.
Payoff		
Appears to avoid unpleasant conflict, tension and confrontation, but only postpones these.	Aggressor vents anger and feels in control of others.	Feel good; respected by self and others; relationships are strong.

Naturally, guidance recognises that adults have wisdom and expertise that children haven't learned yet. Therefore, although we don't boss, we still act as a leader in our families. This is rather like being an orchestra conductor.[55] In an orchestra, the conductor is obviously a highly skilled musician, but knows that he or she is not as capable on the piano as the pianist or on the cello as the cellist. The conductor has an overview of what the ensemble needs to accomplish, notices when the musicians are struggling with a particular passage of the music and offers extra guidance at those points – but, on the whole, trusts the musicians to know their instrument.

So it is in our families. As leaders, we have an overview of what the family needs to achieve, and will offer extra guidance and support when children are struggling with particular tasks – but, on the whole, we will trust children to know their instrument: that is, to know their own minds.

> Rather like an orchestra, family members are equal, with the conductor (parents) being the 'first among equals'. The orchestra conductor faces individuals who are experts in their own instruments (their own lives) but also has some expertise to guide them as they play their life's music.[56]

CONCLUSION

Under the guidance style, while we won't attempt to control children by responding aggressively to their behaviours, neither will we submissively tolerate actions that violate our own needs, or those of other children in our care. Assertion is consistent with the guidance value that we are each separate individuals with our own rights and needs. Rather than a focus on power, the focus is on needs, which I describe in chapter 3.

SUMMARY OF PRINCIPLES

- People who habitually submerge their own needs are indulging demanding thinking. We each have a right to champion our own needs.
- Martyrs give to their children in the hopes of getting something back.
- If punishment were going to work, it would have by now.
- There is no right way to do the wrong thing.
- We are responsible for our own feelings and actions: the only behaviour we can change is our own.
- The right to be assertive is reciprocal.

Human needs   **3**

So far, we have come to understand that parenting is not about using power, but about meeting needs. In this chapter, I describe these.

We can distinguish wants from needs on the grounds that needs are inbuilt: we do not learn that we need to be loved (whereas we learn that we 'need' a device with an *i* in front of its name). Needs are also universal: every person everywhere requires them; and we are happiest when our needs are met and experience distress when they are not.[1] Needs are also consistent across the life span, from childhood to old age.

A MODEL OF HUMAN NEEDS

I have developed a model of human needs, illustrated in Figure 3.1. with a more extensive list of needs in Box 3.1. As indicated by the upward arrow to the right of the tree trunk, the model is hierarchical, which means that we have to meet our lower-level needs before we can focus on meeting our higher needs.

SURVIVAL

The most basic need is for survival. It is so fundamental that, in my model, it is at the roots of the tree. As every gardener knows, if a tree's roots are compromised, the whole plant is vulnerable. Similarly, children's wellbeing suffers if they grow up in deprivation, say in economic hardship or without adequate food or sleep.[2]

SAFETY AND WELLBEING

Next is the need for safety or wellbeing. This refers to both physical and emotional safety, which is 'the safety to be yourself, to be vulnerable, to ask for help, and to be warmly supported'.[3] Children need to feel safe that they can meet our expectations, which implies that we have to take into account their age and other limitations. Research is unanimous that children feel emotionally safe when their parents are sensitive to and respond to their needs[4] and, conversely, that neglect and abuse of children produce a cascade of neurological and emotional damage known as 'trauma spectrum disorders' which are characterised by poor emotional regulation.[5] In turn, emotional dysregulation affects all aspects of abused children's competence: academic, social and behavioural.[6]

FIGURE 3.1 A MODEL OF HUMAN NEEDS

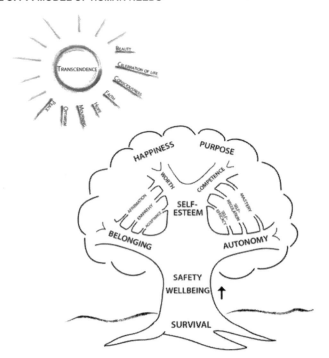

SELF-ESTEEM

In my model, self-esteem is at the centre of the three emotional needs (depicted as the tree's three limbs). This placement reflects the fact that we don't acquire a healthy self-esteem in a vacuum: we develop it through feeling connected to others (belonging) and by exercising autonomy (the need to be in charge of our own lives).

Box 3.1 HUMAN NEEDS

Survival
Air
Clothing
Food
Movement/exercise
Rest
Shelter
Sexual expression
Sleep
Touch
Water

Safety
Fairness
Justice
Order
Predictability
Privacy
Reliable care
Security
Stability
Support
Trust

Wellbeing
Awareness
Clarity
Comfort
Communion
Ease
Harmony
Health
Nurturance
Relaxation
Space

Belonging
Acceptance
Affection
Closeness
Communication
Community
Companionship
Compassion
Connection
Consideration
Cooperation
Empathy
Home
Inclusion
Intimacy
Love
Loyalty
Mutuality
Warmth

Self-esteem
Achievement
Affirmation
Appreciation
Competence
Equality
Independence
Learning
Mastery
Mattering
Presence
Respect
Stimulation
To be understood
Validation
Visibility (to see and be seen)

Autonomy
Choice
Creativity
Discovery
Effectiveness
Efficacy
Freedom
Integrity

Purpose
Authenticity
Challenge
Contribution
Fulfilment
Growth
Inspiration
Participation
Self-expression

Happiness
Celebration
Contentment
Enjoyment
Fun
Joy
Humour
Pleasure
Spontaneity

Transcendence
Beauty
Celebration of life
Consciousness
Faith in self and others
Hope
Mourning
Optimism
Peace

Whereas our self-concept reflects our thoughts and lists our skills and qualities, our self-esteem is how we *feel* about our qualities and achievements.[7] It has two aspects:[8]

- our *competence*, which is the extent to which we achieve at skills that matter to us (our ideals)
- our *worth*, which refers to how much we like, respect and accept ourselves.

Our esteem about our competence has to be *earned* (by becoming competent at some skills that we value); in contrast, our esteem about our worth has to be *given*. It is our birthright: it must have no prerequisites.[9]

Types of self-esteem

Given these two elements to our self-esteem, there are four types of self-esteem, as shown in Figure 3.2. When I'm presenting this material at seminars, I often find that the energy in the audience drops as participants become reflective and sad about their own self-esteem. Therefore, as you read this section, please be compassionate towards yourself and, if your concern is for your children, trust that the recommendations in chapter 4 will be healing.

FIGURE 3.2 TYPES OF SELF ESTEEM

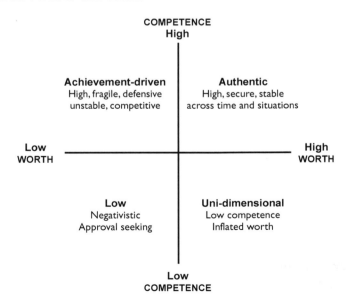

Low self-esteem

Children with low self-esteem are confused about both their competence and their worth[10] (– see Figure 3.3). As you might expect, they are at risk for emotional problems, have poor physical health, are dissatisfied with their lives, are desperate to gain others' approval, and are sensitive to both rejection and failure.[11]

Some children with low self-worth attempt to disguise their self-doubts with displays of conceit, arrogance, intolerance, criticism of others and a lack of empathy.[12] These tactics are commonly aversive to peers. Accordingly, this group is often labelled as narcissistic because they appear to exaggerate their own importance.[13] However, along with Brené Brown, I believe that this label is mistaken: their self-esteem is not in fact inflated but low, while the feeling behind their obnoxious behaviours is a fear of being ordinary.[14] In essence, the feeling is one of shame at not being enough (not good enough, not clever enough, not athletic enough, not good looking enough... or any other imposed standard). But, because of their self-aggrandising behaviour, outsiders are commonly tempted to 'take them down a peg' when, in reality, they are already 'down' – and kicking them while they are there will not help.

FIGURE 3.3 LOW SELF-ESTEEM

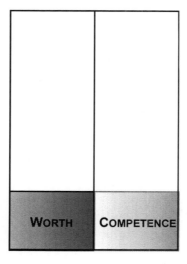

A low self-esteem is stable because, any time these people might start to feel better about their *competence*, their self-esteem is dragged down by their persistent reservations about their *worth*. These deep doubts come about when parents criticise and invalidate children and their feelings, as a result of which the children come to see themselves as unwelcome and unworthy.[15] This sense is more resistant to change than is a sense of incompetence.

Uni-dimensional self-esteem

When children focus on just one element of their self-concept to the exclusion of others, they develop an inflated self-esteem because it notes the highs but overlooks the lows (as shown in Figure 3.4). This is common for children whose self-esteem is based on their possession of power. They see the world in terms of winners and losers; they value dominance and use power to attract the admiration of others.[16] These are the school bullies. They believe that they have worth only when they are superior to others and that, if they cannot achieve this through their accomplishments, they will do so by having more power than others. But, with their self-esteem so reliant on winning, it is stable only as long as they can keep coming out on top.

FIGURE 3.4 UNI-DIMENSIONAL SELF-ESTEEM

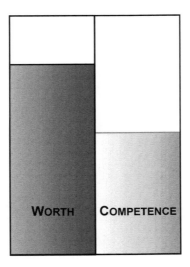

Brené Brown reports that this type of self-esteem comes about because children fear being vulnerable. They have learned this from admonitions to 'Man up' and from being subjected to parental bullying, aggression and violence from an early age.

Other groups with a uni-dimensional self-esteem are those who have learned that to be worthy, they have to be clever. They emphasise ability and are contemptuous towards anyone who seems less able than them. A third group are bigots, who blindly take for granted that their race, gender or religion makes them superior to others.

Unlike those with uniformly low self-esteem (who focus *too much* on any feedback, particularly about their worth), this group attends mostly to feedback about their power, ability or race and therefore fails to notice that they are not as competent (especially socially) as they think they are.[17]

Achievement-driven self-esteem

Individuals with this type of self-esteem doubt their worth and therefore strive to *earn* self-esteem through their accomplishments and by courting others' high opinions of them. This form of self-esteem requires constant validation.[18] Necessarily, then, it is fragile or unstable because fortune is fickle: the next failure or rejection is just around the corner.

This has emotional, academic and social effects. Emotionally, these individuals experience maladaptive feelings and poor coping when challenged.[19] They are highly anxious, depressive and stressed, and experience shame or denial following failure, while bragging about their successes.[20] They often have what is known in gifted education as *Imposter syndrome*. This is usually described as a fear that others will find out that they are not as capable as everyone thinks but, in reality, it is the fear that others will discover that are not as *worthy* as people think they are. They believe themselves to be frauds.

Academically, in an effort to prove their competence (which is the same thing, in their eyes, as proving their worth), the goal of children with an achievement-driven self-esteem is not to learn, but to rescue their self-belief.[21] When children's self-esteem is reliant on how well they do at school, achievement can be an addiction, requiring ever greater success to avoid feelings of worthlessness and emptiness.[22] They feel compelled to succeed, even being willing to cheat because the stakes are so high.[23] They define learning not as acquiring skill but as besting others.[24] They try to outdo or out-perform others to prove their superiority; they avoid tasks where failure is a possibility; when challenged, they give up in an attempt to save face; they procrastinate; and they choke under pressure.[25] As a result, they usually get lower grades in school than people with a healthy self-esteem.[26]

Socially, these individuals are devastated by others' disapproval and accordingly are more willing to change their behaviour (and even to behave antisocially) to be accepted by their peers.[27] In adolescence and beyond, this group retains a 'looking-glass' orientation typical of early childhood which upholds, 'If others approve of me, I will like myself'.[28]

Children develop an achievement-driven self-esteem when controlling parents demand rather than encourage high standards and employ psychological controls such as inducing guilt in their children or withdrawing their love when their children perform below expectations; it also comes from competing for school awards.[29] These 'ceremonies of humiliation'[30] take chastisement about children's mistakes in front of a whole class to another level by shaming non-award winners in front of a whole school. This is supposed to motivate them to work harder – when instead it instils an achievement-driven self-esteem in those who are capable or, in those who cannot excel, a fear and avoidance of learning.

This type of self-esteem is hard (but not impossible) to repair. It is difficult because our evaluation of our worth doesn't work the same way as our judgments about our competence. If we feel incompetent, we have four protective mechanisms. The first is to devalue the skill.[31] For example, I am a poor swimmer, but I don't care because the statistics are on my side: namely, adults who don't swim, don't drown. (You can't drown on dry land, right?) Children who fail at school use this solution: they decide not to care about academic learning. This solution involves changing our ideals.

A second solution is to channel ourselves into something else where we *can* excel. Again, what we have done here is change our ideals so that we can measure up to a different set of aspirations. Some children who are rejected by their peers use this solution: they decide that, 'If I can't be likeable, I'll be powerful', and they become more aggressive.

These self-defence mechanisms mean that we are protected from suffering too dreadfully if we are not competent at something. But we also have a third option: if we want to feel better about our skills, we can learn new skills! And we can work hard enough so that we do not fail at a skill on which our self-esteem is staked.[32]

FIGURE 3.5 ACHIEVEMENT-DRIVEN SELF-ESTEEM

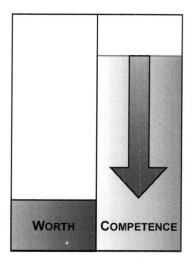

WORTH   COMPETENCE

Fourth, we can take an objective inventory of our skills, perhaps getting feedback from others so that we notice more of the abilities and qualities that we might be overlooking. This expands our self-concept.

However, if we feel unworthy, we do not have these same solutions available to us: we cannot 'not care' (certainly not convincingly) that we have not been welcomed in the world; we cannot find another channel besides our parents for measuring our worth (certainly not easily in childhood, other than a premature orientation to peers and alienation from disapproving parents). This leaves only one route for gaining a sense of worth: namely, to earn it through achievement. However, no matter how successful we become, unless we do some serious emotional work on ourselves beyond the childhood years, we will continue to doubt our worth and this doubt will pull down our overall assessment of ourselves: hence, the downward arrow in Figure 3.5.

Authentic high self-esteem

An authentic high self-esteem (illustrated in Figure 3.6) is secure and genuine. This is because it is balanced: it is made up of roughly equal proportions of worth and competence. As a result, these individuals' self-worth is well anchored, without the need for constant validation and without the compulsion to prove themselves by outdoing others.[33] They feel competent to take achievement risks and worthy enough to sustain a failure.[34] This is because failure – even at skills that matter to them – will not imperil their overall self-esteem, because their sense of worth is not reliant on their achievements. Accordingly, although (as indicated by the double-headed arrow in Figure 3.6), there is some minor fluctuation in their esteem about their competence in response to successes or failures, on the whole they will use failure as a guide to future action rather than as a message about their worthiness.[35] In other words, an authentic self-esteem acts as a reservoir of self-respect that protects us from interpreting failures as a message about our worth.[36] Because this form of self-esteem is not earned, it cannot be taken away.[37] It is neither undeserved nor inflated because it has developed unconditionally.[38]

FIGURE 3.6 AUTHENTIC HIGH SELF-ESTEEM

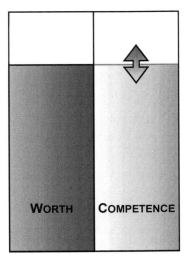

Infants gain their sense of worth from being accepted and receiving empathy and affirmation from their parents. As a result, they mature into adopting the stance, 'If I like myself, others will like me too'.[39] That is, beyond the early childhood years, they become healthily independent of the judgments of others.[40]

As a result of not obsessing about their evaluations of themselves, people with an authentic self-esteem are open to experience, are resilient and trust their instincts.[41] They have a healthy form of perfectionism whereby they strive to excel because of the pleasure of achievement, not to prove themselves to others, are intrinsically motivated, and behave pro-socially.[42] Compared to those with an achievement-driven self-esteem, individuals with an authentic high self-esteem have higher school grades and more positive attitudes and adjustment to school.[43] Given all these advantages, my recommendations in chapter 4 focus on how we can give our children an authentic high self-esteem.

BELONGING

Belonging is the second of the three core emotional needs (depicted in Figure 3.1 as the tree's three limbs). It refers to our need to love and to be loved, to be connected to other people. As we saw in chapter 1, the single most important factor affecting children's outcomes is the quality of their relationship to their parents (– see Box 1.4).[44]

Aside from this research, we know that belonging is a vital human need. Infants and parents from all cultures form loving bonds with each other; people are more satisfied in relationships characterised by mutual caring and frequent contact; and the development of new relationships (e.g. at weddings) elicits joy. In reverse, the dissolution of relationships (e.g. in divorce) creates distress; people think about and seek out new relationships when they feel lonely; the prospect of rejection activates deep fears;[45] and a lack of connectedness leads to many negative outcomes such as higher rates of physical and emotional illness, suicide and delinquency.[46]

Belonging is more than simply fitting in: *fitting in* involves becoming who we need to be for others to accept us, whereas *belonging* is about being accepted for who we are.[47] Children whose peers accept them are emotionally well adjusted and, compared to children suffering peer rejection, are less aggressive and less likely either to bully or to be the targets of bullying.[48] Meanwhile, at a deeper level of intimacy, throughout childhood and adolescence, friendships provide young people with a context for skill acquisition, supply emotional and cognitive resources, and are models for their future relationships. In contrast, sustained friendlessness alters children's beliefs in their own worthiness. This leads, in turn, to emotional difficulties such as depression and loneliness and to pessimistic and distrustful expectations of peers.[49] (I talk more about friendship in the booklet on social skills.)

AUTONOMY

The third emotional need in my model is the need for autonomy. The 'auto' in autonomy is not to be confused with independence, self-centredness, self-sufficiency or detachment from others. Instead, autonomy is the need to be in command of our own lives, to steer our own course in life, to be the initiator of our own actions; it is about intentionality and the exercise of choice.[50] Synonyms are self-determination, or being self-driven and self-governing. (It might help to think of adults with high autonomy needs as being 'control freaks' – although I prefer the term 'control enthusiasts' while, I refer to children with a strong need for autonomy as *spirited*.) Its opposite is either helplessness, or experiencing pressure or coercion to be a certain kind of person.[51] It is the difference between being the origin of one's own actions, or a pawn that is controlled externally.[52]

Evidence that autonomy is vital comes from research that, across cultures (and even across species), when individuals feel out of control of their circumstances, they develop a syndrome known as learned helplessness[53] which comprises an external locus of causality and emotional and behavioural responses typical of depression.

When in chapter 1, I introduced the concept of an internal locus of causality, I argued that no one *can* control anyone else. Given that we are more motivated and better adjusted when in command of our own lives,[54] this means that no one *should* control others. Denial of the emotional need for autonomy will be as devastating as social isolation or a low self-esteem.

When young people are both free *from* unnecessary constraints and are free *to* express themselves, they behave pro-socially and are emotionally healthy.[55] Compared with young people whose parents use controls, their overall self-esteem is higher; they develop appropriate self-regulation skills; are less aggressive; and possess more robust coping skills.[56]

PURPOSE AND HAPPINESS

The lower level of needs provide the engine for our pursuit of purpose and happiness, with our self-esteem about our worth impelling us to do something significant or worthwhile with our lives.[57] These higher-level needs are depicted in Figure 3.1 as being amongst the tree's foliage.

These two needs for purpose and happiness are partners: the theory of positive psychology says that humans are happiest when we are pursuing goals in life that are meaningful to us.[58] Hence, purpose and joy go hand-in-hand, with neither being sufficient without the other. The extent to which we achieve our purpose governs our satisfaction or happiness, whereas a purposeless life breeds resentfulness, listlessness and resignation.[59]

Purpose

Our need for purpose is the need for our lives to stand for something. Pursuing a purpose in life entails engaging in something meaningful *to us*. In other words, our purpose is driven by our values (– see Box 3.2). These are what we stand for in life, which act as an inner compass that keeps our lives on track.[60] Another way of thinking about them is that they are the glue that holds together everything we do. They inspire and motivate us to do what it takes to achieve our goals, and to sustain us as we live our lives.[61] Even so, we can picture placing our top six values on a large dice. Whichever way we hold the cube, we won't see all six faces at once, but they are all still there. At any given moment, those values in the foreground will be our top priority, but our priorities will change with our circumstances.[62]

Values are in contrast to having goals, which involve achieving, possessing or completing something (– see Box 3.3). They focus on outcomes, rather than the process. This distinction means that we will not be happy when our goals are imposed on us from the outside[63] because outsiders' goals will not necessarily align with our own values. We cannot be fulfilled by doing our duty and sacrificing ourselves to live out others' version of who we should be.[64] When we adopt others' expectations, we develop a 'rat-race' mentality where we are just on a treadmill, deferring happiness to some time in the future: after we get good grades, get into a good university, get a good job, get a promotion… and so on.[65] But there is no joy in postponing being true to our own values. Instead, each of us finds joy and will apply ourselves to ideas and skills that we care about.

BOX 3.2 VALUES[66]

Acceptance	Humility
Adventure	Humour
Assertiveness	Independence
Authenticity	Industry
Autonomy	Intimacy
Beauty	Justice
Caring	Kindness
Challenge	Love
Compassion	Mindfulness
Conformity	Open-mindedness
Connection	Order
Contribution	Patience
Cooperation	Persistence
Courage	Pleasure
Creativity	Power
Curiosity	Reciprocity
Encouragement	Respect
Equality	Responsibility
Excitement	Romance
Fairness	Safety
Fitness	Self-awareness
Flexibility	Self-care
Forgiveness	Self-development
Freedom	Self-regulation
Friendliness	Sexuality
Fun	Skilfulness
Generosity	Spirituality
Gratitude	Supportiveness
Honesty	Trust

Having a purpose involves being intentional in our pursuits.[67] Human beings do not find ourselves: we create ourselves. When we pursue a significant goal with resolution, we achieve coherence or a harmony of purpose that unifies our life and gives it significance.[68] It is like a compass setting that helps us steer our way through life, acting as a rudder that prevents us from losing our bearings.[69]

BOX 3.3 EXAMPLES OF THE DISTINCTION BETWEEN GOALS AND VALUES[70]

Goal	To be famous
Value	To contribute to humanity
Goal	To win the match
Value	To play fairly, skilfully, enthusiastically
Goal	To be first in class
Value	To explore new ideas and learn new skills
Goal	To lose weight
Value	To strengthen my body and maintain my health
Goal	To have friends
Value	To be warm, friendly, authentic, outgoing and supportive

---

Happiness

Happiness is not just a permanent good mood, but the experience of joy, contentment or wellbeing in response to a life that is well lived or is satisfying.[71] It is the outcome of a meaningful answer to the question, 'How should I live?'.[72]

Happiness and joy come from within ourselves, rather than from our external circumstances. They don't come from the experience of transient pleasurable sensations, such as watching a fireworks spectacle, because our drive for purpose means that it is not merely pleasure that motivates us, but gratification – that is, our sense of accomplishment when an activity calls on our strengths to rise to an occasion.[73] Also known as *flow*, gratification marks psychological growth.[74] We experience ourselves as doing what we are meant to be doing. This fills us with energy, whereas activities that we dislike quickly drain us.[75]

A close relative of happiness is the need for fun. Humans – and the very young in particular – need fun. Although in childhood, fun is justifiably an end in itself, throughout life enjoyment also signals safety and, therefore, opportunities for growth. Play undoes stress and broadens our intellectual, physical and social resources, building up reserves that we can draw on when under stress.[76] As a result, people who have fun are happier, more productive, healthier, more altruistic and more resilient.[77]

> Feeling positive emotion is important, not just because it is pleasant in its own right, but because it *causes* much better commerce with the world.[78]

TRANSCENDENCE

This final level of need is the uniquely human need to transcend day-to-day experience by appreciating the beauty and possibilities of life. We need optimism or faith in ourselves and others and to have hope that we can set realistic goals and plan to achieve them, in the belief that we can make them happen.[79] We also need to be able to mourn or grieve over unmet needs so that we can heal old wounds.[80]

CONCLUSION

We humans are more fulfilled and productive when our needs are met. The psychology of this is crystal clear. What makes guidance so powerful is that it honours children's needs as well as adults'. Therefore, in the next chapter, I describe how you can be sensitive and responsive to your children's needs.

SUMMARY OF PRINCIPLES

- Every behaviour is an attempt to meet a need.
- An authentic sense of worth is not 'earned', nor can it be taken away.
- Fitting in involves changing ourselves for others to accept us, whereas belonging is about being accepted for who we are.
- Children's need for autonomy is as vital their needs for self-esteem and belonging.
- Our values give our life purpose.
- It is important to hold onto our faith in ourselves and others.
- Fun causes much better commerce with the world.

Meeting children's emotional needs **4**

As you saw from the model of human needs (in Figure 3.1), children learn that they are competent when adults support their autonomy; and they learn that they are worthy when convinced that they belong.

COMPETENCE AND AUTONOMY

The first core ingredient of autonomy is choice. True choices have equally valued options, each of which meets individuals' needs. Although choice is necessary, however, it is not enough. In addition – as shown in Figure 3.1 (on page 50) – for young people to feel both competent and autonomous, they need:

- self-efficacy, which is a belief in their ability to make things happen
- capacity to self-regulate their emotions, impulses and attention
- mastery of skills that are worth knowing.

Self-efficacy

Self-efficacy is our belief in our ability to achieve a particular task in a particular setting. It amounts to trusting ourselves. As such (unlike self-concept), it has nothing to do with social comparison: either I can leap that fence, or I cannot.[1] We can feel efficacious in various domains:[2]

- *metacognitive* efficacy is the ability to manage our own thinking, control our thought processes, and achieve our academic goals
- *social* efficacy is the ability to influence others, to gain support and companionship from others, to resist peer pressures, and to meet social expectations
- *ability to run our lives.* This form of self-efficacy answers the question, 'How effective, competent or powerful am I in my life?'.

Self-efficacy is the reason that children have toys. The real items are too heavy or dangerous for them to use, so we give them something that they *can* manipulate. This teaches them about the object itself and about imaginary play – but the real lesson that they learn that is that they can develop a plan and make it happen.

Self-efficacy is also why children need substantial amounts of unstructured play time, instead of adult-led structured activities. When children are inventing their own play, they learn self-efficacy. This is vital, because when children believe that they can influence the outcomes of their actions (that is, when they have high self-efficacy), they are more intrinsically motivated to invest effort in tasks, are more reflective learners, and are more likely to strive for success, to persist, and to take academic risks.[3]

Our self-efficacy (or belief in our ability to achieve a task) relies on what we tell ourselves about our previous successes and failures. When we have succeeded previously – and particularly when we have failed – we will have generated explanations (or 'attributions') about the cause of these failures and successes. These attributions have four properties:[4]

- where we *locate the cause* of events: whether we believe them to be due to internal versus external forces;
- whether we see these forces as *durable* (e.g. personal traits such as ability) or *temporary* events (e.g. lack of effort);
- whether the causes are *pervasive* (e.g. an inability at maths) or specific (e.g. not understanding fractions); and
- how *controllable* we believe events to be.

For children to feel effective at managing themselves, they need to explain outcomes as being due to something that is internal; temporary; specific to the event rather than as a sign of a general or all-pervasive failing on their part; and in terms of their actions (or strategies), not their personality.[5] To help them to do this, we can highlight the strategies they are using by giving children feedback about the processes that they used, rather than the outcomes – see Box 4.5.

Specifically, when you hear your children blame their personality for failings (e.g. when they say 'I'm hopeless at this') or when they assume that the problem is permanent ('I'll never be able to do it'), first you can reflect their disappointment, but then gently correct their statements with something like: 'You're right: It hasn't worked out ... What could you do to fix it?' or even, 'Do you have to fix it, or can you leave it as it is?'.

Self-regulation

The capacity for self-regulation is the second process that contributes both to children's self-esteem about their competence and to their sense of autonomy. Self-regulation means that children can balance others' needs and values with their own and with the demands of the situation.[6] Nevertheless, guidance does not expect children always to put other people's needs ahead of their own, because never considering oneself is just as thoughtless as never considering other people.

Self-regulation requires that children are aware of their own emotional state and can use that information to exercise choice about how they express their feelings, without exploding uncontrollably on the one hand, or denying or repressing their feelings on the other.[7] This gives them a 'dimmer switch' on their emotions, as it were, rather than only an on-off button.[8] It is not a question of having self-control (as if our own instincts cannot be trusted), but of having choice.[9]

Learning self-regulation skills is the core task of the early to middle years of childhood. It allows children to behave in ways that are in tune with others – but, even more importantly, to be able to use their feelings to help them to live a rich, spontaneous and joyous life in which outbursts of uncontrolled emotion do not block them from achieving their life's goals. The capacity for self-regulation will help children to be resilient when they experience setbacks, because they know that they can stay in control of how they feel and how they behave by staying in command of what they think.

The guidance approach teaches self-regulation by listening to children's cues that they are distressed and by supporting them to soothe themselves. (I detail these methods in chapters 5 and 8.)

Mastery

The third aspect that contributes both to children's self-esteem about their competence and their autonomy is mastery (or accomplishment). To ensure that children master skills that are worth knowing, we need to present them with challenging tasks that are personally meaningful *to them*. Real and meaningful success at something that matters *to us* is the most reliable route to a high self-esteem about our competence.

This means that school curricula should emphasise depth rather than breadth, so that young people can master worthwhile content to a level of competence that empowers them.[10] To achieve deep knowledge, children need opportunities for experimentation and reflection, rather than rote learning.

Third, we need to give children *time* to integrate their learning and to develop deep understandings. Unstructured play time is important here, because downtime allows children to process what they have learned during the day, resulting in better recall of the information and concepts later. Play time and sleep time both allow children to 'park' information in their memory so that they can retrieve it later.

Finally, we must have a reason for what we are asking children to learn. This reason cannot be just to prepare them for the next stage of their education. When planning to enrol them in extracurricular activities, for example, we should ask:[11]

- Would this skill be worth knowing as an adult, and would it contribute to the child's quality of life or wellbeing in adulthood?
- Is the skill relevant to young people now?

That is, we need to be concerned about the quality of both the present experience, and its likely contribution to the child's future happiness. This means that extracurricular activities must allow children to pursue their own passions, rather than to fulfil our ambitions for them. Young people's after-school activities cannot be yet another exercise in self-improvement, but a way that they can learn a skill that they value and in a style that is natural for them.

WORTH AND BELONGING

As I show in Figure 3.1, three core processes help children to feel both worthy and connected to others: acceptance, receiving empathy and receiving affirming feedback.

Acceptance

Our brains are 'should' factories. In our efforts to make sense of our world, we are genetically wired to form judgments. As an expression of this, we praise 'good' behaviour when children please us, and chastise them for being 'naughty' when they don't. We judge children's emotions, as if feelings *can* be good or bad, moral or immoral, acceptable or unacceptable, when instead feelings cannot obey rules: they happen automatically, like breathing.[12] And we judge even when the emotion is positive – for example, when we try to suppress children's exuberance by telling them not to be 'silly'.

Judgments give outsiders the power to tell us who we are. Even 'positive' judgments (such as 'You're a good girl' or 'You're so clever') involve using labels. Negative labels in particular are inaccurate, hurtful, partial (in the sense of overlooking positive examples that contradict the label) and can be self-fulfilling. Judging others incites conflict with them.

BOX 4.1 JUDGMENTAL VERSUS COMPASSIONATE STYLES[13]

Judgment	Compassion
Denies choice	***Acknowledges choice***
I have to. I must. I can't.	I choose to. I want to. I can.
There's only one way to meet needs.	There are many ways to meet needs.
Perceives scarcity	***Perceives abundance***
There's not enough to go around.	There's enough when we share.
We can't meet everyone's needs.	Everyone's needs can be met.
Life is competitive.	Life is cooperative.
It's you or me.	It's you and me together.
Evaluates and judges	***Observes and expresses***
You're too...	Here's what happened...
He's mean; she's rude	I see, I hear, I remember.
Blames others ***Blames self***	***Takes responsibility for my*** ***own feelings and needs***
I feel... because you...	I feel... because I need...
Makes demands	***Asks for what I would like***
You have to...	Here's what I'd like...
If you don't...	If you're willing...
Listens selectively	***Listens empathically***
Suggests, lectures, advises,	Are you feeling...?
argues, fixes, analyses.	because you need...?

Instead, as I described in chapter 1, children need us to accept them as separate and unique individuals with their own lives, opinions, interests, needs and values. We need to accept and validate their feelings, understanding *that* they feel as they do, even when we don't understand *why*. When we validate even negative feelings, we teach children that all emotions are valid – indeed, that *they* are valid. In this way, guidance employs a compassionate style, which differs from a judgmental style in the ways listed in Box 4.1.

One way to communicate non-verbally to children that you accept and trust them is not to interfere in what they are doing. This is hard for parents to do, because we want to teach our children how to do things well and can feel disappointed for them when they make mistakes. We also want to be proud for them with the result that, out of concern for what others think of them, we encourage them to perform well. Finally, of course, we just like to be needed. But letting them do things their way tells them that we believe in their abilities.

Acceptance also means accepting children's mistakes. We must teach children that it is not a failure when we try but do not succeed: it is a failure when we do not try. In this vein, I often tell children that if you are not making mistakes, this means that you already knew the skill – and if you already knew it, that is not called *learning*, it is called *practising*.

At heart, acceptance is about respecting children. We can demonstrate respect in everyday ways: by making sure that we introduce children when greeting others and that we don't talk about children in front of them as if they can't hear or don't care what we are saying.

Empathy

Empathy has been aptly described as emotional resonance with others.[14] It is the ability to appreciate how others feel and to respond in a caring way to alleviate their distress.[15] This requires both the ability to see the world from other perspectives and the emotional sensitivity to appreciate someone else's feelings.

I describe skills for showing empathy in chapter 5. For now it is enough to know that children develop empathy when their parents give them support during times of distress.[16] This support helps the children to understand their own emotions and gives them experience of how it feels when someone else understands us.[17] As a result, children who have received empathy from their parents are both more understanding of others and more altruistic or helpful.[18]

You will need to be empathic when your children are talking or behaving in ways that signal that they have a problem. This is easier to do when they are distressed or sad, but you also need to be empathic when their feelings are producing behaviours that are troublesome to you. Even disruptive behaviour is an attempt to meet a need, while its intensity tells you how important that need is to the child.

Affirmation

We all thrive and become more motivated when people who are important to us give us compliments or feedback about our achievements.[19] However, feedback has two elements: it can either be judgmental and controlling, or it can supply information. And these two facets have opposite effects.[20]

Judgmental feedback in the form of praise or other rewards (such as stars or grades) has many detrimental effects.[21] In terms of children's self-esteem, praising children for their accomplishments teaches them to link their self-esteem to their achievements, instead of to their worth. They come to define themselves by what they do, not by who they are. Even 'positive' judgments (such as 'Good girl/boy; You're clever; Good work') imply that we approve of children only when they meet our standards. In young child speak, if they are good for getting things right, this means that they would be bad if they got them wrong. Not being willing to take that risk, they will do exactly what you reward – and no more. They will develop an achievement-driven self-esteem and a dysfunctional form of perfectionism.

Meanwhile, because these artificial rewards are so shallow, children need more and more praise – that is, they can get addicted to it. Yet babies don't ask for praise for being born properly: we *teach* them to depend on our judgments rather than their own.

Rewarding children for their ability teaches them that they are worthy only when they are clever. In that case, they can develop a uni-dimensional self-esteem, imposing on others the same high standards that they apply to themselves and showing disdain for any who do not measure up.

When we praise [a child], are we not perhaps honing in on his accomplishment, stealing a little of his glory, edging our way into the limelight, praising ourselves for having helped turn out such a smart child?[22]

Emotionally, praise of the person imposes on children an obligation to continue to act in a praiseworthy manner. This makes children anxious that they might not be able to live up to our expectations. As a result, their thoughts, feelings and behaviour all mimic helplessness. In turn, these negative feelings impair both their engagement and work quality while their achievement-driven self-esteem means that they cannot be seen to fail and therefore they will choose safe tasks and avoid challenge.

As well as impairing children's willingness to engage, controlling feedback for their accomplishments (in the form of rewards, grades, praise, and so on) leads to a decline in their intrinsic motivation and achievement. This is because when we receive an external reward, we shift our focus away from wanting to be competent at the task itself, to wanting to earn the reward. But once a reward looks unlikely, we stop applying ourselves. In technical terms, our motivation has shifted from internal to external.[23] In turn, focusing on the rewards rather than the task leads to less enjoyment of the activity, reduced conceptual learning and weaker persistence.

A final effect on motivation is that rewarding children for a particular activity implies to them that the task is noxious: otherwise, they would not have to be bribed into doing it. That is, delivering a reward for a particular behaviour *decreases* the attractiveness of the behaviour and *increases* the attractiveness of the reward.[24] When, for example, parents reward children (say, with ice-cream) for eating their vegetables, the children come to dislike vegetables more.[25] Similarly, rewarding children for learning makes the task *less* not more attractive. This is because giving children rewards for learning does not teach them to like learning, but to like rewards.

These negative effects come about because praise links children's competence or compliance to their *worth*. This, as we know, leads to an achievement-driven self-esteem, with all of its emotional, social and academic costs. Therefore, guidance upholds the following principle.

> When you want children to develop
> an authentic high self-esteem,
> do not praise them.

But of course, like everyone, children *do* need affirming feedback that they have achieved something worthwhile or that they have made a difference to someone else. *Information* (in contrast with judgments) inspires a greater investment in a task[26] and will foster an authentic high self-esteem. Therefore, we must give children specific information about what they have achieved, without judging them personally or judging their accomplishments. This 'acknowledgment' differs from praise in the ways listed in Box 4.2.

In short, compared with judgments, information leaves children's innate sense of worth intact (because it does not link their worth to their achievements), and it inspires a greater investment in or motivation towards tasks. Therefore, guidance advises:

> When you want children to develop an authentic high self-esteem,
> acknowledge and celebrate (but do not praise)
> their efforts and accomplishments.

BOX 4.2 DISTINCTIONS BETWEEN PRAISE AND ACKNOWLEDGMENT

Praise	Acknowledgment
Approves of work that meets adults' standards.	Guides children to evaluate their own efforts.
Judges children or their efforts.	Gives our opinion (sparingly).
Prescribes what children must do to earn our respect.	Describes qualities that children display which we already respect.
Is delivered in public as a way to manipulate children into repeating a desired behaviour, or to encourage onlookers to copy a child who has been praised.	Is a personal event that does not show children up in public or compare them to each other but shares in and celebrates their achievements in private.

HOW TO ACKNOWLEDGE

When I am teaching participants at my seminars how to acknowledge rather than praise, I tell them that it is the easiest thing in the world – but hardly anyone can do it. It is easy because everyone already uses acknowledgment with the adults in our lives. However, almost everyone I teach finds it very difficult to use the same language with children. It might help to realise that you don't have to patronise children as if they cannot think for themselves, but neither do you have to talk to them as if they were adults; instead, you can talk to them as *people*.

Invite the children's evaluations

The first and most vital way to acknowledge children is to ask them what they think about their achievements. Can they assess themselves? Of course they can. Every one-year-old who ever learns to walk thinks she's neat. She's been working on walking for 13 months and has finally nailed it. She doesn't turn to her parents and ask for a merit certificate for good walking behaviour.

However, many children have been so well trained to ask for our judgments that they have lost the skill of self-assessment. So when you first ask them for their evaluation, they might not know how to answer you because no one has asked their opinion before. Therefore, you might need to prompt them and give a few hints.

BOX 4.3 THE RISKS OF PUBLIC PRAISE

Many years ago I worked with a gifted 12-year-old whom I'll call Sarah who, until the age of 10 had topped her class in all school subjects but who, for the past two years, had been lucky to get a C grade in a tail wind.

Her parents and I traced her academic decline to an event two years previously when she had done an exceptional project – and the principal had displayed it at school assembly. Presumably, his intention was to reinforce Sarah for her good work and to encourage onlookers into being similarly diligent.

However, you don't have to be a genius (although Sarah was) to figure out that if you don't want to be made a spectacle of in front of the whole school, never again do good work. This is what Sarah had set about doing ever since.

Meanwhile, because giftedness means that you're in the top 5 percent of ability, 95 percent of students looking on that day knew they would never be able to produce work of that quality. Now they feel badly about themselves and blame Sarah for this, and will want to get back at her later, perhaps by excluding her from their friendship groups.

Praise and public acknowledgment do not always have these negative outcomes – but they *can*. And the risk is unnecessary, because all the principal had to do was call Sarah into his office and say, 'Sarah, thanks for coming over. I called for you because your teacher showed me your project. And I just want to tell you that I think it's stunning and to say that I hope you're very proud of it. I just wanted to congratulate you, and shake your hand'.

To my mind, this authentic and personal form of feedback has at least as much chance as public accolades of keeping Sarah engaged academically, with none of the risks that public praise poses to her intrinsic motivation, the self-esteem of her classmates or to Sarah's social inclusion.

Respond to children's own signals

Sometimes children will come to you beaming, asking if you like something they've produced. If you start with, 'I like the colours you've used' that will be too cold, but if you go into raptures of praise, although that matches their emotional tone, it will be judgmental. Instead, comment on their body language: 'You look delighted with that! Tell me about it.'

Verify, highlight and expand on achievements

When children have evaluated their efforts positively, you can *verify* this by adding your opinion; *highlight* an aspect of the achievement that they might not have noticed; and *expand* on that: 'Not only is your block tower really really tall, but you also had another go when it fell down the first time'.

Focus on the process

If you comment on the artwork or other items that children produce, you cannot be honest. You are never going to tell children that their painting is horrible; conversely, it is patronising to go into raptures over everything they put onto paper.

And, even more important, if you praise children for their abilities, they come to believe that ability is a fixed commodity. It's an all-or-nothing thing: you either have it, or you don't. Armed with this 'fixed mindset', they will avoid challenge because having to make an effort proves that they lack natural talent. Worried about being judged, they become obsessed with proving that they are superior to everyone else. And if they do fail, they will blame outside events and will believe that they cannot do anything about it. To them, failure is not an action ('I failed') but an identity ('I am a failure').[27] Therefore, instead of trying to repair a failure, they try to repair their self-esteem.[28] This mindset leads to declining performances over time.[29]

In contrast, we need to teach children that they can turn failure into success by changing their strategies. That way, in their minds a failure is just information about what didn't work. Instead of worrying about how they'll be judged for the outcomes, those who believe that skill improves with effort are concerned with the process, with whether they are improving.[30] This 'growth mindset' leads to improving performances over time.

BOX 4.4 TRAIT PRAISE AS INTERPRETED BY A CHILD WITH A FIXED MINDSET[31]

What the parent says	What the fixed mindset child hears
You learned that so quickly! You're so clever.	If I don't learn something instantly, I'm stupid.
The way you swim, you'll be our next Olympic champion.	I'd better quit swimming so that they don't find out I'm not that good.
Wow! Aren't you brilliant? Such a high grade, and without even studying!	I had better not study in future; otherwise, they will think I'm not that clever after all.

BOX 4.5 LEARNING PROCESSES[32]

- *Creative* dispositions: being imaginative; being open to new ideas and experiences; having tolerance of ambiguity; being curious, adventurous, playful; exploring new ideas and approaches; seeking alternatives.

- *Reflective* skills include the use of metacognitive strategies of self-awareness, self-regulation of their impulses and attention, and self-monitoring to regulate their own thinking.

- *Critical* thinking skills include being planful, strategic, inquiring, investigative, intellectually rigorous and logical (seeking truth, reason and evidence).

- *Emotional* dispositions:
  - *Motivation*: taking a risk; approaching a task with confidence; trusting oneself; having passion for a task; and enthusiasm for learning.
  - *Goal-directed behaviours*: engagement, diligence, persistence (trying again), patience, independence, cooperativeness, and delay of gratification.

Therefore, you can comment on the strategies they use as they develop mastery, such as those listed in Box 4.5. This teaches them that their abilities will develop with effort. Giving children specific information about the strategies they used highlights to them that they know how to learn, with the result that they will know they can use those strategies next time. In short, a growth mindset gives your children room to grow into individuals who can be passionate about learning and about the contribution they make to others.[33]

Commenting on the process also means that you can give even-handed feedback to children of differing ages or ability levels. The older or more able child's products will always be superior, causing the one who overhears the praise to feel inferior. However, both children can (at their age level) try again, try something new, work together, work alone, concentrate and so on.

Of course we can feel proud when our children work at something and finally master it. But we should be proud *for* them, not proud *of* them. *Proud of* means that they make us look good; *proud for* reflects the fact that they cannot claim any credit for their talents because these are largely genetic, but they (and we) can take pride in how well they use them.

Give an opinion

You can add an opinion if you think that will help. This will be in the form of 'I-verb': 'I admire... I respect... I value... I'm impressed... I appreciate...' This tells children about you and your values, not about themselves. Nevertheless, give an opinion sparingly, because it will be powerful and might over-ride theirs, when instead children need to be able to trust their own assessments. Only they know what they had in mind when they set out to do a task and they are the best judges of whether they achieved that. Moreover, we won't always be there to make evaluations for them. Given that they are the only constancy in their lives, they are the best source of evaluations.

Keep in mind that children already want to be competent and therefore they don't need incentives to develop skills, particularly since there are natural incentives for much of what they do (such as climbing some stairs gets you to where you want to go, and eating satisfies your hunger). Therefore, these behaviours don't need to be 'reinforced' with praise. Children can notice these achievements for themselves. Accordingly, avoid giving a running commentary on their every action.

> Self-esteem is not a trivial pursuit that can be built by pepping children up with empty praise, extra pats, and cheers of support. Such efforts are temporary at best, and deceptive at worst. Our children need coaches, not cheerleaders.[34]

We can, of course, celebrate with them when we see their pleasure in their accomplishment or follow up their evaluations with an opinion, 'Wow! I agree that you can be really proud of that'.

Intend to congratulate

When your child has achieved something that she is excited about, you can exclaim, 'You're a star!'. Strictly speaking, this is a judgment (they can be a star, or not be a star), but when your intention is just to share in their excitement, the children will receive it in that way.

On the other hand, an apparent acknowledgment such as, 'I like to hear such lovely manners' or, 'I like the way you're packing up' is intended to incite them to do it again and therefore is praise. Unlike praise, appreciation has no agenda.

BOX 4.6 TIPS FOR ACKNOWLEDGING CHILDREN'S ACHIEVEMENTS

- Ask children how they feel about what they have achieved:

  Are you pleased?
  What do you think of *that*?
  Are you happy with that?

- When children are saying or giving non-verbal messages that they are pleased, reflect that:

  You look delighted!
  You seem very proud of yourself.
  You look very pleased.

- *Verify* children's own assessment that they have achieved something worthwhile, *highlight* their successes so that they notice these, and *expand* on what they have achieved:

  I agree that it's quite an achievement (*verification*).
  Did you know you could do that? (*highlighting*).
  And not only have you finished it, but you worked on it for ages (*expansion*).

- Focus on the process (or strategies that children have used), rather than the product:

  I admire that you planned that so carefully.
  I'm impressed that you had another go.
  I respect that you took the chance and tried something new.

- When appropriate, add your opinion sparingly:

  Well, I agree with you!
  I agree that you can be very pleased with yourself.
  I think it's special too.

- Give information or feedback in the form of *I-verb*:

  I admire...
  I respect...
  I value...
  I'm impressed that...
  I appreciate...

- Intend to congratulate, not manipulate:

  Congratulations!
  Hey! You did it!
  Wow! Look at that!

- Express appreciation:

  Thank you!
  I'm grateful that...
  I appreciate that because...

- Use natural manners, without patronising. For example, in response to a child's thanks:

  You're welcome!
  It's a pleasure.
  I hope you enjoy it.

BOX 4.7 EXAMPLES OF PRAISE AND ACKNOWLEDGMENT

Praise	**Acknowledgment**
You're a good helper.	Thanks for helping.
	I appreciate your help.
	Thanks: that made my job easier.
	Thanks: it was fun to do that together.
Good boy/girl for using your manners (when the child has thanked you for a biscuit).	It's a pleasure.
	You're welcome.
	I hope you like it.
I'm proud of you for doing so well at ballet.	Congratulations!
	I'm proud for you.
	I think you can be proud of all the effort you put in to practice.
That's a beautiful painting.	You look delighted with that.
	Looks like you enjoyed doing that.
	What do you think of *that*?
Your school play was excellent!	I enjoyed your play very much.
	I admire that you practised so much to learn all those lines.
	You put so much passion into your play that I appreciated it in a whole new way.

Express appreciation

When a friend does you a favour such as picking up your children from school when you are delayed at work, you don't tell her she's a good girl for helping, but instead simply thank her. We can do the same with children.

Use natural manners

When you order a meal in a restaurant and the waiter delivers it and you thank him, he doesn't come back at you with, 'Good girl for using your manners'. Instead, the waiter says something such as, 'You're welcome' or, 'I hope you enjoy your meal'. Similarly, when your child asks for a biscuit and you give it to him and he thanks you, you don't need to praise with, 'Good boy for using your manners' but instead use the same language as the waiter.

THE BEST RESPONSE TO 'GOOD BOY'

RESPONDING TO CHILDREN'S DISAPPOINTMENT

Carol Dweck tells the story of a child who has a natural talent and a love for gymnastics and who performs well in a competition but does not win any events. As a parent, Dweck asks how you should respond:[35]

- Tell the child that *you* thought she was the best.
- Tell her that the judges are blind fools who robbed her of an award that was rightfully hers.
- Reassure her that gymnastics is not that important.
- Tell her she is very capable and will win next time.

The answer, of course, is none of the above. You both know that the first response is insincere because, if she had been the best, she would have won; the second blames other people; the third teaches the child to devalue something unless she can be successful at it instantly; and the fourth emphasises natural talent instead of effort.

While it is understandable for us to want to protect our children from disappointment, in a scenario such as this, they need to hear that they didn't yet deserve to win. They need feedback that will inspire continued effort. A tactful version of this would go something like, 'I know how disappointed you must feel to have done your best and not won. But, you haven't really earned it yet. Many of the others have been working at it for much longer than you. If this is something you really want, you'll need to keep working for it'.[36] The theme of your message is that if a child wants to do something for fun, that is fine, but to excel will take effort. This does not mean that effort should be regarded as unpleasant, however. It is important that children enjoy the *process* of developing more skill, rather than focusing only on the *outcome* (of winning).[37]

Keep in mind, however, that if children are to receive your feedback as inspirational rather than punitive, it is vital that they have a growth mindset; otherwise, children with a fixed view of ability just feel that their character or ability is being judged.[38]

If children are disappointed in something they have produced, you can question them about that: 'You seem a bit disappointed in that. How come?' Next, you would empathise with their disappointment. If you agree with their assessment, you can say, 'Yes. I can see that it didn't work out the way you hoped'. After a pause, you can ask if they are happy to leave it as is, or what they could do to fix it, perhaps now or later.

Alternatively, if you think their judgment is too severe, you can say so. 'Mmm. I wonder if you're being too hard on yourself?'. If a child is, say, six years old and expects to be as good at something as her nine-year-old sibling, for example, you could ask, 'I wonder if you're trying to be as good as someone who's nine, when it's not your turn yet to be nine? At the moment, it's your turn to be six. And six is a good age to be'.

LIMIT COMPETITION

Meanwhile, when giving children feedback, be sure not to compare them to each other. In competitive settings, children are more tense and anxious and they lose self-confidence.[39] Competition is detrimental for those who habitually lose, but also for those who habitually win because they often develop an achievement-driven self-esteem and a mindset that ability is fixed (and a lot of it makes you superior to others). The question then becomes: 'Did I win?' when it should be, 'Did I make my best effort?'.[40]

In competitive settings, success is measured not as an increased level of knowledge or skill, but by beating others. In this way, competition causes children to regard each other as rivals[41] and contributes to hostility and ill feeling towards their peers.[42] It corrodes the cooperative climate, weakening group cohesion and producing increased aggression and disruptive behaviour.[43] As Kohn observes, 'Competitiveness cannibalizes cooperation'.[44] It reduces empathy for others and makes it less likely that children will be altruistic.[45]

In contrast, cooperative settings minimise status differentials such that children's worth is not dependent on their achievements, and certainly not on defeating others.[46] Although social comparison is inevitable as a way of measuring ourselves against a standard, seeing ourselves as better than or deficient compared to others is not inevitable. A difference in competence does not have to mean a difference in *worth*.

Imposing a competitive culture on children is an ethical issue. Very few adults would persist at an activity at which they constantly lost; yet we impose losing on some children every day of their lives – and still expect them to remain engaged and hopeful.[47]

PERFECTIONISM

Perfectionism generally has a bad name, but it is detrimental only when children have an achievement-driven self-esteem. In that case, it is a bully that tells them that they *must* do things perfectly, *have* to get things right the first time, *must not* make mistakes and that, if they can't do it well instantly, there is no point in trying.[48] People who believe these rules and that they have to prove their worth by outdoing others are known as socially prescribed perfectionists.

They fear failure and, consequently, avoid tasks where failure is a possibility; they are highly anxious and depressive; and they treat themselves harshly when they think they have performed below expectations.[49] If they sense that they are failing (compared with others), their emotions become increasingly negative, they give up and they become off-task, with the result that their performance declines. And their external motivation leads to procrastination. This protects their fragile self-esteem because if they do less well than expected, they can blame a lack of time or effort, rather than any lack of ability.

In contrast, children with an authentic high self-esteem have a form of perfectionism that is self-referenced, where they strive to do well for the pleasure of being competent.[50] These perfectionists are willing to persist when challenges are high, regardless of how others perform. They are intrinsically motivated and therefore generally have a strong work ethic: they are organised and thorough in their study habits.[51]   In some respects, this form should not be labelled as perfectionism at all, because the children strive for excellence, not perfection.

This distinction provides a further reason to use acknowledgment rather than praise: namely, that informative feedback encourages self-referenced perfectionism. In turn, the combination of a healthy self-esteem, intrinsic motivation and a functional form of perfectionism emboldens children to persist at tasks, rather than giving up in the face of challenge. Confident learners can live by the mottos:

- Strive for excellence, not perfection.
- On worthwhile tasks, strive to do your best, not to be the best.
- Have the courage to be imperfect.
- Don't let failure go to your head.

MOTIVATION

Participants at my seminars often ask (in some horror), 'If I don't praise and reward and I don't make activities competitive, how will I get my child to do anything?'. I give the long answer to that question in the booklet on *Guiding children's learning*. Here, the short answer is that all human beings are motivated – to meet their needs. Therefore, if children are not motivated to perform a particular task, this means that the task does not meet their needs. (Children refer to these tasks as 'boring'). To help us understand what might be going on for these children, Jones and Jones propose the following formula:[52]

Motivation	=	expectation of success
	x	anticipated benefits of success
	x	the emotional climate.

In other words, if children believe that they cannot achieve the task, they will not engage. If they believe that success at it will not meet their needs now or (for older children and adolescents) in the future, they will not engage. If they are being taught in an atmosphere of judgment instead of trust, they will not engage.

And once children are old enough to decide that something is pointless now but will benefit them in the future, those potential benefits will have to justify the sacrifices the children have to make now. That is, the cost must not be not too high. While it is true that we should not give up what we want *most* for what we want *now,* neither should we sacrifice our present, unless the anticipated future benefit *is* in fact what we want most.

> **BOX 4.8 SUMMARY OF THE BENEFITS OF ACKNOWLEDGMENT**
>
> - Acknowledgment gives children information about who they are and what they are capable of being: it adds to their sense of competence.
>
> - It does not imply doubt about their worth, or tie their worthiness to their ability to satisfy our expectations. In this way, it fosters an authentic high self-esteem, rather than an achievement-driven one. Children learn that what they do does not define who they are.
>
> - Because it is authentic, it is credible, meaningful and, therefore, influential at low doses.
>
> - It maintains children's intrinsic motivation in which they strive to achieve for the satisfaction of becoming competent, rather than trying to earn a reward.
>
> - Acknowledgment fosters self-referenced perfectionism, in which children strive to do well out of a desire to develop skills, rather feeling compelled to prove to others that they are good enough.

PHASING OUT REWARDS

A second question that participants often ask (this time with some guilt) is how to phase out rewards. If, for example, you have been giving children a sticker or sweets (candy) for using the toilet during toilet learning, you can continue to do so. However, instead of giving the sticker as a reward for being 'good', you can give it simply as a physical reminder to the children about their achievements: 'Let's put a sticker on your chart to remind you that you did it! You must be very pleased with yourself'.

Alternatively, you can invite children to get a sticker from the container, and put it on their own chart, or on a piece of work they have completed. You might say, 'Would you like to put a star on that to remind yourself that you were pleased with it?'. After a short time, the children typically lose interest in this visible form of reward because they prefer instead your authentic congratulations and natural celebration of their achievement.

Recovery time

A third question that parents often ask me is how long children take to adjust when parents stop giving artificial rewards, including praise. The question reflects the reality that children get addicted to praise, largely because it is so empty that they crave more and more of it and because they have learned not to trust their own evaluations.

In my experience, it takes about one week per year of life: four-year-olds take four weeks; six-year-olds take six weeks, and so on. But in fact the issue is not how long the *children* take to adjust, but how long it takes the *adults* to change their habits. Luckily, you do not have to learn any new language to use acknowledgment – because you already acknowledge adults – but it takes a change of mind set. And *that* takes time, patience and forgiveness of your own mistakes.

Meanwhile, when you are first practising giving acknowledgment, be reasonably strict with your language because judgments come so automatically to us. (We heard in childhood a thousand times that we were 'good' and the old tape in our heads just churns out the same comments without thinking.) But after a while, when your intention is to celebrate, you will get away with something like 'You're a star!' (which is actually a judgment). And of course, any time you just want to tell your children that you love them to bits, you can do so. But this spontaneous expression of affection is not intended to manipulate them into doing anything in particular.

Inconsistency

Fourth, parents often ask me how children will cope when school or their grandparents – in fact, the rest of society – continues to reward them whereas their parents don't. This is my favorite question, because the answer is so powerful. First, we can trust that our opinion is more important to our children than anyone else's. Therefore, they will dismiss the praise of others and instead trust our messages that they do not have to perform in a particular way to earn our respect.

Second, we have to remember that the loss of praise is no loss at all, because it is both meaningless and detrimental to children's self-esteem. I have literally seen children stand taller after receiving acknowledgment.

Third, if schools (for example) continue to use rewards such as student-of-the-day awards, achievement certificates and stars, you can give your child the *I believe in you* speech. The speech says, 'If you've tried your best and your teacher doesn't notice by giving you a star, I want you to know that *I believe in you* anyway.' You can repeat this for the opposite scenario, 'And if you make a mistake and get into trouble, I want you to know that *I believe in you* all the same'. And, if there is another parent in the picture, 'And your father wants you to know that *he believes in you* anyway'. This speech separates out the receipt (or non-receipt) of a reward from any message about the child's worth – because you think he or she is worthy regardless. After that, the reward system becomes irrelevant to the child.

Fourth, if other people praise your children, from around the age of five or so, you can teach them to translate others' feedback from a message about them, into a message about the speaker. If, for example, her grandmother tells your daughter that she looks pretty, she can tell herself that this means that her grandmother likes her dress. (We don't want to teach girls that the way to get ahead in life is to be decorative!) Or if his grandfather tells your son that he is 'good' for doing as asked, the child can tell himself that Granddad is grateful.

The 'fine line' argument

Finally, some participants are confused about the differences between praise and acknowledgment. Naturally, neither one is neutral: acknowledgment does express our values and opinions. But people can have different opinions. I don't like musical theatre, but my friends do. If I were to say that musicals are bad, they might feel reluctant to contradict me, whereas if I say that I don't enjoy them, they are equally free to declare that they do. The same is true when we give an opinion about a child's accomplishments. Of course, our opinion is powerful in our children's eyes and therefore it is wise it give it sparingly, but when we express an opinion, this still permits them to hold a different view.

The fact that we are rendering an opinion instead of judging means that we can also say when we don't like something. We will do this rarely if it is about a piece of work that children have produced, because they will be very sensitive to our negative opinion. A more benign scenario is if my daughter asks what I think of her outfit. If I don't like it, I can tell her that it isn't my favourite, but that she is free to have her own opinion. After all, she is the one wearing it.

Particularly for women, our confusion comes about because we have been thoroughly trained to believe that when we please others, we are good people (instead of that they are grateful). As a result, we mistake informative feedback that we have pleased someone with a judgment about our worth. And then we think our children won't be able to tell the difference either. Let me assure you: they can. And if they never receive praise, they never get confused.

Some still protest that it's a fine line between praise and acknowledgment and we are just splitting hairs. My response is that in life, there is a fine line between a lot of things (such as between being healthy and unwell) but that is a line we care about deeply. As for hair splitting, language is powerful. It *matters*.

CONCLUSION

The greatest gift that we can give our children is an unwavering belief in their own worth. They will have to earn a sense of competence by striving to achieve skills that matter to them, but they need to know in their hearts that what they do does not determine their worth. The single most effective way to teach this is to acknowledge rather than reward their achievements. It is the most powerful technique that I have learned as a child psychologist. It is a difference that makes a difference.

SUMMARY OF PRINCIPLES

- It is not a failure to try and not succeed. It is a failure not to try.
- If you're not making mistakes, that is not called learning: it is called practising.
- When you want children to develop an authentic high self-esteem, acknowledge and celebrate (but do not praise) their efforts and accomplishments.
- Children need coaches, not cheerleaders.
- Guide children not to try to outdo others – but to fall in love with what they are doing.
- Giving children rewards for learning does not teach them to like learning – but to like rewards.
- Competition destroys cooperation.
- Strive for excellence, not perfection.
- Have the courage to be imperfect.
- Don't let failure go to your head.

Listening to children   **5**

Relationships with children are no different from any others: they require mutual respect and communication. This entails three skills, of which listening is the first. In this chapter, I will be describing how to listen to children both when they are distressed and when their distress is provoking behaviour that is troubling you. You would use the second communication skill of assertiveness when you are distressed but your child is not, and the third skill of collaborative problem solving when both your own and your child's needs are not being satisfied. I discuss these last two skills in chapter 7.

As you read this chapter, please avoid beating up on yourself over your listening skills. You know more than you realise. Because we are all human, we each know the qualities of communication that we appreciate, and those that shut us down. That is, we already have a wellspring of knowledge about compassionate communication.[1]

NEEDS AND FEELINGS

Pleasurable feelings tell us that our needs are being met. Satisfaction of our needs gives rise to a range of pleasant emotions, as listed in Box 5.1. These feelings signal that we are safe and, therefore, that we have an opportunity for growth.[2]

In contrast, the 'negative' feelings, although unpleasant, serve a vital survival function of signalling when we need something that we are not receiving. Box 5.2 lists our emotional responses to unmet needs. The purpose of unpleasant emotions is hinted by the very word *emotion*: these feelings mobilise us to take action to meet our needs.[3] For example, fear tells us that we need to do something to make ourselves feel safe again. Therefore these so-called 'negative' feelings are actually our allies in our goal to satisfy our needs.

ACCEPTANCE OF EMOTIONS

When children's negative emotions give rise to behaviours that inconvenience or upset others, we can be tempted to focus on our own needs and forget to listen to and validate the children's feelings. When they are communicating their feelings in ways that are objectionable to us, it is easy to think that *they* are the problem. This can cause us to make the mistake of assuming that we have to be assertive. Anger, irritation and annoyance are likely to result when we focus on ourselves and how the behaviour affects us.

Instead, the children's distress during behavioural outbursts means that, at these times, we have to suspend our own needs for the moment and supply compassion, listening to the children's words and actions to detect what these communicate about their needs. Giving children understanding in this way is valuable in its own right because it helps children to resolve their feelings and enhances our relationship with them. It has the secondary gain of helping children to return to behaviour that no longer disturbs us.

As I mentioned in chapter 4, when we validate even negative feelings, we teach children that all emotions are valid – indeed, that *they* are valid. This is a powerful message about their worth and will contribute to an authentic high self-esteem. In contrast, when we dictate what children should feel, it will shut down communication between us. And when their parents control their emotional expression, children learn to suppress emotions such as sadness, anger and fear.[4] Girls in particular have been shown to be especially vulnerable to emotional constriction when their parents censor their expression of negative emotions.[5]

CHILDREN'S EMOTIONS

To be able to accept children's feelings, it will be helpful to understand the difference between their emotions and adults'. First, many adults mistakenly think that 'little people have little feelings'[6] and that this moment's distress will be forgotten in a few minutes, and therefore it isn't important to listen to children when they are upset. However, children's feelings change suddenly not because the emotion is insignificant but because children are 'serial emoters'. Until they are 8 to 10 years of age, they do not realise that they can feel two conflicting emotions about the one event.[7] (For example, on the last day of the

Box 5.1 FEELINGS IN RESPONSE TO FULFILLED NEEDS

Affection
adoring
affectionate
caring
charmed
compassionate
desirous
fond
friendly
loving
moved
open hearted
sympathetic
tender
touched
trusting
warm

Calmness
calm
carefree
centred
clear headed
comfortable
composed
contented
fulfilled
mellow
peaceful
pleasant
quiet
relaxed
relieved
rested
sated
satisfied
serene
settled
still
tranquil

Confidence
adamant
adept
adventurous
assured
bold
brave

Confidence *(cont'd)*
capable
certain
confident
definite
determined
empowered
encouraged
firm
open
optimistic
safe
secure
skilled
sure
vital

Delight
amused
animated
bubbly
buoyant
cheerful
delighted
ecstatic
elated
enchanted
euphoric
glad
happy
joyful
jubilant
overjoyed
playful
pleased
positive
rapture
thrilled
upbeat

Engagement
absorbed
alert
attentive
aware
captivated
challenged
committed
curious

BOX 5.1 FEELINGS IN RESPONSE TO FULFILLED NEEDS *(cont'd)*

Engagement *(cont'd)*

dedicated
eager
energetic
engaged
engrossed
enthralled
enthusiastic
entranced
fascinated
fervent
immersed
intent
interested
intrigued
involved
keen
lively
motivated
passionate
rapt
riveted
spellbound
stimulated

Excitement

amazed
animated
ardent
aroused
dazzled
energetic
excited
giddy
invigorated

Exhilaration

blissful
ecstatic
elated
electrified
exhilarated
exuberant
fervent
pleased
radiant
rapturous
thrilled

Gratitude

appreciative
grateful
gratified
honoured
pleased
thankful
touched

Hope

expectant
encouraged
hopeful
optimistic

Inspiration

admire
amazed
astonished
astounded
awe
enthused
impressed
inspired
invigorated
marvel
respect
wonder

Refreshed

enlivened
recharged
rejuvenated
renewed
rested
restored
revitalised
revived

Box 5.2 Feelings in response to unmet needs

Anger

angry
enraged
fuming
furious
incensed
infuriated
irate
livid

Annoyance

annoyed
bothered
cross
disgruntled
disillusioned
dismayed
displeased
dissatisfied
exasperated
frustrated
impatient
irritated
irked
peeved
piqued
thwarted

Anxiety

anxious
cranky
distressed
distraught
edgy
fidgety
frazzled
irritable
jittery
jumpy
nervous
on edge
overwhelmed
restless
stressed
tense
uptight

Aversion

abhor
animosity
dislike
hate
hostile
loathe
repulsed

Confusion

ambivalent
baffled
bemused
befuddled
bewildered
confounded
confused
dazed
deceived
diffident
disoriented
divided
doubtful
dubious
hesitant
lost
mystified
perplexed
puzzled
questioning
stupefied
tentative
tenuous
torn
uncertain
unconvinced
undecided
unsure
vague

Disconnection

alienated
aloof
apathetic
bored

Disconnection

(cont'd)

cold
conspicuous
detached
different
distant
distracted
estranged
indifferent
lethargic
listless
lonely
longing
numb
remote
removed
reserved
uninterested
withdrawn

Disquiet

agitated
alarmed
disconcerted
disturbed
flustered
frantic
jumpy
nervous
perturbed
rattled
restless
startled
surprised
overwrought
tense
troubled
turbulent
turmoil
uncomfortable
uneasy
unnerved
unsettled
upset
wary

Box 5.2 Feelings in response to unmet needs *(cont'd)*

Embarrassment
apologetic
ashamed
contrite
culpable
embarrassed
foolish
guilty
humiliated
mortified
penitent
regretful
remorseful
repentant
self-conscious
shamed
sorry

Fatigue
beat
burnt out
defeated
depleted
drained
empty
enervated
exhausted
helpless
lethargic
listless
sleepy
tired
weary
worn out

Fear
afraid
anxious
apprehensive
cautious
concerned
delicate
dread

Fear *(cont'd)*
fearful
foreboding
fragile
fretful
frightened
frustrated
guarded
insecure
leery
mistrustful
nervous
panicked
petrified
scared
sensitive
shaky
suspicious
tense
terrified
threatened
uneasy
vulnerable
wary
worried

Pain
agonised
anguished
bereaved
crushed
devastated
distraught
distressed
disturbed
heartbroken
hurt
lonely
pained
regretful
sore
tormented
troubled

Sadness
bereft
bleak
blue
dejected
desolate
despairing
despondent
disappointed
discouraged
disheartened
dismal
down
forlorn
gloomy
glum
grieving
heavy hearted
hopeless
hurt
inconsolable
low
maudlin
melancholy
miserable
morose
sad
sorrowful
suffering
unhappy
wretched

Yearning
aching
brooding
grief-stricken
homesick
longing
nostalgic
pining
wistful

school holidays, older children might feel disappointed that the holidays are over at the same time as being excited about seeing their school friends the next day.)

Instead of feeling combinations of emotions, young children feel emotions in succession, each one real at the time. They might declare to a best friend, 'I hate you. You're not my friend any more' but, within 30 minutes the two are walking around holding hands. Seeing this, we might dismiss their earlier feeling as insignificant. But at the time they could not feel two things at once, and therefore their distress was not diluted by the knowledge that the relationship would heal. They truly believed it was all over. Therefore, their pain at the time was real. (This phenomenon is also why three-year-olds cry plaintively when a parent is angry with them, 'You don't love me any more, do you?': Because they themselves cannot feel two things at once, they do not realise that we can be angry with them and love them at the same time.)

Second, babies' survival *requires* that they tell us everything that they feel so that we can meet their needs. They *have* to tell us when they are tired, hungry, in pain, cold, frightened, overwhelmed, and so on. To babies, feeling something and communicating it are one and the same thing. This keeps them safe. In contrast, adults' wellbeing relies instead on our ability to filter and regulate our emotions. When we can do this, our feelings will enrich our lives, rather than block us from achieving our goals.[8]

Third, because their survival depends on their feelings being responded to, children's emotions are more intense than are adults'. As evidence of this, picture a park on a sunny day, when a two-year-old drops her ice-cream. You know that her parents are now in for a ten-minute despair session, whereas last time you dropped some ice-cream, you didn't need to despair over it.

The fourth thing we know about children's feelings is that they have a limited vocabulary to explain to themselves what they are feeling. They also have less experience with managing emotion. Both these qualities make children's feelings all the more disturbing to them. This is why children need understanding, not criticism for how they feel.

Fifth, as far as we know, we are the only species that has feelings *about our feelings*. We might be nervous about speaking in public and embarrassed that we cannot hide our nervousness. We similarly see two layers of emotion when children are having meltdowns: the problem starts out being that they are not allowed a treat at the shops... and then a switch flips, as it were, and they become hysterical. The problem now is not that they want the treat, but that their feelings are scaring them. Adults have the same experience when we have lost someone we love through death or desertion. We feel sad, but that is not surprising: we expect to feel sad. And it is not even unfamiliar: we have been sad previously in our lives. But what makes grief so distressing is that we can be so intensely sad that our feelings scare us. We think we're going crazy. In a similar way, when children's feelings become intense, they can panic and become frightened and overwhelmed, unsure that they know how to recover.

For their future wellbeing, because the skill is not hard-wired, children need to *learn* how to regulate their feelings. They will learn this when their parents provide sensitive support, in contrast with using controls to suppress children's emotional displays. To support children, you will need to:

- ensure that you do not blame, shame or humiliate your children for their feelings or resulting behaviour
- express your own emotions appropriately to show children how to do so
- help children to recognise and understand their own feelings by labelling and reflecting these for them
- help children who are overwhelmed emotionally to feel safe by giving them support while they calm down. With us on hand to comfort them, they will learn that they can stay in command of the intensity and duration of their feelings and therefore will find them less distressing. This recommendation accepts that being able to regulate our feelings is not hard-wired into humans, and therefore will take considerable practice and inevitably will entail many mistakes in the form of lapses (or 'meltdowns').

To be able to defuse emotion, we need some emotional literacy skills. It will help, therefore, to know the difference between thoughts and feelings. This is important for two reasons: first, we mistakenly believe that we cannot control our feelings because these 'just happen'; and second, therefore, we think that other people should change what they are doing when their actions seem to be causing our feelings.

THOUGHTS AND FEELINGS

Thoughts include memories, images, fantasies, beliefs, ideas, attitudes, assumptions, values, goals, plans, visions, dreams, desires, predictions and judgments.[9] Or, put more simply, they are words and images in our mind.

Feelings involve physical sensations (such as a chemical release in the brain and changes to our heart rate, blood pressure and so on). However, we cannot interpret and understand what these physiological changes mean, without *thinking* about the external events going on around us. What we choose to think about those events will determine both the type and intensity of our resulting emotions. In other words, our emotions start with thoughts.

Our understanding of our feelings can get muddled when we mistake thoughts for feelings. One way to tell the difference is that we can non-verbally demonstrate feelings (such as excited, happy or sad), whereas we cannot act out our thoughts. Another way is to identify the three types of 'fake' emotions: demanding thinking, thoughts-in-disguise, and victim language.

Demanding thinking

The first type of fake emotion is generated by *demanding thinking*. This uses words such as '*should, should not, ought, ought not, have to* and *must*' to demand that we or someone else act in particular ways. (Ellis provocatively called this *must*urbating!)

The sequence begins when we experience an original feeling – such as hurt or fear – and then we generate demanding language ('I shouldn't have to put up with *this*'). In turn, this demanding thinking intensifies our original feeling. With our feelings inflamed, we then see threats that do not exist, underestimate our ability to cope, and exaggerate the outcomes of not coping. (Ellis termed this *catastrophising*.)[10] The outcome is that our feelings become more difficult to resolve.

In comparison, thoughts that accurately express our desires are less likely to provoke exaggerated emotions and therefore they make it easier for us to focus on what we need. We may still have unpleasant emotions such as sadness, regret, sorrow, annoyance or frustration, but these are healthy, realistic or 'workable',[11] in that they are more likely to propel us towards solutions. These two pathways are illustrated in Figure 5.1, with common demands listed in Box 5.3.

Some words which indicate that we are adding demands to feelings include:

aghast	appalled	bitter
contemptuous	disappointed	depressed
disgusted	envious	horrified
indignant	jealous	offended
outraged	resentful	revolted
scornful	shocked	sickened
spiteful		

Beneath these experiences is an original feeling, such as hurt or fear, but this emotion becomes exaggerated by our demanding and judgmental thinking. We sometimes even apply judgments to ourselves, such as guilt, shame, judgments of failure or worthlessness; or, their opposites of arrogance, conceit, righteousness, smugness or vanity.

FIGURE 5.1 PATHWAYS TO EMOTION

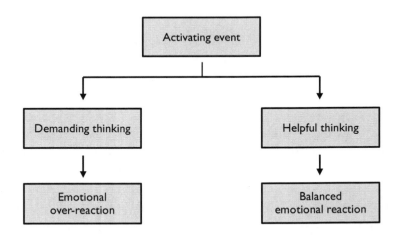

Thoughts in disguise

A second type of fake emotions are what Rosenberg terms *thoughts in disguise*.[12] These are *I-feel* statements that are followed by words such as *that, as if,* or *like*:

Box 5.3 Common demanding thoughts[13]

1. *Demand*: I must be loved, or at least liked, and approved of by everyone I meet. I am bad and unlovable if I get rejected.

   Accurate thought: I want to be loved, liked or approved of by the people who are important to me and I may feel sad and lonely if I am not. However, I can cope with these feelings and take constructive steps to build and keep better relationships, without submerging my own rights.

2. *Demand*: To be worthwhile, I must be completely competent and achieve in every possible way.

   Accurate thought: I would like to do well as a parent, worker, partner, son/daughter, friend. But, like everyone else, I will occasionally make mistakes. I know that I will feel disappointed when I do, but I can cope with these feelings and learn from the experience so that I grow over time.

3. *Demand*: I should have the solution to every problem.

   Accurate thought: I do not know everything. I can open myself up to learn things that I need to know and can apply this knowledge conscientiously and with the courage to be imperfect.

4. *Demand*: Other people in my life must always be happy, or it is my fault.

   Accurate thought: Other people are responsible for their own feelings. I am not responsible if they choose to live unhappy lives.

5. *Demand*:   I should look after others, never myself.

   Accurate thought: Other people will feel disappointed if they want me to do something for them and I do not. They may choose to reject me, but I can cope with my feelings about that and can accept myself and my decision.

6. *Demand*: It is a catastrophe when things aren't how I want them to be. People *must* treat me fairly and give me what I want.

   Accurate thought: It is disappointing, sometimes very disappointing when things aren't how I would like them to be, but I can cope with that. I can take steps to change my circumstances and manage my own thinking so that I do not exaggerate or catastrophise my disappointment.

7. *Demand*: If there is ever anything to be done, I must not relax until it is completed.

   Accurate thought: I am allowed to rest when I wish.

8. *Demand*: I should worry a good deal about anything that could go wrong for me or other people in my life.

   Accurate thought: Worrying about things that could go wrong will not stop them from happening. I can prepare for possible problems without dwelling on them, can live without guarantees, and can focus on the good that is present in my life now.

BOX 5.3 COMMON DEMANDING THOUGHTS *(cont'd)*

9. *Demand*: I need someone stronger than myself to rely on. I cannot survive alone.

   Accurate thought: I like to have support from other people when I want it, although I can survive on my own. The only person on whom I need to rely is myself.

10. *Demand*: I have problems now because of what happened to me in the past. That is outside my control, so little can be done about it now.

    Accurate thought: I cannot change events in the past but I can control how I think about them now so that I grow in ways that will be effective and rewarding for me.

> I feel *that* I'm being asked to do too much.
> I feel *as if* I'm the only one willing to go the extra mile.
> I feel *like* I'm under pressure.

One way to tell that these are not feelings is that we could not mime them or act them out in a game of charades. Another is that they would make just as much sense if we said:

> I *believe* that I'm being asked to do too much.
> I *consider* that I'm the only one willing to go the extra mile.
> I *am* under pressure.

When we give these statements the status of feelings, we believe that we are justified to act on them and to make others suffer for 'causing' them. Instead, we must realise that these are only thoughts, which we have chosen to invite in and entertain.

Victim language

The third type of thinking that generates excessive or fake emotion is when we focus on how others 'should' be treating us. These thoughts place us in the role of victim and give power to others by placing them in the role of the enemy or our oppressor. Victim language makes us a prisoner of our own thinking and includes words such as:

abandoned	abused	attacked
betrayed	bullied	cheated
coerced	condemned	cornered
deserted	distrusted	dominated
ignored	imposed upon	intimidated

invisible	isolated	left out
let down	manipulated	misunderstood
neglected	overworked	patronised
persecuted	pressured	provoked
put down	rejected	rushed
taken for granted	threatened	trapped
unappreciated	unfair	unheard
unseen	unwanted	used

This victim language cons us into thinking that other people 'make' us feel as we do and therefore are to blame for our misery. When we believe this, we try to make them stop it; believe that they deserve to be punished for what they are doing; and exaggerate the outcomes if they don't stop. Instead, how we *feel* about others' actions depends on what we *think* about these. We have a choice about the thoughts we invite into our heads. This choice is liberating and will not breed resentment of others.

BOX 5.4 EXAMPLES OF THOUGHTS AND FEELINGS

Feeling in disguise	Actual feeling
I feel that you should tidy your room.	I am frustrated at this mess.
I feel like a failure.	I am disappointed in myself.
I feel as if I have to do everything around here.	I am exhausted.
I feel that she is being bossy.	I am annoyed that I'm not allowed to make my own decisions.

LISTENING SKILLS

When we want to understand children and what they are feeling, we will need to listen to them. True listening requires generosity, because it is something we do for someone else; it takes willingness to see another's point of view, particularly with younger children who might lack a vocabulary to describe their feelings; it takes patience to decipher more than the verbal messages alone; and it takes courage, as we might hear something that causes us some discomfort.[14] It also requires us to abandon the notion that we are responsible for our children's feelings and the idea that we are the boss, so that we don't try to impose solutions on children to 'fix' their problems. We need to be able to let go of the impulse to manage their lives for them and to recognise that there are many strategies for meeting the same needs.

Listening is essential when children are talking or behaving in ways that signal that they have a problem. This is true even when the way they are communicating their feelings upsets us – say, when they are being aggressive, disrupting an activity or inconveniencing us. Listening works even in these circumstances because it sets up a conciliatory relationship that helps children to discharge their strong feelings and to think through their emotions to achieve a resolution. This has the added side-benefit of ensuring that they return to considerate behaviour, which meets our needs.

Conditions needed for listening

Listening to young people requires, first, that they are not so upset that they cannot talk yet and, for our part, that we accept children as people and are willing to allow them to be themselves and to feel whatever they do.[15] As I mentioned in chapter 1, this attitude reflects our commitment to granting children the freedom to be themselves. Second, we need to intend to empower children's own problem solving, rather than instructing, compelling, advising, or solving children's problems for them.

Third, we will need to be able to manage our own emotional reactions. When our children are in pain, as mammals it is our job to get feral and to try to protect them. However, we need to rein in these feelings so that we can focus on the children, not ourselves. We might need to deal with our own emotions – but later.[16] In the meantime, we can console ourselves with the knowledge that pain does not equal trauma. With support, children will be resilient. Our fear on their behalf is justified only if they lack that support.

When children's feelings and needs give rise to thoughtless behaviour, we have to resist judging either the children or their actions. Instead, we need to silently empathise with ourselves so that we can identify what our feelings are telling us about which need of ours is not being met. If we feel annoyed, it might be that our need for a sense of order and control (autonomy) is not being met; while anger means that there is an original unmet need, plus demanding thinking that is inflaming our emotions. (I talk more about anger in chapter 8.)

With our own feelings under control, we will be able listen, rather than talk. If listening fails, it is seldom because we have listened too much and more commonly because we have done most of the talking.[17]

Listening skill 1: Attention

When you want your children to know that you are paying attention to them, you will need to use the following skills.[18]

- Define your availability: if you cannot talk then, make a commitment to discuss their concerns later.

- Create a suitable space, with privacy and minimal distractions.

- Be present: As Rosenberg advises, don't just do something, *stand there*.[19]

- Tune in and attend to the most immediate needs first, connecting to what is alive for the child in the moment.

- Maintain appropriate eye contact and assume a posture that communicates non-verbally that you are paying attention, such as by matching the child's tone of voice, gestures or facial expression.

Listening skill 2: Empathy

Empathy is a respectful understanding of what another person is feeling.[20] It is being connected to their experiences, feelings and needs. As I mentioned earlier, it is easier to be empathic when children are sad or distressed, but you also need to be accepting and empathic when they are acting in ways that are inconvenient for you. Even disruptive behaviour is an attempt to meet a need, while its intensity tells you how important that need is to the child at this time.

When we offer children compassion, help and connection, they will feel understood, will experience a release of their pent-up feelings and will become familiar with what it is like to receive empathy. The result will be that, in turn, they are more likely to offer this to others.

BOX 5.5 LISTENING TO CHILDREN'S PHYSICAL PAIN

When children have hurt themselves, they cry to tell us that they are in pain. But because their pain hurts us too, we might scold them: 'I told you to be careful' (even though we know that accidents can still happen even when people are careful) or tell them not to cry. As a result, they can feel criticised and not receive the comfort they need. Instead, you can:

- Acknowledge that it hurts: say so.

- Tell them that it will hurt for a while. Because they know this to be true, they will believe the next thing you say.

- Point out how strong and healthy they are, or that they have 'good, red blood'. This tells you that they will heal quickly and the pain will go.

When you can accept their experience and their right to express their feelings, they will feel safe, will know that they can trust you to be there for them and, with your support, will have learned that in future they can recover from hurt.

Listening skill 3: Decoding

Behaviour is children's loudest form of communication. Therefore, instead of focusing on *what* they are doing, we need instead to care about *why*. Or, more specifically, on the understandings that all behaviour is an attempt to meet a need, and that needs are always legitimate, our task is to discover what need they are trying to satisfy.[21] Once you know what need inspired the behaviour, it will be easier to find a different strategy for meeting that need.

Listening skill 4: Reflection

Listening entails being reflective, in two senses. First, like a mirror, we will reflect what the other person feels and needs; and, second, listening requires us to be in a reflective, contemplative frame of mind that accepts others and 'lets them be'.[22]

BOX 5.6 STEPS FOR GIVING EMPATHY[23]

Inner processing

Step 1. Be present. Focus on the child's needs. At the moment, it is not about you. Connect with what is alive in the child at the moment.

Step 2. Observe without judgment so that you can form a careful, tentative impression of what the child might be experiencing and needing.

Give empathy outwards

Step 3. Connect with the child's needs and feelings. Use minimal encouragers and reflection to gain a deeper understanding of the needs, values and feelings that the child is expressing. (Some tips are given in Boxes 5.7 to 5.9.) You might ask, 'Do you feel (x) because you (need, hope or value y?' Verify if your guess is accurate. The message here is that you want to be sure that you understand what the child needs. Even when your guess is slightly off target, it will still be helpful because it demonstrates that you care and it helps children to think through and understand their feelings.

Step 5. Check. Keep reflecting your impression of what the children feel and need, until they give off a sense of relief and are quietened. These two signs mean that they have received the empathy they require. Once the relief is felt, check with them, 'Is there more that you'd like to say?' Shift your attention away slowly. Move on only once you are sure that they are finished.

Step 5. Identify the child's request. When individuals are upset, they want to know that they have been understood. Therefore, to signal your understanding, you can ask, 'Right now would you like...?' or 'Would you like to hear what I think about what you said?'.

Occasionally, children will want some advice. However, our almost reflexive impulse to solve children's problems for them means that we will probably be too quick to give advice. Therefore, Rosenberg recommends that we should never give advice to children unless they request it in writing, with a lawyer's signature![24]

When reflecting, we must always focus on the child's own experience, rather than on the actions of others. For example, instead of saying, 'Samantha is mean, isn't she?', reflect what the upset child *needs:* 'Sounds like you want Samantha to let you play because you need to be part of the fun'.

BARRIERS TO COMMUNICATION

In summary, listening requires that we accept children, their feelings and needs; empathise with these; attend to what they are telling us, decode their message when it is disguised or unclear, and reflect the meaning and content of what they are telling us.

Sometimes, however, although we intend to listen and think that's what we're doing, we are actually responding in ways that shut down communication and discourage our children from talking with us. Tom Gordon identified twelve of these common habits, which he termed 'roadblocks' to communication. They form three clusters: judging children, attempting to fix their problem, and avoiding feelings.[25] These barriers to communication send children the following messages.

- I don't validate you ('Don't be silly').
- I won't validate you ('I don't care…').
- I want you to be someone else ('Your brother is so clever at this.').
- I want you to feel differently ('Don't worry').
- I want you to *be* different ('If you were more careful, it wouldn't have happened').
- I know better than you what you need.

Mostly when we use barriers to communication, we don't intend to be destructive. Most of our errors come about with good intentions, in

---

BOX 5.7 COLLOQUIAL REFLECTION OF NEEDS[26]

Need	Reflection
Acceptance	You'd like people to accept you just as you are?
Autonomy	You'd like some choice about what you do?
Belonging	You want to be part of the group?
Consistency, order	You want to be able to count on things happening when you need them to?
Contribution	You'd like to be able to help/share?
Ease	You need this to be easier for you?
Inclusion	You want to be part of what's happening?
Mourning	You need to show how sad you're feeling?
Purpose	You want something worthwhile to do?
Security	You need to know that you're going to be okay?
Self-esteem	You want to feel good about yourself?
Validation	You want to be heard how special (or hard) this is for you?

that we falsely believe that we can only be helpful if we know all the answers, come up with the solutions ourselves, or make the other person feel better.[27] As a result of these false beliefs, we use fake listening skills that become habitual because:

- we are repeating how our parents and other adults spoke to us when we were children
- we may be down on our reserves at the time and, rather than telling children that we feel exhausted, we instead tell them about themselves.
- we might falsely believe that criticism will motivate children to mend their ways
- we want to prove that we are right.

The roadblocks imply that we want to change or influence our children to act differently. They disrespect children by telling them what they are and are not experiencing and feeling.[28] In turn, the children can experience this lack of listening as threatening, manipulative, frustrating or condescending. As a result, they may avoid telling us anything personal. But, even more important, the roadblocks miss an opportunity to help children when they are in need.

Accordingly, the problem can escalate in three vital ways. First, when young people feel misunderstood, they can become even more distressed and out of control of their emotions. Second, our impatient or intolerant responses convey subtle negative judgments which children will resent. Third, by communicating that we do not understand, children are left with their original feelings, plus the sense that they have no support. The resulting fear, shame or panic will add to the intensity of their original emotion.

BOX 5.8 TIPS FOR REFLECTION[29]

- Listen for the thoughts, feelings and meaning behind what the children are saying.

- Encourage them to continue talking, using silence and minimal encouragers ('Mmm... Uh-huh... Okay... And..?')

- Reflect the need underlying the feeling: 'Because of... you need...'

- Sum up what the children said, translating it into your own words, to make it clearer and more real.

- Check that you have understood and interpreted the children's meaning accurately.

- Reassure children that they are being heard, that you 'get it'.

- When children are expressing mixed feelings or separate ideas, include them all: 'You feel... and you also feel... (because you need...)'

- Vary your reflective statements. Do not use the same phrase, e.g. 'What I hear you saying is...' or 'So you need...'. Repeated formulaic responses can be perceived as a maddening word game.

- Ask very few questions — especially ones that call for a yes/no answer — because questions will direct, rather than follow, what the children say, and can make them feel that they are being subjected to an inquisition instead of being listened to.

- Avoid attempts to diagnose or interpret what the children are feeling, because interpretations are intellectual tools that distance us from being present and prevent us from offering emotional connection (empathy).

As I mentioned a moment ago, the three barriers or roadblocks to communication are: judging or inducing shame; sending solutions or attempting to fix a problem; and avoidance.

Judging/Inducing shame

This first group of communication barriers involve judging children, comparing their behaviour with our own internal standards of rightness and wrongness. The judgmental responses interfere with expressing compassion and therefore damage our relationship with our children. They can have devastating effects on children's self-esteem because they induce shame and make children afraid of getting things wrong and of being reprimanded.

> **Box 5.9 USEFUL REFLECTIVE PHRASES**[30]
>
> When you think you understand the child accurately, you might use reflective statements that start with:
>
> - It seems that you need...
> - It sounds like you feel...
> - Are you feeling... because you need...
> - From your point of view...
> - You're feeling... (name the emotion)
> - You believe...
> - You mean that...
> - In other words...
>
> When you are not certain that you understand the child accurately, use your ignorance constructively, trying reflective statements that start with:
>
> - Let's see if I understand: you feel...
> - I get the impression that you need...
> - Is that what you mean?
> - I'm sorry. I'm lost. Tell me again.
> - Do you feel...?
> - Maybe I've misunderstood, but it seems...
> - Is it possible that...
> - Maybe it seems to you that...
> - Maybe you need...
> - Perhaps you're feeling...
> - You seem to be feeling...
> - It appears that you need...
> - What I think you're saying is...

The four judgmental roadblocks are the following.

Criticising, blaming, name calling, comparing children negatively to others, *ridiculing,* and *making fun* of children all communicate to them that they are unloved, unworthy or not good enough. If the children believe these disparaging comments, the labels can become like seeds in children's minds[31] that grow into self-doubts that eat away at their self-esteem. Alternatively, they might retaliate against the criticism and 'answer back'. Sometimes, we use ridicule if the children challenge our negative messages. Examples of negative judgments include:

- You never do anything. You're too lazy for your own good!
- Don't be ridiculous.

- Give that back, you selfish little brat.
- You're acting like a baby.
- You can't take a joke, can you?
- Don't be silly. I didn't mean it.

Emotional blackmail or *martyrdom* tries to blame and induce guilt in children for how we feel. It overwhelms children with responsibility for things over which they have no control and therefore they feel powerless; alternatively, they reject the implication of fault and, with it, the person who is blameful. Examples include:

- Look how angry you've got me!
- It makes me sad when you do that.
- How could you put me to so much work?

Praising or *agreeing with* children is patronising, manipulates children into behaving the way we want and creates anxiety and fear of criticism in children, in case in future they don't live up to our standards. Examples include:

- You're such a good child that I know you'll do the right thing.
- You're so clever. I know you'll figure it out.

Diagnosing, analysing or *interpreting* what children are experiencing is an attempt to tell them what their 'real' problem is, ignoring their experience of it. This can be threatening and frustrating, causing children to feel trapped, exposed, misunderstood or disbelieved. They can become afraid to say anything in case it is turned around and used against them. Examples include:

- Maybe you're just still upset over what he said to you yesterday.
- Perhaps you're jealous that she was playing with someone else?

Sending solutions (fixing)

The second group of communication barriers involve telling children what they should do about their problem. Mammals are *supposed* to protect their young from threat or pain. This means that, when children are hurting, we will want to leap in and solve the problem for them. This is natural. However, we will need to deal with those feelings later.[32]   Right now we need to rein in the temptation; otherwise, we will limit children's growth and confidence in their ability to solve their own problems. (That is, it affects their self-efficacy – see chapter 4). Also, solving problems can *be* a problem because it does not resolve the original difficulty. Giving your solutions takes the following five forms.

Ordering, directing, commanding or *demanding* that children stop feeling or doing something, tells them that their needs aren't important and that you do not care about their objections. Given that your solutions are often backed by coercion, they demonstrate that you do not accept or respect children, and imply that their judgment is unsound. Examples include:

- Do it now – *or else*!
- I don't want to have to tell you again!
- I don't care what you want: you're going to your grandmother's!

Threatening, warning or *delivering negative prophecies* will make children feel unaccepted, scared and meek; or, alternatively, resentful to the extent that they are prepared to test us to see if we will carry out our threat. Threats and ultimatums also remind children that they are not living up to our expectations. Examples include:

- If I have to talk to you children about this again, I'll take the computer off both of you.
- Be careful! You'll fall!
- You'll never make any friends if you keep this up.

Preaching or *moralising* are an attempt to tell children that they should feel differently while at the same time 'putting a halo' around our advice, giving it moral authority.[33] This can make children feel guilty, and implies that that they do not know right from wrong. As a result, they will either retreat or become defensive, with reactions such as, 'Who says I have to?' or 'You shouldn't either'. Examples of preaching include:

- You ought to know better.
- That wasn't very nice. How would you like it if someone did that to you?
- What you have to understand is that other people have rights too.

Interrogating, probing, questioning or *grilling* involve asking children a series of questions aimed at 'getting to the bottom' of the problem so that you can find a solution to it, instead of trusting children to find their own. In response to an interrogation, children will withhold information for fear that what they say will get them into trouble or will lead to being told what to do. They learn not to disclose anything significant or to tell half-truths or lies. If they are not sure where we are going with our questions, they feel intimidated and scared, while losing sight of the original problem. Examples include:

- What's making you so upset, do you think?
- How long has this been going on?
- Are you sure that's what she meant?
- What started it?

Giving advice is an attempt to impose a positive solution. Although the advice is meant positively, it tells children to get over their feelings before they are ready. And, because you did not wait to hear what the real problem was, advice demonstrates that you are not listening: if the answer were that obvious, they would have thought of it already. But at the same time, children are unlikely to follow your suggestion because it wasn't their idea. In turn, this means that you will have to enforce your solution, which the children will resent.

Giving advice also devalues the problem-solving skills that children already possess and deprives them of an opportunity to practise solving problems, which can make children dependent. (Bolton calls giving advice an 'interfere-iority complex'.)[34] Examples include:

- How about you do...?
- I think you should try...
- What if you did...?
- What you ought to do is...

Avoidance

A third and final group of roadblocks tries to avoid the other person's feelings, usually because these upset or irritate us. However, when we avoid their feelings, children receive the message that it is not alright to be upset and we deprive them of the opportunity to resolve their emotions. Avoidance also implies that their problems are not real or important, and stops them from being open with us about their concerns. If we use avoidance often, children learn not to tell us about what matters to them in their lives. The three avoidance methods are the following.

Distracting, diverting, trivialising, story telling, one-upping and *'me-too'isms* make light of children's problems and imply that if something is too hard, we should avoid it. Examples include:

- Try thinking of something cheerful so you feel better.
- I had that happen to me when I was your age.
- Don't worry. Be happy.
- You think *you've* had a bad day? *Try mine!*

Persuasion, education or *logical argument* can generate more argument, or cause children to switch off and stop listening to us. It sends the message: 'Don't feel: think'. Examples include:

- You know you'll enjoy it once you get there.
- If you got ready on time, we wouldn't have this last-minute rush.
- Give it a try. It will probably be more fun than you think.

Reassuring, sympathising, commiserating or *consoling* cause children to feel misunderstood and alone – that is, feeling unsupported adds a second layer of emotion to the original feeling. Examples include:

- Cheer up!
- You'll feel better in the morning.
- That's really too bad. You poor thing.
- At least it could be worse.

Guilt and blame. Robert Bolton, who wrote one of my favourite books on communication skills, added a thirteenth communication roadblock to Gordon's 'dirty dozen'.[35] He says that accusing other people of using the roadblocks on us (blaming them), or feeling guilty ourselves for using them, is itself a barrier to communication. If while reading this section, you (like most of us) have been groaning as you recognise yourself in this list, take heart. Just as your muscles grow stronger with exercise, so too your listening skills will improve with practice. But, instead of trying to change all of your habits at once, you could notice the roadblock that you use most, and work on using that one less often. Then work on your others in turn. As Calvin Coolidge said, 'You can't do everything at once – but you can do something at once'.[36]

LISTENING TO CHILDREN'S ANGER

Sometimes children will declare that we never listen to them, that they hate us, or that we are the worst parent in the whole world. It is tempting to dispute the facts (Don't be silly: Have you met every parent in the whole world to know that I'm the worst?') or to dispute their accusations (e.g. by responding to 'You never let me do anything I want!' by pointing out an instance where indeed you did give them something that they wanted). However, this focus on the surface invalidates children and dismisses their feelings.

Instead, we need to translate children's anger into a message about their needs. For example, when they say, 'I hate you', this means that they are feeling angry because their needs are not being met, and that they do not know how to meet their needs at the same time as keeping us happy with them.[37]

NEEDS VERSUS STRATEGIES

By now you are familiar with the idea that at all times, every one of us is attempting to meet our needs. Most conflict with others comes about because the strategy they are using to meet their needs happens to block our ability to meet ours. In that case, the solution is not to abandon or compromise our needs, but to identify the need that the strategy is intended to satisfy, then replace that strategy with a different one that does not hinder us but still satisfies the other's need.

Sometimes, when children express a need, such as, 'I need you two to get back together' (when the parents have divorced), we can feel stuck because we can't do what they say they need. But reuniting is not the need, it is the *strategy* for meeting the need. In that case, you can ask about the need:

- In what way would (us getting back together) be good for you?
- How would that help you?

The young person might respond, for example, that it would 'make us a family again', which tells us that he or she feels that the family as it is now is broken or fractured somehow. So our next step is to ask what other things could happen that would help the child to feel that it is a family again, even though you remain separated as a couple.

CONCLUSION

Listening is not just an added skill, but a way of *being* a parent. It demonstrates to children that we value them. Listening to them affirms that we accept both them and what they feel – even when we do not understand why they feel as they do. This is the foundation of a strong sense of worth. Children will possess a certainty that they and their feelings are valid and that they can express what they want and need without fear of judgment. As a result of being heard, they will come to understand and be able to manage their own emotional life.

Nevertheless, listening is not appropriate for every situation. Sometimes, children just want a straightforward answer to a question such as, 'Have you seen my phone?'. When all they want is information, reflecting that they seem worried about the whereabouts of their phone will just enrage them.

Another occasion when listening is not relevant is when the children are too upset to talk right now, or it is not a pressing problem and they need to get on with something else. Or, we ourselves might not be in a frame of mind to listen to them, which makes it more likely that we will try to impose our own agenda on them or will become angry or irritated by their problem.

The last circumstance when listening is not appropriate is when something someone else is doing is violating our own needs, in which case we will need to be assertive. The even more likely scenario is that neither of us is getting our needs met, in which case we will need to solve the problem collaboratively. I describe those two communication skills in chapter 7. Prior to that, we need to understand the origins of children's disruptive behaviours, which I outline in the next chapter.

SUMMARY OF PRINCIPLES

- Respect is something adults earn through being respectful towards children and making wise decisions that can be admired.

- Our feelings are our allies: they mobilise us to take action to meet our needs.
- When we focus on how other people 'should' be treating us, we place them in the role of our enemy or oppressor.
- When we validate even negative feelings, we teach children that all emotions are valid – indeed, that *they* are valid.
- Little people have big feelings.
- Developing self-regulation takes practice. Children are still learning it.
- When listening, don't just do something: stand there.
- We can't do everything at once, but we can do something at once.

Origins of disruptive behaviours 6

Every behaviour is an attempt to meet a need. This is the chant that we have to repeat over and over to ourselves, especially when something our child is doing is troubling us: *Every behaviour is an attempt to meet a need.*

Guidance focuses on needs. Therefore, in this chapter I outline what I have learned about the needs that trigger children's disruptive behaviours. For one-off events, you can ask the child – or for pre-verbal children, you could mentally scan the list of needs in Box 3.1 – to determine what need might be behind a given behaviour. In this chapter, however, I focus mainly on the causes of persistent behavioural difficulties.

A focus on needs means that we will avoid judgment. The default stance of the judge is to establish who is at fault. Driven by the need to be correct rather than to connect, compassion and safety are lost when we judge, and is replaced with a climate of fear.[1] Therefore, in order to understand children's behaviours, we need to observe rather than judge these.

OBSERVATIONS VERSUS JUDGMENTS

We are genetically wired to try to make sense of the world around us so that life is predictable. This tendency means that we interpret outside events and other people's behaviour before deciding how to respond to it. However, our interpretations go through a number of filters, as it were: our emotions at the time colour how we interpret events, our previous experience leads to biases in our interpretations, and our beliefs (especially our demanding thoughts) cause us to judge rather than merely to observe events.

In chapter 4, I argued for eliminating praise and other rewards because, although intended positively, these judge children. I recommended replacing judgmental messages with information about children's accomplishments, which I termed *acknowledgment*. Here, the focus is on replacing negative judgments with pure observation. The aim is to understand the need behind a particular behaviour.

Under a controlling style, when children are disobedient, we become judgmental: caught up in black-and-white thinking about right versus wrong, moral versus immoral, correct versus incorrect, proper versus improper, and so on. We get all puffed up by moral outrage, on the assumption that the children are being willfully defiant and that they 'should' know better. This sort of thinking refers to thoughtless behaviour as *inappropriate, misbehaviour, naughty, bad,* or *unacceptable*. Other judgmental words include:

attention seeking	bad mannered	bossy
bullying	destructive	evil
horrible	inconsiderate	irresponsible
lazy	manipulative	mean
messy	nasty	rude
stupid	thoughtless	wasteful

This language alone will set us down a path of trying to punish children for their actions. Yet adults who use judgmental language about children's behaviour don't label their spelling mistakes (for example) as inappropriate, misbehaviour, naughty, bad, or unacceptable. A grade two teacher *understands* that spelling mistakes are inevitable at that age. At the same time, though, she doesn't leave it at that. She doesn't tell the children's parents: 'I'm sorry to report that your children can't spell properly. So my plan is to wait the year and hope they outgrow it'. Instead, in the knowledge that learning to spell is a useful skill, the teacher sets about teaching it.

This teaching will include correcting mistakes. But how we correct the likes of spelling mistakes is often very different from how we correct behaviours. Let's imagine that a child has misspelled a word: *recieve*. In that case, the teacher doesn't reprimand:

> Now LISTEN HERE! *How many times* do I have to tell you that, for the sound ee, i comes before e except after c? Now, go and sit on that chair over there and think about what you've done wrong. When you're ready to apologise, you can come back and talk to me about it.

> But, after today, I don't want to have to speak to you about this again. *Am I making myself clear?*

Although this is a parody, I'm sure that, like me, you have heard some adults reprimand children in this way about their behaviours (even if only in a shopping centre). But we don't reprimand children like this when they make developmental errors. I've never heard the parent of a toddler say:

> Look at yourself: falling over every five steps! Do you see *me* falling over every five steps? Now, go and sit over there on that chair until you can get your balance. I'm sick of looking at you!

We never chastise children like this for their developmental mistakes, because we understand that these are natural. Guidance understands that behavioural mistakes are natural too.

Box 6.1 lists the opposite attitudes that we have to developmental versus behavioural errors. Some examples might help illustrate the difference. First, when a child is learning to ride a two-wheeler bike, falls off and skins her knee and we give her a bandaid, we don't see this as an instance of 'bandaid-seeking behaviour'. We don't punish her, but accept the mistake for what it is – a lack of skill – and offer more opportunities to practice. The mistake is an accident. But when two children are having trouble taking turns, we assume that, because we have to step in to them to help them sort it out, they are doing it deliberately to get our attention. This is a case of confusing motive with outcome: the *outcome* might be a bandaid or parental attention, but the *motive* in both cases is just a lack of skill.

Second, when an eight-year-old is learning to play the piano, we know that he will need many lessons and lots of practice and will inevitably make many, many mistakes before becoming a virtuoso. But when the same child is learning to share (for example), we assume that he should not need to be taught it, he should not need to practise it to get it right, and he should never make mistakes.

Third, when children are learning about their physical world, we know that they need to explore: to find out how frogs feel on their hands, discover how damp sand has to be for a sandcastle to stay put, and find out what dirt taste like. But in their social world, we think they should not explore what we stand for, but should simply *know* what we expect of them.

Fourth, when a child with a significant vision impairment was enrolling in an educational program, her teachers would ask her parents about her residual vision: what kind of lighting helps her to see best?... What distance should she sit from the teacher at group times?... Does she have enough vision to notice hazards or do they have to clear the walkways of small blocks and vehicles so that she does not trip over them? In other words, when children have a developmental disability, we do as much as we can to adjust the environment to help children to function despite their impairment.

Box 6.1 ATTITUDES TO DEVELOPMENTAL VERSUS BEHAVIOURAL ERRORS

Developmental errors	Behavioural errors
Children are trying to get things right; any errors are accidental.	Children are trying to get things wrong; their errors are deliberate.
Errors are inevitable.	Mistakes should not happen.
Learning requires exploration.	Children should not explore limits: they should obey them.
Children who have learning difficulties need extra support.	Children who have behavioural difficulties should be punished.

But when children have a behavioural difficulty – say, impulsiveness – instead of adjusting the *environment* to make it easier for that child to function, we usually try to change the *child*, to make him stop the behaviour. I've heard many adults say to impulsive children, 'Oh, James! For goodness' sake, *control yourself!*'. This is equivalent to saying to the child who is blind, 'Oh, Amy! For goodness' sake, *use your eyes!*'.

Amy would use her eyes if she could... and the impulsive child would control his impulses if he could. But, whereas we assume that children with developmental difficulties cannot help it, we believe that children with behavioural difficulties are doing it deliberately – and then we set about punishing them to make them stop.

In contrast, whatever the type of mistake (behavioural or developmental), guidance adopts the same compassionate understanding.[2] It accepts that everyone does the best they can and that, like us, children are just trying to meet their needs. Instead of judging them for using a strategy that happens to bother us, we use compassion and listen for the need behind the behaviour.

Instead of judging, our job when trying to understand children's behaviour is to observe what actually happened, to describe what onlookers would see or hear. The clue to the distinction between judgments and observations can be what a videocamera would record, as that would record events without evaluation.

> Observing without evaluating
> is the highest form of sensitivity and intelligence.[3]

Avoiding judgments does not mean, however, that we tolerate every behaviour: that would be permissiveness, not guidance. When our goal is to teach children to be considerate, we should not tolerate inconsiderate behaviour. Doing so could teach the children an antisocial habit, attract for them a negative reputation, and unfairly inflict their behaviour on others. If they are behaving thoughtlessly, we have to find a solution to it – but without blaming them for it.

IDENTIFYING THE SOURCE OF CHILDREN'S OUTBURSTS

The controlling style believes that children behave disruptively because of consequences:

- Desired behaviours are not being rewarded enough. Controlling discipline has a slogan that you must 'Catch children being good' and reward this. The assumption, of course, is that children would not think to repeat the behaviour unless we manipulated them into doing so.
- Undesired behaviours are not being punished enough.
- Undesired behaviours are accidentally receiving rewards (e.g. attention).

This faith that behaviours are being caused by the rewards and punishments that they attract is actually based on an error in logic. This error is illustrated by the example that if some medication helps your headache, you nevertheless don't assume that your headache was caused by a lack of medication. Similarly, if consequences bring about a change in children's behaviour, this does not mean that the behaviour was being caused by the consequences that were in place at the time the behaviour began.

Instead, guidance believes (as I have repeated already) that every behaviour is an attempt to meet a need. The question here is why children are repeatedly acting in disruptive ways, when there are more positive ways to meet their needs. In that case, we can use Figure 6.1 as a guide to identify what might be going on for them.

FIGURE 6.1 THE SOURCES OF BEHAVIOURAL OUTBURSTS

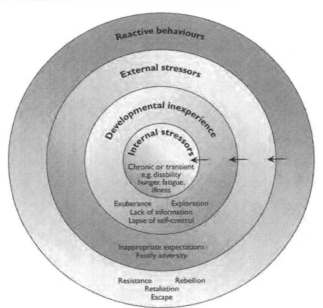

Reactive behaviours

Working from the outer circle of Figure 6.1 inwards, we will start by asking whether children who are displaying repeated emotional or behavioural difficulties could be protesting about our efforts to control them. We start here because my research showed that this is the most common cause of children's disruptive behaviours.[4]

These behaviours are children's reactions to how adults handle an original incident. In my research, I discovered that when adults used guidance methods, the incident was usually resolved peaceably. However, when the adults tried to punish children for the original behaviour, the children would respond in ways that 50 years ago Tom Gordon labelled as the *Three Rs*: the children *r*esisted, *r*ebelled and *r*etaliated. Then they would escape.[5]

Box 6.2 gives an example of one of the incidents that I witnessed during my research. The teachers' explanation for this sequence was that the child had (in fact *was*) a behaviour problem. However, my interpretation was that Katy was being fidgety because she was a four-year-old with a four-year-old's attention span. Her teachers could have honoured that by inviting her to leave the group session once she had had enough. Instead, they tried to punish her with time out.

When I saw scenarios such as the story in Box 6.2 being played out over and over again during my research observations, I realised that, whereas adults might get away with using controls with compliant children, the controlling style leads to escalating difficulties with that group of children whom we might call *spirited*.

To explain these children, we need to recall what we know about children's emotional needs. Referring back to Figure 3.1 (on page 50), it shows us that our self-esteem is an amalgam of our sense of belonging and our ability to be in command of our own lives (autonomy). As I mentioned in chapter 3, substantial research has shown that these three needs are universal.

In contrast, what I'm about to tell you next has not been researched. It is simply my experience – namely, that we can divide the population into an 80/20 split. (The proportions differ between cultures, but the exact numbers aren't important: it's the distinction that matters.)

That is to say, 80 percent of children gain most of their self-esteem from having their belonging needs met. These children want you to like them and will behave well most of the time for fear of disappointing you. (You might find it useful to think of their self-esteem branch in Figure 3.1 (on page 50) leaning over to the left, because the main source of their self-esteem is belonging.) When they do make the occasional behavioural mistake, they are upset, are remorseful, and are willing to make amends. These children do not need punishment to 'teach them a lesson' – because they have already learned from what happened.

In contrast are the (roughly) 20 percent of non-conformist or *spirited* children whose self-esteem comes mainly from being in command of their own lives. (You might find it useful to think of their self-esteem branch in Figure 3.1 (on page 50) leaning over to the right, because the main source of their self-esteem is autonomy.) These spirited children are willing to risk your displeasure to prove to you that you can't make them do stuff. Their mantras are:

BOX 6.2 A TALE OF A SPIRITED CHILD

During a group story session at preschool, a child (I'll call her Katy) became fidgety once her attention span had been exceeded. The teacher who was leading the session repeatedly reminded Katy to sit still and to keep her hands to herself. Finally, in exasperation, the teacher told Katy to go to the time out chair at the side of the room, until she was 'willing to listen' to the teacher.

At that point, being about as eager to be humiliated in front of her peers as you or I would be, Katy flopped onto the floor. (When young children don't want to move, they can impersonate a puddle.) Seeing that Katy was refusing to move and fearing the disruption to the rest of the group, the boundary rider came forward (that is, the teacher at the back of the group making children stay there when it was the last place they wanted to be). This teacher tried to cajole Katy to go to the chair. At this point, Katy declared, 'I'm not going! You can't make me!'. In desperation, the teacher eventually tried to drag Katy to the chair, upon which Katy hit out at her. Not being paid enough to put up with *that*, the teacher let Katy go. Now free, Katy ran away, with the teacher in hot pursuit.

Meanwhile, the other four-year-olds had the options of either listening to one more verse of 'Twinkle, twinkle' – or watching this circus. No points for guessing what their vote was. The result was that group time completely disintegrated.

Freed now to help her colleague, the group leader also set off in pursuit of Katy. But to Kate's relief, when she reached the back of the room, she discovered a large table and dived under it, refusing to come out.

Now, in the belief that children listen with their eyes, the teachers wanted to pull Katy out to give her a stern talking to. And that might have worked, except that it was summertime. You might wonder what the climate has to do with all this. Well, in summer, we tend to wear short-sleeves shirts – and if you place bare forearms near a child who is this upset, you will be pinched, spat on, and scratched. When this inevitably happened, the teachers turned to me and announced, 'You see? She's a behaviour problem!'.

- You're not the boss of me!
- You can't make me.
- You can't stop me.

As I've mentioned, 'belongers' don't need punishment because they are already remorseful and if you were to use it, its side-effects would be fear of abandonment and dependence. On the other hand, spirited children don't profit from punishment. When we we try to control spirited children, their behaviour deteriorates – and rapidly. We get into a 'dance' of escalating coercion on our part being met by escalating defiance on theirs. This is illustrated in Figure 6.2.

FIGURE 6.2 THE 'DANCE' OF ESCALATING COERCION AND DEFIANCE

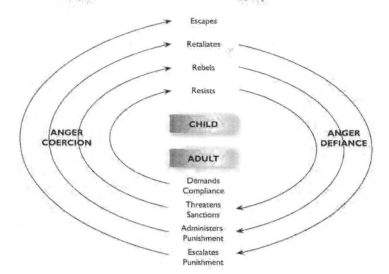

In this dance, we insist that children do things our way and they resist... So we threaten some form of sanction, and they rebel... In response, we administer a punishment, and they retaliate... Until, finally, we escalate the punishment, and they escape if not physically at least emotionally: they stop listening to us. The interaction becomes more unmanageable – perhaps even to the point of labelling the child as having 'Oppositional-defiance disorder'. However, the problem is not the dancers: *it's the dance*. That is, the problem is not the child, and it is not you: it's your coercive interaction pattern. Research is very clear on this: children are not born inherently oppositional; they become so when parents use restrictive control over them.[6]

We see this in the story in Box 6.2. Instead of inviting Katy to leave the group session once her attention span had been exceeded, her teachers tried to punish her for having the attention skills of a four-year-old. Once they tried to punish her, Katy did exactly as Tom Gordon predicted (and I love it when four-year-olds have read the same text books as me): she refused to leave the group (resistance), declared that the adults couldn't make her (rebellion), hit out at them (retaliation), and then ran away (escape). She did not have a behavioural problem: she was a spirited child – that is, one for whom autonomy is her main need – who therefore was reacting against attempts by the adults to control her.

We can think of this dance as being like a tennis rally, with the ball lobbing back and forwards between us and our opponent. Gasping of thirst on a hot summer's day, we just want the match to finish. To end it, we could try talking your opponent into stopping – which is harder to do if she is winning... or we could just put our racquet down.

Similarly, in this coercive dance between an adult and a child, we could try talking the child into stopping... or we could stop being the force that the child is opposing. As well as being more efficient, when the dance is occurring between us and a child, it is also our responsibility to act like the grown-ups and be the ones to end it. This means that we will stop using all punishments and rewards, and instead will support children to manage their emotions and impulses themselves. If we do not present ourselves as a force, the children have nothing to oppose.

With these spirited children in particular, as Gordon said, 'If you use power, you will lose influence'.[7] This is because being in command of themselves (having autonomy) is their most important need. Therefore, when you impose controls on them, you deny them not only their autonomy but also the main source of their self-esteem. This is such an existential crisis that they *will* resist:

> When we make children obey by force, threats, or punishment, we make them feel helpless. They can't stand feeling helpless, so they provoke another confrontation to prove that they still have some power.[8]

External stressors

Referring back to Figure 6.1, once we are clear that we are not attempting to control children (and they are also clear about that), a second possibility is that children with persistent behavioural difficulties might be stressed at home or elsewhere (such as school).

In families, only six events will derail children's emotional development: child abuse; domestic violence (partner abuse); mismanaged mental illness of a parent; parental drug or alcohol abuse (because this leads to neglect of the children and increases family violence); death of a parent during childhood; and poverty – if it affects parents' capacity to be responsive to their children.[9] (Marital separations and divorce will temporarily distress children while they grieve – but only the Big Six adverse events distort children's emotional development in the long term.) The mechanism is that adversity raises children's levels of stress hormones (particularly cortisol) and, through a chemical process known as methylation, actually heightens the brain's sensitivity to cortisol and reduces its ability to regulate the stress response.[10] In this way, adversity in the absence of parental support produces an array of social, emotional, behavioural, learning and physical health problems in children.[11]

In schools, children can be stressed when they spend their days afraid of failing because they know that failure would disappoint their parents and teachers.[12] A confusing torrent of words and explanations and a constant expectation to learn – that is, to do something they are not yet good at – is painful because, like us, children want to know what they are doing and do not like to be confronted with their ignorance any more than we do. They dutifully persist at confusing and often boring academic work that offers little intellectual nourishment[13] – and all this occurs within a complex social setting in which their wellbeing is often under threat from loneliness, isolation or bullying. To them, school can feel like a dangerous place where escape and safety are their main concerns.[14] Instead of thinking about the world, they are worrying about their position in it.[15] However, rather than admire the courage of children who hang in there day after day, we typically criticise, reprimand and humiliate those children (often publicly in front of their peers) whose tension, boredom and anxieties cause them to find it difficult to focus on their work and who do not conform to our expectations.

Developmental inexperience

Against a backdrop of a belief that children are wicked by nature, the controlling style of parenting often assumes that children who are behaving thoughtlessly should have foreseen – and therefore must have intended – the outcomes of their actions.

In contrast, guidance believes that when children make mistakes, they are not deliberately attempting to be malicious or disruptive or to 'get at us'. Referring to the third circle in Figure 6.1, guidance believes that children occasionally act thoughtlessly because are developmentally inexperienced, as a result of which they:

- get exuberant or excitable
- are exploring what you will tolerate
- lack information about how they should be acting
- are experiencing a lapse of self-regulation.

Natural exuberance

Mistakes can come about because children are naturally exuberant. This is aptly summarised by a group of researchers who, after five years of observing young children, concluded that, 'Kids do stuff'.[16] By way of examples, when children are one year old and self-feeding, they smear their food in their hair, up their nostrils and in their ears; when they are two, they have meltdowns; when they are three, they whinge (or whine), usually including a complaint that 'It isn't fair'; when they are four, they experiment with bold words like *poo* and *bum*; and when they are six, they think they are the only person ever to discover how to make their armpits fart. If you don't want irritating behaviour like this in your life, don't have children. (*'Too late!'* I hear you cry.)

We all also know that children get excitable and that they are sillier in packs than when alone. This is why we serve savouries before sweets at children's birthday parties, and the reason for the advice to early childhood teachers: 'Never ever serve sugary snacks on a rainy day'.[17]

These examples tell us that we need to *understand* normal childishness. But, as I said in chapter 1, this is different from being patient with something that is unfair. If it is unfair, we need to act to put a stop to it.

Exploration

Second, children learn best by exploring. When it comes to their social world, they don't come to you with a clipboard and survey to discover your attitude to a range of potential behaviours such as jumping on the bed. Instead, they jump on the bed – and *find out* what your attitude is. Sometimes, they already know your attitude, but they perform the behaviour to find out what you will do about it. The controlling style calls this 'testing' but I like to think of it as trying to find out if you will 'walk the talk'. They need to know if you are authentic.

Lack of information

A third developmental reason for disruptions is that, sometimes, children don't yet know any better. They lack information about what is expected of them. However, a lack of information is not as common a cause of disruptions as you might think. By three years of age, most children have either been told directly or have overheard a companion being told that that they must share with a playmate, be gentle with littler children, wait for a turn, and so on.

You can test whether your children are likely to know how they should be behaving by asking yourself two questions:

- How many times have I told this child about this particular behaviour?
- How many times would I have to tell this child where I had hidden some chocolate?

If your answer to the first question exceeds the number in answer to the second, you know that they know how they should be behaving, because the second question is a measure of their memory capacity. In that case, their behaviour is not being caused by a lack of knowledge – but by a lapse of self-regulation.

Lapse of self-regulation

This, then, is the fourth type of developmental incompetence. In many cases, children know what they should be doing, but cannot get their act together to do it. This happens to all of us every now and then. When we're on a low-fat diet but give in to the temptation to eat some fries on a cold winter's day, we don't need someone to ask: 'Do you *realise* the fat content of those hot chips?' Of course we are aware of their fat content. We are not eating them because we lack *information*.

Parents using a controlling style commonly overestimate their children's ability to regulate their own feelings and impulses. As a result, the parents see children's outbursts as wilful and defiant. In turn, blaming the children for their behaviour justifies these parents' use of punishment.[18] Instead, guidance realises that the ability to self-regulate is not inbuilt in our species and takes time for children to learn. During lapses, guidance advises that we support children to regain self-control, using the approaches that I recommend in chapter 8. Guidance also accepts that too much self-control is as harmful as too little[19] and seeks only for children to have the capacity to manage their emotions and impulses at those times when a failure to do so would interfere with their own wellbeing or the needs of others.

Health status

Finally, when children have ongoing behavioural or emotional outbursts that cannot be explained by the outer layers in Figure 6.1, we have to consider the possibility that they may not be well. Perhaps this is a temporary state, such as with tiredness or hunger, or it could be that a chronic health issue is affecting their wellbeing in the longer term.

Digestion problems

Problems with digestion are at the core of chronic health issues because they produce inflammation. This sounds merely painful but when it is systemic and when it affects the brain, it is especially troubling because it can impair and even destroy brain cells and impede the function of neurotransmitters.[20] Given that the brain only thinks, feels and behaves, when brains are inflamed, their owners will think morbidly, feel emotional (often explosively) and behave (at times) uncontrollably. Signs of an irritated nervous system are listed in Box 6.3.

Food intolerances

Food allergies result when B cells of the immune system produce antibodies that attack partially-digested proteins,[21]   whereas intolerances occur when T cells produce an inflammatory response.[22] (Only the former are detectable by blood tests.)

When the small intestine cannot properly digest the proteins in grains (gluten) or in milk, these remain in an opioid form that is a cousin of morphine, which enters the bloodstream and crosses the blood-brain barrier.[23] As a result, the brain can be inflamed and irritable, even if there are no gastrointestinal symptoms.[24] This is borne out by findings that children with celiac disease are at increased risk of schizophrenia in adulthood,[25] while children whose mothers are allergic to gluten are at increased risk of mental illnesses in later life.[26] If a gluten sensitivity can lead to this most serious of mental illnesses, lesser emotional effects are also possible.

Milk or soy protein intolerances are a second common culprit,[27] as is an inability to digest lactose (milk sugars). Lactose intolerance is common because, to be able to produce the digestive enzyme (lactase) past the age of four, children need a recessive gene.[28] Without this gene, they will have poor digestion of lactose beyond early childhood. The resulting inflammation can target any organ, including the brain.

Infections

Infants' brains are especially vulnerable to infections because their blood-brain barrier still lacks full integrity. Luckily, the brain contains more immune cells than our lymph system whose job it is to protect the brain from damage. Once a bacterial or viral infection crosses the blood-brain barrier, these immune cells within the brain release hydrogen peroxide to kill the pathogen. However, this would damage brain cells and therefore the immune cells also release nitric oxide to safeguard nearby brain cells by putting them into effective hibernation.[29] (Hence the 'brain fog' seen in chronic fatigue syndrome.) Both these chemicals are toxic free radicals that produce inflammation which affects both the development and functioning of the nervous system.[30]

When the brain is affected, the most suspect pathogens are:

- The *herpes* viruses: cold sores, chicken pox and glandular fever (or Epstein-Barr virus).[31]
- *Influenza,* particularly in children whose mothers contracted the flu during the fifth to seventh months of pregnancy,[32] when the mother's antibodies somehow alter brain development in the fetus.[33]

- *Streptococci* infections. In addition to their role in ear, nose and throat infections, these viruses can affect the brain, leading to learning difficulties, obsessive-compulsive disorders, and hyperactivity.[34]
- *Lyme disease*. Infection of a mother in early pregnancy or infection in the early childhood years increases children's risk of an autism spectrum disorder.[35]

BOX 6.3 SIGNS THAT HEALTH PROBLEMS ARE AFFECTING THE BRAIN[36]

Emotional signs

- The children are often morbid, ruminating over bad things that may happen in the future, or over events that are long past but which, when upset, they still report being troubled by.
- They are fearful of benign events.
- The children can 'go from zero to a hundred in microseconds' – that is, there is little build up to their emotional outbursts. (These children can be said to have the temperament of car alarms.) The smallest frustration sets them off into despair or rage.
- They often declare in despair that they can't help it and are remorseful or embarrassed after an outburst.
- They complain that there is something wrong with them or their brain.
- They have low self-esteem despite being loved and capable in most other respects.

Physical signs

- The children have known or suspected food intolerances, including those they have appeared to have 'outgrown'.
- They are very fussy eaters and restrict themselves to only a few food groups (which typically have high allergenic potency, such as wheat or milk).
- They have a history of diaper (nappy) rash; colic; gastric reflux; ear, nose, throat or respiratory infections; eczema; or digestion difficulties such as constipation or diarrhoea.
- They over-react to and become stressed by sensory input.
- They self-soothe excessively, perhaps by rocking, head banging or with genital stimulation.
- They have longstanding difficulties falling or staying asleep, sleep too deeply, require more sleep than normal, and/or are still tired in the mornings (that is, sleep is not restorative).
- They sleep so deeply that they wet their bed beyond the usual age.

> **BOX 6.3 SIGNS OF HEALTH PROBLEMS THAT AFFECT THE BRAIN** *(cont'd)*
>
> **Family history**
>
> - Family members have known or suspected food intolerances.
> - The mother had a viral infection (particularly influenza) during or just prior to the pregnancy with this child.
> - The mother had post-natal depression following a pregnancy. This signals low zinc levels for herself and potentially for the child also. Given that zinc is needed both for digestion and to metabolise serotonin, this raises the possibility that children's emotional issues can be due either to poor zinc metabolism or to an outright zinc deficiency.[37]
> - Family members have auto-immune illnesses, such as mature onset diabetes, multiple sclerosis, thyroid conditions or celiac disease.
> - Extended family members have a history of emotional disturbances such as depression, anxiety or addictions. These signal that, in this family, the brain is the target organ.
> - There are no serious external stressors in the family that could derail children's emotional development, such as child abuse, domestic violence, parental drug abuse, mismanaged parental mental illness, or abject poverty.
> - The parents use caring and what ought to be successful parenting methods (guiding, rather than controlling the child) and yet the child's behavioural outbursts are persisting.

Nutrient deficiencies

Nervous tissue is more sensitive than any other to nutrient deficiencies.[38] Even prenatal deficiencies can be devastating, with famine followed twenty years later by increased rates of schizophrenia in the young adults who were deprived of nutrients in utero, for example.[39] In particular, a deficiency of the nutrients needed to manufacture neurotransmitters (– see Figure 6.3) will compromise brain function, while omega-3 fatty acids are vital for both the structure and function of all cells in the body, including nerve cells.[40]

Toxicity

As a byproduct of metabolism, the body produces a constant stream of toxins; as well, we are exposed to toxins within our food and our environment. Given that many of these toxins have an affinity for fat cells and that the brain is substantially comprised of fat cells, once the body is toxic, the brain will be affected. The most toxic substances for the brain are alcohol, lead and mercury (mainly from amalgam teeth fillings).[41]

Children are especially vulnerable to an overload of toxins because their detoxification systems are still immature; because compared with adults they ingest more toxins for their body weight; they breathe more than adults per kilogram of body weight and therefore inhale proportionately more airborne toxins; and they are closer to carpets and other surfaces that outgas chemicals.[42] Children with weak methylation (a biochemical process that is the basis of many cellular functions) will also have reduced ability to detoxify.

FIGURE 6.3 NUTRIENTS NEEDED TO PRODUCE NEUROTRANSMITTERS[43]

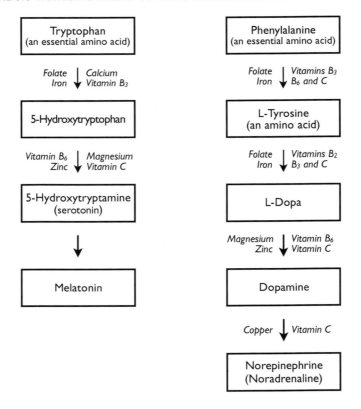

THE 'ATTENTION SEEKING' MYTH

You might have noticed that, in this description of the origins of disruptive behaviours, I did not mention that children do things to get attention. This is because I do not believe that children are so deranged that they would prefer to get into trouble than to be ignored. None of us ever misbehaves at work so that our boss will pay us attention by reprimanding us, so it is ludicrous to think that children would.

In a hundred years of research, not a single study anywhere has shown that children do things to get attention. Yes, when we deprive them of attention by ignoring them or sending them to time out, they might stop behaving disruptively, but that's not because we're withholding our attention, but because being abandoned is so devastating that the children compulsively comply. As I described earlier, when medication helps our headache, that does not prove that the headache was caused by a lack of medication. So too if children's behaviour improves when we ignore it, that does not mean that the behaviour was being caused by our attention.

Second, given that so many children nowadays are under watch 24 hours a day, it is hard for me to *imagine* a child who would need more attention than that. But let's say there is a child out there somewhere who needs extra attention. If we believe that a behaviour is attention seeking, we will think that we should ignore it. Let me say this in a slightly different way: What we're saying here is that this child needs attention, but we are not going to give it to her because she isn't asking for it properly. (You can almost hear the *Na na na na na* on the end of that sentence.) Guidance believes that, if children need something, whenever possible we should supply that.

In purely practical terms, whereas the concept of 'attention-seeking' behaviour implies that you should ignore the behaviour, in my experience ignoring a well established habit does not work. Children who are needy can persist until their behaviour becomes so dangerous, disruptive or annoying that you have to pay attention to it in the end, in which case you might as well have done something about it in the first place.

The concept of attention-seeking behaviour was proposed early in the 20th century by Alfred Adler. He actually said, however, that children were *affection* seeking but his disciplines changed affection seeking to *attention* seeking (along with identifying three other causes of children's behaviours, all of them negative: seeking power, revenge or to withdraw).[44] None of those other three causes have been proven either.

In one respect, the concept that children seek adults' attention is right in that everyone wants affection and affirmation. However, if children are attempting to recruit these by behaving thoughtlessly, my assumption is that they lack the skills to gain them any other way.[45]

It is true that, when you are looking the other way, children will occasionally do things that you have asked them not to, such as jumping on the sofa. The classic case is that the sofa gymnastics begin as soon as you get on the phone. This might look as if it is attention seeking, but I think it reflects the reality that the children realise that you cannot do two things at once: you cannot complete your phone call and respond to their behaviour at the same time. Therefore, you will need to put the call on hold and ask the children to consider your needs, returning to your call once they are ready to do so.

'TESTING' BEHAVIOUR

When children are constantly producing disruptive behaviour as if to test how we will react, this tells us one of three things. The first possibility is that they cannot find you: they do not know what you stand for and what you will not stand, because this seems to change day to day. When you are authentic with them and admit to being more sensitive today than usual, they will not need to test out your mood. And when you are steadfast that they will consider you, they will not need to act up to find out if you will have the courage to lead them.

A second potential explanation is that in the past you resorted in desperation to threats and punishments. These communicate that your love is conditional, in which case the children are attempting to find out the 'terms and conditions'.

A third possibility is that you have been alternating between being too permissive and using controls, or have been emotionally explosive, as a result of which the children cannot read what you want from them. Using guidance instead of controls will allow the children to know your needs, in which case they can consider them.

CONCLUSION

Every behaviour is an attempt to meet a need. For occasional meltdowns, a scan of the list in Box 3.1 might identify the need that your children are trying to satisfy. The most common will be that they are protesting at being denied the opportunity to be in command of their own lives (that is, they are trying to meet their need for autonomy).

For persistent behavioural difficulties, if using guidance to satisfy children's autonomy needs is not working, it can help to reduce stressors and to understand children's developmental capacities so that you can adjust what you expect of them. You will also accept that childish behaviours are normal for children.

Finally, when you are using guidance methods but these are not working as well as you'd expect, refer back to Figure 6.1 to try to figure out what might be going on. When children's outbursts are excessive (otherwise known as having the temperament of car alarms), consider the possibility of a health problem – because the human body in fact cannot go from zero to a hundred in microseconds. If your children are explosive, they are not functioning at zero but at simmering point. The question then is, what is keeping them simmering? If they are unwell, no amount of ideal parenting or self-regulation strategies will solve it. Neither parenting skills nor willpower will fix an inflamed appendix – and neither will they fix an inflamed nervous system. Unwell children need physical treatment. In that case, naturopaths, homeopaths, enlightened medical practitioners or a biophysical treatment known as bioresonance could assist children's physical health, so that the children's emotions and behaviours settle.[46]

Now that we have an understanding of what might be causing children's emotional or behavioural outbursts, in the next chapters I will describe how you can respond – without, of course, using punishments.

SUMMARY OF PRINCIPLES

- Observation without judgment is the highest form of sensitivity.
- If you use power, you will lose influence.
- The problem (with repeated disruptive behaviour) is not the dancers: it's the dance.
- We all need to be in command of our own lives. Spirited children are just more determined about this than others.
- Children do stuff.
- If we punish children for normal behaviour, we would be punishing them for *being* children.

Everyday practices 7

When our children's behaviour interferes with our capacity to meet our needs, conflict arises between us. This is sometimes referred to as a conflict of needs. But that label is not accurate – because everyone needs the same things. Therefore, the conflict is not over *needs*. Instead, it arises because of conflicting (or competing) solutions – or a *conflict over the strategies* individuals are using to meet their needs. The strategy that the children are using to meet their needs happens to block our ability to meet ours.

At the heart of all conflict is fear that we will not be able to meet our needs.[1] However, in a family where there is an implicit agreement that everyone has a right to get his or her needs met, this fear is unnecessary. Because there are more strategies than needs, we can maintain the faith that we will be able to find a strategy that satisfies everyone.[2]

Listening skills (as detailed in chapter 5) are your first tools for solving problems. Listening reflects the fact that, 'Every moment of every day, your children are doing their best to meet their needs'.[3] The everyday practices that I recommend in this chapter reflect the second fact that, similarly, 'You are also, at each moment, doing the best you can to meet your needs'.[4]

SELECTING A RESPONSE

It is unrealistic to apply fixed rules or rigid standards about children's behaviour. This is because, with the exception of truly abnormal acts (e.g. head banging and self-mutilation), virtually every behaviour is appropriate at certain times and places. Even violence can be legitimate, such as when a child is trying to escape from a would-be kidnapper. Second, different individuals can have differing opinions and reactions to what children do. What troubles one person may not bother another. Furthermore, we can each react differently at different times. Something that did not interfere with our ability to meet our needs yesterday may provoke problems for us today. Moreover, our reactions can depend on our emotional state: when we are unwell, tired, worried, stressed, or overwhelmed, we are less able to tolerate particular behaviours and more likely to need extra consideration. Our reactions can also be a product of the environment, context, or timing: loud noise will disturb us more when it is indoors than when it is outside, or a behaviour may bother us more when it is the fifth disruption compared with when it is the first.

If we think of our coping capacity as a cup, when our cup is filled by other pressures in our lives, our children's behaviours can exceed our capacity to cope: our cup runneth over, as it were (see Figure 7.1). In comparison, Figure 7.2 shows that when we are not already stressed by other factors in our lives, the same series of behaviours by our children are within our coping capacity. The problem, then, isn't the behaviours, but our depleted resources at the time.

Therefore, what defines a given behaviour as a problem is not the act itself, but whether it is suitable to the occasion or whether it happens to interfere with someone's needs. That is, the actual or potential outcomes of the behaviour will determine whether and how we respond to it.

FIGURE 7.1 BEHAVIOURS THAT OVERWHELM OUR COPING CAPACITY

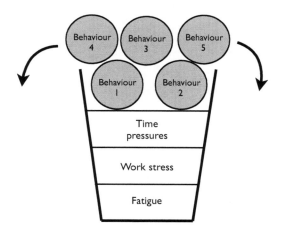

FIGURE 7.2 BEHAVIOURS THAT ARE WITHIN OUR COPING CAPACITY

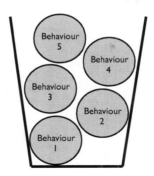

This awareness generates the following five scenarios (as illustrated in Figure 7.3).

- The behaviour troubles no one. It has no effect on ourselves, the child or bystanders. Therefore, it is a non-problem and requires no response.

- The behaviour is annoying, irritating or disruptive and may even interfere with meeting our needs, but we recognise that the children do not have the capacity to do what we are asking of them. This may be because of their age, tiredness, or a learning difficulty, for example. In this case, we need to understand the children's limitations and modify our demands to make it easier for them to achieve expectations.

- The behaviour interferes with meeting the child's own needs, in which case the child needs compassion. Our task is to listen.

- The behaviour troubles us and we are tempted to try to put a stop to it, despite the fact that it has no tangible effect on us and does not interfere with meeting our needs. For example, we might want to protect our 12-year-old (and ourselves) from embarrassment at his or her thumb sucking in public. Our temptation to do something about the behaviour (even though it does not affect us) tells us that the child's behaviour conflicts with one of our values.

- The behaviour has negative effects – or the risk or potential for these – on ourselves or other children in our care. The behaviour troubles us because it violates a need. It has a material or concrete effect on us and, therefore, we will be assertive. Or, more commonly, the behaviour troubles us *and* the child performing it is also in some distress. Given that we have a shared problem, we need to collaborate to solve it.

FIGURE 7.3 SELECTING RESPONSES TO CHILDREN'S BEHAVIOURS

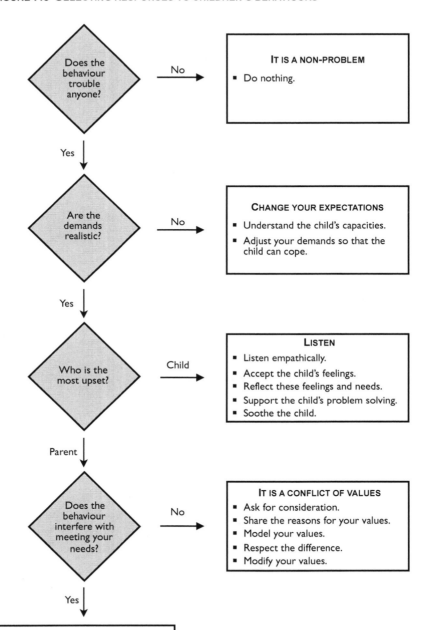

PREVENTION

It is far more humane to prevent conflicts than to have to resolve them once people have been upset. Preventing problems protects both our children and ourselves. Therefore, it is the first of the everyday responses.

Change your expectations

When children are not able to produce a behaviour that you would like, rather than finding ways to force them to change, you can honour their limitations and change your expectations. This will make it *easier* for children to consider what you need, while your consideration towards them helps them to be more *willing* to cooperate with your needs in return.

One of the most common mistaken expectations of parents is that they assume that, just because toddlers can talk, they are able to use language when they are distressed. Instead, this skill doesn't emerge until 3½ years of age. Before this age, although they can talk, they cannot use language to solve conflicts.[5] Instead, they commonly use aggression. Accordingly, the human species is most aggressive between the ages of 24 and 42 months.[6] After 3½ years, aggression begins to decline steadily in both frequency and severity. This is made possible by the children's developing ability to use language when emotionally roused. Therefore, while they are very young, we need to guide them not to hurt others, but we cannot punish them, even for hurtful behaviours – because if we punished children for what are normal behaviours, we would be punishing them for *being* children.

Another mistaken assumption is that young children's behaviour is under verbal command. Instead, although very young children might understand an instruction, they cannot yet interrupt their train of thought on command, or translate a verbal instruction into a physical action. In these cases, it can help to move across to them and help them to get started – say, by holding their hand and drawing them to you, rather than calling for them from across a room.

A third mistake is that we expect children to be able to persist at adult-led tasks (such as sitting at a meal table, or shopping) for the same length of time that they can concentrate on activities that they have selected for themselves. Instead, you think of their attention span as being three minutes times their age in years (up to a maximum of 20 minutes). When this is played out in a supermarket, for example, it means that you have nine minutes to get your shopping done if accompanied by your three-year-old. And you've used up those nine minutes just commuting to the shops. It's no wonder, then, that young children often 'lose it' when we take them on protracted shopping expeditions. That so few do is a testament to children's goodwill.

Another developmental limitation is that children naturally congregate in groups whose size is one more than the number of their birthdays:

Child's age	+ 1	=	Natural group size
0 year	+ 1	=	1 child
1 year	+ 1	=	2 children
2 years	+ 1	=	3 children
3 years	+ 1	=	4 children
4 years	+ 1	=	5 children

This means that when we place children in larger groups, many will find it difficult to participate, with the result that their behaviour will either become disorganised or 'ratty', or else they will retreat to a quiet space to be by themselves.

Change the environment

Rather than trying to change a child or change your demands, a third option is to adjust the environment. This will make it easier for children to achieve what we need. Modifications can span the following measures.[7]

- *Child proof the setting* – for example, by removing items that we do not want children to touch so that we do not have to keep reminding them to leave the items alone. Although some believe that children have simply 'got' to learn to avoid temptation, child proofing the setting is the same strategy that we would use if a disabled relative were living with us: we would adjust the environment to reflect the person's diminished capacities.

- *Enrich the environment:* for example, by giving children more (or more interesting things) to do than the behaviour they are presently producing.

- *Restrict the environment:* give children less inappropriate responsibility, or fewer distractions so that it is easier for them to function.

Another useful practice is to alternate doing something that you want, followed by something child-focused. For example, first, you do the grocery shopping; then your child gets a ride on the mechanical toy in the shopping mall; then you go to the health food shop; then he gets a snack; then you call into the bank; then your child gets to watch the nearby fish tank... and so on.

GIVE POSITIVE INSTRUCTIONS

When giving instructions, be sure to tell children what *to do* rather than what *not to do*. When I say, 'Don't think about pink elephants', now that I have mentioned them, you are thinking about pink elephants, when you wouldn't have otherwise. If I tell children not to run, they will think about running. Instead, if children are on wet tiles, you could say, 'Take small steps on the wet tiles'.

Make sure that your instructions are specific. Instead of telling children to be careful, suggest that they hold onto the hand rail; instead of telling them to be polite or play nicely, let them know what you want them to do. If you can't figure out what you actually mean by these instructions, your children won't be able to either, in which case your instructions are redundant. Therefore, say nothing. Assume instead that your children know how to behave, because you've shown and taught them in the past.

When you regularly visit certain friends or relatives, it can be useful for you all to establish ahead of time that the homeowner will be the one to child-proof the house and to ask children not to touch his or her own precious items. Alternatively, you might arrange that your friends will tell you if they are bothered by something that your child is doing or touching, so that you can deal with it. This saves you from worrying constantly that your child might be upsetting your host when the host is not actually bothered, or not intervening when your host *is* concerned.

Give visual instructions to visual learners

Around two-thirds of children learn best by listening. These children think logically, attend to details, respond well to verbal instructions, plan ahead and are organised. They get lots of practice at thinking sequentially because language conveys one idea at a time.

The remainder, however, learn by forming visual images of concepts. They cannot hear you when watching the TV; miss details as they focus instead on the bigger picture; tend not to be able to follow long sequences of instruction; cannot be reasoned with verbally, especially when distressed; and find it difficult to change tack when they have a fixed plan of action in their minds.

I talk more about these two learning styles in the booklet on children's learning. For now, the implication is that if you are an auditory-sequential learner, you might find yourself frustrated when your visual-conceptual children fail to listen to you, do not anticipate the outcomes of their actions, or appear to be disorganised and obstinate. In fact, these problems occur because visual children need to be able to picture what you are asking them to do, not just hear about it.

- Before giving an instruction to visual learners, make sure you have eye contact. Place an upright pointer finger within their line of sight and move it towards your eyes, or stand between them and the TV. Then give them a moment to change out of picturing mode into listening mode, so they can take in what you are about to tell them.

- Give instructions in visual language. Rather than: 'Get your pyjamas and a book from your room' try, 'Picture your room… Can you see where your pyjamas are at the moment?… Okay, now can you see yourself, wearing your pyjamas while you choose a book for me to read to you?… Okay, call out to me when you've done that.'

- Sometimes these children have a fixed picture that they need, say, to complete their model space station, but this conflicts with your imperative that they get ready for school. In these situations, you do not have to force them to abandon their picture entirely, but just to set it aside temporarily. You might instruct them to 'change channels' in their head – just as they change channels on the TV – to shift their focus onto another picture, reminding them that they can return to their own picture later – say, after school.

- Because they can be disorganised, to prevent having to nag them when getting ready to leave the house, have them help you to take photos of the tasks they have to do each morning: breakfast, toothbrush, hairbrush, clothes, their made bed, school bag, lunch box, and so on, and put these photos on a chart or onto a series of index cards which the children can independently check to remind themselves about what they have to do next.

Make requests

There will be dozens of times each day when you ask children to do something. Being assertive means issuing requests, whereas demands attempt to control others by threatening, bossing, manipulating or shaming them. Demands attract either submission or rebellion, as our children feel forced into doing what we want because otherwise we can make their life miserable by blaming or punishing them.[8] The more that listeners hear demands, the less they will want to be around us and the more controlled they feel.

In contrast, requests take the form:

- 'I understand that...
- and I feel... (Disclosure of feelings is optional and may at times be unwise, for reasons that I give shortly.)
- because I need/value/hope...
- therefore, would you be willing to...'

Box 7.1 distinguishes between requests and demands. We can tell from our reaction whether we are issuing a demand: if we try to make children feel guilty for not complying or we attempt to force compliance, we are making a demand. Instead, when we are making a request, we are willing to listen to children's objections to doing as we asked.

Sometimes, even when we are clear that we are making a request, children hear a demand. With older children and adolescents, we can undo this by asking for their advice:[9]

- Would you be willing to tell me how I could say what I want so it wouldn't sound like I didn't care about what you'd like?
- How could I tell you what I want so that it didn't sound like I was bossing you around?

When children object to doing something that you ask, it will be because they cannot see how the task would meet their needs. Therefore, when you hear a 'No' to a request, listen for the 'Yes' that is behind it. This 'Yes' is a different strategy for meeting a need. For example, they might refuse to turn off their computer because they are visual learners and need the chance to learn in their native mode, having had to learn by listening all day at school. Once we know the need, we might be able to discover a way that they can meet that need while still considering others.

In response to children's objections, we can change our request; express understanding; or, in rare cases, ask if they would be willing to do as we asked anyway because it is an emergency.

Box 7.1 Differences between demands and requests[10]

Demands	Requests
Aims	
Our objective is to change others' behaviour.	We want others to consider us willingly, out of compassion for our needs.
We want to meet our needs.	We want to find a strategy that meets both people's needs.
Our thinking	
Contains judgmental thoughts about others and assumes that we are justified in demanding compliance. (*'She should... He's supposed to... I have a right... I deserve...'*).	Contains observations of others' actions that allow us to see them as human beings who, like us, are attempting to meet their needs and to make their life enjoyable and satisfying.
Our responses	
We react to non-compliance with outrage and an attempt to punish in order to secure compliance.	We respect others' needs and are willing to listen empathically to their objections.
Our expressions	
Do this right now, or else!	I'd like us to find a solution that works for everyone.
Don't make me ask you again!	I'd like to hear how this sounds to you.
Just do as you're told!	I'm wondering what you need right now?
Don't talk back at *me*!	Would you be willing to...?
How many times do I have to tell you?	Can you explain what is your problem with (or objection to) doing it?
I don't care what you think.	Please help me understand what you have in mind.

ASK CHILDREN

Many of us believe that we must have the solutions to other people's problems (especially our children's). However, we are not the ones experiencing the problem. Moreover, people know more about themselves than outsiders ever will.

Therefore, given that every behaviour is an attempt to meet a need (and that parents aren't mind readers), one of the most useful things we can do when children's behaviour has had a negative effect on others, is to ask the children about it. However, we cannot ask them *why* they acted as they did, because a request for insight will only confuse them.

Besides, we already know why they did it: they were trying to meet a need. We just might not know which one until we ask *what* need the behaviour fulfilled. You will adjust these questions to the circumstances and the age of the children, but will always deliver them in an enquiring tone (rather than the outraged '*What* do you think you're doing?').

- In what way did you hope that would help?
- What did you have in mind when you did that?
- What is your objection / problem with (doing what I asked)?
- What did you hope it would achieve for you?
- What do you need right now?
- What can I do to help you?
- What can you do right now to feel better?

Child as consultant

Asking children can be formalised into having them act as your consultant, either over a specific issue or just in general as they enter a new life stage. Children change so rapidly that it is impossible for parents to anticipate and plan for the kind of parenting that they will need.[11] However, children can teach us what they need.

By asking children for their ideas about what they think will work for them, we honour that they know themselves better than we do. Our questions could be:

- I haven't been a parent of you (at *this* age / when you've been in high school / when you are getting ready to leave home), so I need you to let me know what you need from me nowadays.

- What's going on for you at the moment? Can I help?
- I'm worried about you. Do I need to be?

When asked this last question, children will often deny that there is a cause for concern. In that case, unless you're alarmed, wait. Ask the question again later (in a few days or weeks, with the time frame depending on how serious the issue is). If the children still say they're fine but you are now alarmed, as the executive or leader in your family, you can decide to take action. In rare circumstances, this will mean over-riding the child's protests that you should stay out of it. In that case, you can express your judgment that it has gone on too long now for you to stand by, but you can still ask your child about what steps you will take.

EXPLAIN THE EFFECT OF A BEHAVIOUR

Sometimes, children do something that they did not know would harm someone else. During my research observations, a child fell off his bike and two nearby toddlers laughed at him. The teacher just said calmly, 'It hurt Michael's feelings when you laughed at him for hurting himself'. This is very different from becoming outraged and declaring:

> WELL! *That's not very nice, is it?* How would you like it if he laughed at you if you feel off your bike?... How would you like it if *I* laughed at you?... Would you like me to push you off your bike so you can see how it feels?

This tirade is clearly judgmental: you could end it with 'you horrible human being'. Judgment won't work, but empathy might be enough, especially when we have previously empathised with children so that they have experienced it and truly learned how it feels.

OFFER CHILDREN CHOICE

Given that autonomy is one of the three vital emotional needs, it is crucial that we give children choices over as many aspects of their lives as possible. Not only is this a fundamental human need, but children are less likely to assert themselves aggressively when they are already being given control of their own lives. Being self-governing will also empower them to resist abuse and will improve their self-efficacy in general.

Children learn to make good choices by making choices, not by following directives.[12] Often instead we deny them choices because we want them to do things a particular way or we find it quicker to do things for them. But, without opportunities to exercise choice, it is difficult for children to see themselves as capable and competent.[13]

It is important to be clear that fake choice is no choice at all. It is deceptive to pretend that 'My way or the highway' edicts offer children meaningful choice. For example, 'You have chosen not to go to Stephen's party because you did not behave' − as if a child *would* voluntarily choose to be excluded from social events. These unequal choices disguise the threat of punishment as a 'choice' that the child is making.[14] In reality, the only choice on offer here is, 'Behave or else!'.[15]

> In this smoke and mirrors game, the children are 'causing' everything to happen and the [parents] are the puppets of the children's choices. The only ones who are not taking responsibility for their actions are the adults.[16]

Instead, true choices have equally valued options and are guided by children's interests, not by their desire to avoid humiliation, to protect their self-esteem, or to minimise effort.[17] Choice is real only when the various alternatives offer authentic opportunities for children to select between personally meaningful options.[18]

The fundamental factor here is volition. This means that our actions emanate from ourselves, rather than being pressured from without. I might, for example, do housework (which I don't enjoy) for the pleasure of having a clean home; or I might do housework because I worry what my visitors will think of me if I don't.[19] In both cases, I am focused on the outcome (in the jargon, my motivation is said to be instrumental rather than intrinsically enjoying the task), but the first is freely chosen, whereas the second is controlled or compulsive.

When an activity is voluntary, children can have an option of *whether* to do it. If, however, it is compulsory (which will usually be for safety reasons), it is dishonest to pretend otherwise. Nevertheless, we can still give children limited choice of *how* to do it or, as a last resort, *how to feel* about doing it. For example, if you are going shopping, you won't ask young children *whether* they would like to come if there would be no one at home to look after them. Instead, you could ask *how* they accompany you: do they want to sit in the front seat or the back seat of the car? But if they are very young and their car seat is anchored in the back, even this limited choice is not available. In that case, they have a choice of how to feel about it: 'I need you to sit in your car seat. You can sit there happily or you can sit there miserably. It's up to you'. Used mainly for safety issues, the message here is a compassionate one that they should not put themselves through getting upset, because it will not change what they have to do.

BE ASSERTIVE

Assertiveness employ I-messages. These tell our listeners about ourselves, in contrast with you-messages that tell them about themselves. The usual three-part assertive message of:

> When you (do x),
> I feel (whatever)
> because...'

is a mixture of both. As a result it is often ineffective, because it amounts to blaming others for our feelings, as a result of which listeners can become defensive. Young children might produce a swagger or an eye roll, while older children might even come back at you with a verbal response such as, 'Well, I'm sorry, but you've mistaken me for someone who cares!'. These reactions are the inevitable outcome of using the 'you' part of the message.

Instead, the intent of I-messages is not manipulation or control, but honest communication. I-messages are authentic and describe our inner reality: they do not contain evaluations, judgments or opinions of others. There are five types: declarative, positive, preventive, empathic, and problem solving, whose intent is to disclose to listeners:

- how we feel
- what we value or need, and why
- how we experience the other person's behaviour (while taking responsibility for our own reactions, rather than blaming them for provoking these).

Declarative I-messages

This first type of I-message has no agenda. It just expresses your thoughts, feelings, values, opinions and ideas in the here and now.

Declarative I-messages foster mutual understanding. Examples include:

- I like that song.
- I feel discouraged about my work.
- I don't enjoy musicals.

Positive I-messages

This type of I-message simply describes your positive feelings about children, with no intent to 'reward' or manipulate them into repeated a desirable behaviour, but just to appreciate them for who they are:[20]

- I'm having fun doing this with you.
- I like listening to you play your music.
- I admire you.
- I love you to bits!

Preventive I-messages

Preventive I-messages can prepare children for situations where they have experienced problems in the past, with the aim of preventing them from happening again. These messages can also flag a future need so that you create an opportunity for your children to cooperate or change in ways that will fulfil your needs. For example:

- I'll need the car tomorrow to get to the airport.
- I will need some time alone tonight to work on my presentation for next week.
- We're going over to your grandmother's now. What do you need so that you can remember not to touch her special glassware?

Empathic I-message

This simple I-message has three parts:

- Reflect the child's needs: *I understand that you*
- Express your own needs, assertively: *However, I need*
- Solve the problem jointly: *So what can we do about that?*

For example:

- 'I understand that when you're cross it's hard to use your words.
- But I need to keep everyone safe – and I wouldn't let him hurt you, so I can't let you hurt him,
- So what can we do now so that everyone feels better?'

Problem solving I-message

This final type of assertive message is relevant when children's actions are interfering with meeting our own needs. When we express that this is happening, it is important that we are clear that our children are not responsible for looking after us and that neither they nor their behaviour are causing our feelings. These are a result of our thoughts or interpretations of events.

This type of I-message is considered to be effective if it has a low risk of damaging the children's self-esteem or harming your relationship, promotes children's growth and produces helpful change.

Part 1: Assertion

The following steps for sending problem-solving I-messages are illustrated here with the scenario that, as you drive your child to school, he realises that his school project is due today but he has left it at home and he wants you to drop him off at school then go back home to collect it and then deliver it to school. You are on your way to work. Applied to this scenario, you will use the following steps.

- *Self-empathy*: silently in your head, identify what you feel and need... breathe. Let's say that you feel anxious about being late for work, or irritated at the inconvenience.
- *Empathy for the other*: Then out loud say: 'I understand...' (that you worked hard on your project and want to hand it in on time and that it's easy to forget things at your age).
- *Disclosure of feelings*: 'Although it feel...' (anxious about being late for work / irritated at having to go back and drive further in this traffic).
- *Statement of need*: 'Because I need...' (to get to work on time because people are relying on me to be there).
- *Request*: In this step, you ask for what you predict will meet your needs and check if that will work for the child as well. 'So what about when I drop you off, I meet with your teacher and tell him that you finished the project on time but have to hand it in tomorrow?'. Or, 'How about I take

lunch time off to go and get it then?' Or, 'What if I call my office and your school to let them both know that we'll be a few minutes late and we turn around now to get it?'.

In this five-part sequence, disclosing your feelings has the advantage of helping children to recognise that you are human and to identify feelings and their triggers. But it runs the risk that children will perceive it as a criticism for 'making' you feel as you do and therefore can incite parent watching, submission, defensiveness or resistance.

Also, many of us can find it difficult to name any feeling other than anger or sadness, especially in the heat of the moment. Therefore, it might pay to leave out the expression of feelings. This can be safer, especially if you are not calm enough to express your feelings non-judgmentally or without using emotional blackmail. Another option when you are upset, is to let children know that you are having difficulty controlling your feelings right now and want to take a few moments to calm yourself.

Part 2: Change gears to listen

After we have delivered our assertive message, we have to be ready to switch back to compassionate listening. This is because, even when we do not intend to accuse or blame other people, listeners can sometimes react as though we have. Regardless of the intent of the speaker, the meaning of any communication is how it is received by the listener.

Responses that signal that children now have a problem include:[21]

- defensiveness: 'So?…Who cares… So what?'
- hostility: 'And I care because?…Tough… Boy, you're in a bad mood'
- questioning (e.g. whether you had to do this kind of thing at their age)
- debating: 'Why do I have to?'
- becoming hurt and tearful or using a quivering voice
- withdrawing, avoiding eye contact
- becoming silent.

These responses simply mean that the children now fear that their own needs will not be met. We do not have to worry when we hear these reactions: we just need to listen (– see chapter 5).

Part 3: Recycling

Because listeners' feelings block their ability to understand our point of view, after their feelings are resolved through listening to their reactions, we will need to repeat our assertive message, clarifying our statement and checking that they have understood it. The key is persistence, and engaging in a repeated rhythm of asserting then reflecting the listener's response.[22]

BOX 7.2 DIFFERENCES BETWEEN LISTENING AND ASSERTIVENESS

When a child is upset	When I am upset
I am a listener.	I am the sender.
I am a counsellor.	I am an influencer.
I want to help the child.	I want to help myself.
I am interested in the child's needs.	I am mainly interested in my own needs.
I am a sounding board.	I want to sound off.
I help the child to find his or her own solution.	I need to find a solution myself.
I can accept the child's solution: I do not need to be satisfied.	I must be satisfied with the solution.
I am more passive.	I am activated.

Teach children to be assertive

We need to be clear with children that the right to be assertive is mutual. This will mean listening to children when they assert their needs. We teach children to be assertive by using I-messages ourselves, so that they learn from our example how to disclose their feelings without upsetting others. We can also actively coach children to express their needs in ways that do not press our own buttons or trigger an unproductive reaction in us.

COLLABORATIVE PROBLEM SOLVING

Collaborative problem solving combines the dual skills of listening to others and asserting our own needs (which are contrasted in Box 7.2), and adds a structure for jointly generating solutions. It is useful when both we and our children are distressed or bothered by a behaviour; for persistent problems, which assertiveness has not resolved; and when a solution will require a change in the child's behaviour.

As with the other communication skills, the people involved need to be motivated to solve the problem, and both parties need to be calm: you cannot reason with people while they are being unreasonable.

In contrast with controlling discipline, which imposes solutions on children, guidance trusts young people to know their own minds and to be able to generate workable solutions. When we recruit their ideas about what they think will work, we increase the chances of finding relevant and vibrant solutions, not just because two heads are better than one, but because contributing to the solution makes them more willing to put it into action.

Guidance also takes account of the differences in power between adults and children so that attempts at resolution do not put children at a disadvantage.[23] It keeps sight of our core purpose, which is to find a solution, not a culprit. And it accepts that, even though we are feeling upset, because we are the adults, we have the greater capacity to postpone our needs. Therefore, in most cases the children's needs will take priority.

With this in mind, our goals are, first, to solve an issue in a mutually satisfactory manner so that the solutions we arrive at are durable.[24] The aim is not for us to find a compromise – which meets no one's needs – but to find a strategy that honours and meets everyone's needs.[25] Our second goal is to teach children skills including taking another's perspective, listening to others, expressing their needs, managing their own emotions and solving problems. Collaborative problem solving gives children opportunities to learn and practise these skills in real-life situations that concern them.[26]

Using the anagram SOLVED,[27] the basic steps for problem solving are:[28]

S   *Specify the problem*. Use I-messages to disclose your needs and listen empathically to children's expression of their needs: 'I get upset when I see you getting so frustrated that you throw things across the room'.

O   Invite children to contribute to generating *options* for solving the problem: 'What's your ideas?' Brainstorm all possibilities and listen to all suggestions.

L   Consider the *likely outcomes* of these options.

V   Choose the solution that seems *viable* (or, for younger children, the *Very best one*) – that is, one that is realistic (which means that it is achievable by the child and in the circumstances) and mutually satisfactory. This stage recognises that the solution is not pre-determined.

E   *Enact* it: carry it out and *evaluate* how it is working.

D   *Do it again:* re-negotiate. If subsequently the solution fails, this simply signals that the previous plan did not capture the original problem, or the solution was too ambitious. You will need to repeat the process to generate a different strategy until one is found that everyone *can* achieve and which works to meet both their needs.

Collaborative problem solving can go wrong when, instead of stating our concern, we attempt to impose our solution. This can lead to 'duelling solutions'[29] that, in turn, can result in the two people involved meeting halfway. However, this is rarely an ideal solution, because neither one's needs have been met. Instead, durable solutions will typically entail one of three options: giving the child some help; giving a little in your expectations; or doing things differently.[30]

A second mis-step comes about because, out of sheer goodwill, children sometimes agree to something that later proves too ambitious or difficult for them to do. To prevent this, when you hear an agreement but are uncertain about a child's commitment, you can say,

'I'm feeling uneasy with your 'Okay'. Can you reassure me that you're happy with what we've decided?' or 'I'd like you to take a moment to check that you're happy to do what we've agreed'.

Problem solving between children

When children are in dispute with each other and appear to be unable to resolve it themselves, the following steps can be useful.

- *Discover what the conflict is about by asking:* 'What's going on?' (in an enquiring tone that seeks information in order to help, not in an accusatory tone that seeks information about who is at fault and therefore who to blame and punish).
- *Restate the problem:* 'I can see your problem. There are two of you and there is only one ball'.
- *Guide the children to find their own solution:* 'What can you do?' Suggest solutions if the children are too young to generate their own. (This is typically not necessary past the age of four years.)
- *Ask them to choose and commit to a solution* that satisfies them both.
- *Invite them to ask for further* help if they need it: 'If you have any more trouble, come and ask me for more help'. (This last step may be unnecessary with older children and adolescents.)

Contracts (pacts, or deals)

If you think it will be useful, you can formalise the solution that you generated through the collaborative problem-solving process into a contract, pact or deal. By their very nature, contracts are reciprocal: if I buy your house, I pay you the asking price, and you give me the title deeds to the property. That is, we each do something. But most controlling contracts with children (particularly in schools) specify how the children must behave – and that is all.

Instead, you can negotiate a deal with your children that specifies what they have agreed to do, and what you will do to help them achieve that. While shopping, for example, you might have a deal that they will not run away from you, and that to help them you will pause in the middle of the shopping to give them something to eat.

You offer this support on the understanding that the children would already be producing the behaviour if it was easy for them; they are not producing it; therefore, it must not be easy for them. In that case, they need extra support.

CONFLICTS OF VALUES

While most conflicts between parents and children will be over behaviours that interfere with each person's ability to meet his or her needs, some will be about differing values. Unlike needs, values are *learned* and, if someone else does not abide by our values, this has no tangible effect on us. We can still breathe, work, eat, walk… and so on. Gordon gives the example that if you declared to your neighbour that you didn't like her car and she should buy a different one, she will not be willing to do what you want, on the grounds that it's none of your business what type of car she drives, because it does not affect you.[31]

Because conflicts over values do not interfere with meeting our needs, any fear in us that our needs will not be met is misplaced. Instead, conflicts about values have to do with autonomy – that is, about being self-governing and choosing our personal behaviour for ourselves.

As parents, it is our duty to teach our children values that we believe will help them to live their lives both now and in the future. However, our duty is to teach them *how* to think morally, not *what* to think. Just as we filtered our own parents' values, our children will be selective about which of our values they adopt. This is how societies make progress. Therefore, while we can model and teach our values, we cannot impose them on our children. Instead, we can try the options listed in Box 7.3.

> **BOX 7.3 RESPONSES TO CONFLICTS OF VALUES**[32]
>
> - Ask for consideration of your values (e.g. not to use certain swear words in your company). When your relationship is responsive to their needs, children may voluntarily observe your standards out of courtesy, even when they have no obligation to do so.
>
> - Share with children your life's lessons that cause you to be concerned about their behaviour. (This is suitable only for recently emerging difficulties; it will not work if delivered as a repeated lecture.)
>
> - Model your own values in the hopes that children will come to cherish them also.
>
> - Respect that young people's values differ from your own and decide not to turn the difference into a point of contention.
>
> - Listen to your children's reasons for their beliefs and, when persuaded, change your own attitudes.

RECOVERING FROM CONFLICT

Many people fear conflict because they don't know how to recover from it afterwards. They fear it will do irreparable damage to their relationship. Instead, after a conflict with your child, you can normalise your relationship by chatting afterwards about something unrelated to the earlier issue, 'I forgot to ask what your teacher thought of your idea for the school play?'. This, however, can seem to be glossing over the conflict and the child might not be ready to move on as quickly as you are (because, as you will recall from chapter 5, children's emotions are more intense than ours). Therefore, my preferred method is to address the conflict directly, saying something such as, 'We both got really upset before, too upset for my liking. I want to know if *we're* okay and, if not yet, what can we do to get okay?'.[33]

DO NOT SHAME CHILDREN

Shaming young people for their actions as a tool of discipline teaches them that they are unworthy and threatens them with rejection; in response, they will either:

- *move away* from us by withdrawing, hiding and silencing themselves;
- *move towards* us by becoming compulsively compliant in an effort to appease us; or

- *move against* others by trying to gain power, being aggressive and shaming others in retaliation.[34]

In contrast, remorse that is given freely can motivate restitution. As Brené Brown states, 'Recognizing we've *made a mistake* is far different from believing *we are a mistake*'.[35]

To give children a way to save face, you could say things like:

- 'Sometimes people forget to think first. You'll probably remember next time. What do you think?'.

- 'Looks like that was an accident. What could you do next time so that it doesn't happen again?'.

- 'I'm sure you wouldn't have done that if you had known it would hurt her. Now that you know, I reckon you won't do it again.'

Because children cannot always anticipate the effects of their actions, the result can startle them enough to teach them not to do it again, and you would only humiliate them if you preached about something they had already realised.

APOLOGIES

Rosenberg says that it is a particularly vicious kind of violence to demand that others apologise when our needs have been violated.[36] Seeking an apology and insisting that other people feel remorseful implies that we are judging them to be in the wrong. We are addicted, he says, to making others suffer and feel badly for their mistakes.

When we have been hurt, the actual issue is not to induce remorse in others but to grieve for our unmet needs.[37] When we are in touch with an unmet need, we will feel sadness, but not depression or anger.

There are three occasions when apologies can seem justified: when children have said or done something that hurts us; when they have hurt a peer; and when we have wronged children.

When children have said something hurtful to us, we have to remember that we choose how to feel about that. It is important not to take it personally. It is not children's job to look after us, but ours to look after them. If we have unmet needs, we must look to the adults in our lives to fulfil these. Therefore, we cannot seek an apology from children. If they offer one, it is a credit to them, given the power difference between adults and children. It is also a signal that your relationship is healthy, because children find it impossible to offer a sincere apology to adults who exercise control over them.

When children have hurt a peer, your first step will be to empathise with the target, with the perpetrator alongside you. The victim deserves an apology but you will not force perpetrators to apologise because if you tried to, they might refuse, tell a lie by saying they are sorry when they are not, or offer an apology grudgingly – upon which we have to demand, 'Now say it like you mean it!'.

Instead, you are big enough to apologise on the perpetrator's behalf. 'I see that Harry hurt your arm. And I see that you are crying, so that tells me he hurt your feelings too. He must have been very cross. And he's probably still to cross to say *Sorry*. So I'll say it for him... I'm sorry that Harry hurt your arm. And I'm sorry that he hurt your feelings'. When we don't blame, shame or humiliate perpetrators, they will often apologise willingly while you are comforting the victim, in which case the apology will be heartfelt.

When we recognise that we have failed to meet someone else's needs, we can feel sad, but not guilty or ashamed. Depression, anger, guilt and shame are blameful. Nevertheless, when we have wronged children, we will gain their respect if we can find the courage to apologise. The children already know that we have hurt them; they don't yet know if we are heroic enough to admit it.

CONCLUSION

The practices that I have outlined here will ensure that both we and our children can each safeguard our needs, and that as parents we remain accountable for maintaining and repairing our relationship with our children. However, the methods are effective only when everyone is calm; when children are in meltdown, you will need the practices that I recommend in chapter 8.

SUMMARY OF PRINCIPLES

- Rather than giving instructions about their behaviour, assume that your children know how to behave.
- We can try to change our child, or we can change our demands.
- Children learn to make good choices by making choices, not by following directives.

- Guidance trusts young people to know their own minds and to be able to generate workable solutions.

- Conflict is over strategies for meeting needs, not over needs themselves.

- Recognising that we've *made* a mistake is very different from believing that we *are* a mistake.

- Punishment seeks retribution for past misdeeds. Guidance teaches in order to prevent future ones.

- People know more about themselves than outsiders ever will.

Teaching self-regulation   **8**

As I mentioned in chapter 5, babies' survival demands that they express everything they feel, whereas adults' healthy adjustment requires that we do not, because sometimes impulsive actions will get in the way of meeting our goals.[1] Given that it is not inbuilt, this capacity for self-regulation has to be learned. Doing so is the most important task of childhood.[2] It begins in infancy,[3] with children's ability to regulate their emotions continuing to undergo important changes into middle childhood. By school entry, most children can manage their emotions effectively most of the time[4] and from then till 10 years of age they become less emotionally intense and less expressive of all emotions, particularly anger.[5]

Nevertheless, guidance does not expect children always to regulate their feelings, as if humans were so wicked that we must suppress all of our desires. It recognises that our emotions enrich us and that people are best adjusted when they can be spontaneous, warm and expressive.[6] Indeed, compulsive self-control is unhealthy. Therefore, the aim is simply for children to be able to express themselves without infringing on others. The purpose of this chapter, then, is to describe how you can support children to integrate their emotions and to exercise choice over how they express their feelings.

TEACH HELPFUL THINKING

As I described in chapter 5, almost all of our feelings are generated by our thoughts. An example here might help.[7]

> Let's say that as you are driving one day, you pass a lifelong friend whom you are delighted to see but who, upon seeing you, leans out her window and hurls a long string of abuse at you, ending with a declaration that she never wants to see you again.

If your friend is leaning out of her car window, you are likely to feel distressed and hurt, especially when you have no idea what you did to upset her.

If instead she is leaning out of the window of a mental hospital, you are more likely to think, 'The poor dear: she's clearly disturbed and in the best place to get help'.

This story tells us that, despite the fact that the friend's actions were the same in both scenarios, what you felt about her behaviour depended on what you thought it meant. That is, our thoughts generate our feelings. Therefore, if we want to change our feelings, we will have to change our thinking.

Instead, some people mistakenly believe that they cannot do something until they feel better. To explain this error, psychiatrist Bill Glasser notes that there are four parts to our behaviour: thoughts, actions, feelings, and our physical state.[8] He likens these to the four wheels of a front-wheel-drive car. The front two (or driving) wheels are our thoughts and our actions, and these pull along behind them our feelings and our physical wellbeing. (Younger children might prefer the simpler concept of elephants pulling each other along.)

When we want to drive somewhere, we don't wait in our driveway for our car's rear wheels to 'get in the mood' to move – but instead we engage the front, driving wheels to pull the rear ones along. Likewise, if we want to feel better, we have to change what we think and do. In turn, this will change our feelings and physical state.

To change what we think, we can teach children (and ourselves) to disconnect or get unhooked from the ongoing chatter in our minds. We can do this in three steps: notice it, name it, and neutralise it.[9]

Notice the thought

The good thing about our minds is that they are constantly churning out thoughts that help us plan for the future and learn from the past.[10] But the downside is that our minds evolved to anticipate danger, such as the presence of predators. Therefore, as a species our minds are wired to be pessimistic and judgmental of ourselves and others, reminding us of our flaws and failings.[11]

> Our mind is like a radio... it's always got something to say. It's always got an opinion, an idea, a prediction, a judgment, a criticism, a comparison or a complaint.[12]

These negative thoughts are not a problem in themselves. In fact, they are normal (because in past eras, they kept us alive). But negative thoughts become a problem when we *believe* them and allow them to control what we do.[13]

In other words, the issue isn't whether the thoughts are true or false, but whether they help us to live a full and enriching life. The first step, then, is to notice that we're having an unhelpful thought. Once we can notice the thought, we create a bit of space between it and us. We no longer hold it to be the *The Truth*.

Name the thought

Our mind is great at generating a whole range of reasons for not being able to take charge of our own actions.[14]

- *Obstacles*: our mind points out all the difficulties that prevent us from taking action.

- *Self-judgments*: our mind tells us all the ways that we're not up to the task. As Harris says of self-criticism, if beating ourselves up were a good way to change, we'd all be perfect by now.[15]

- *Comparisons*: we tell ourselves that we are inferior to others, who are more capable or talented than we are.

- *Predictions*: our mind predicts failure, rejection, humiliation and other unpleasant outcomes.

For adults, when we are naming these types of thoughts, we can tell ourselves, 'Ah, yes, here's *Reason giving* again' (for example). For children, we could give them the names of some unhelpful thinking patterns, such as those listed in Box 8.1.

Box 8.1 COMMON UNHELPFUL THINKING PATTERNS OF CHILDREN[16]

Theme	Self-talk	Emotion
Robot thinking It's not my fault.	I can't help it.	Sense of failure.
I'm awful It's all my fault.	I can't do anything right. I'm no good.	Low self-esteem. Fear of risks.
You're awful Everything's your fault.	I'd be able to do this if you weren't so bossy/stupid/etc.	Belligerence. Anger.
Fairy tale thinking It's not fair.	I wish things would get better.	Hurt, victimhood, helplessness.
Defeatist thinking I can't stand it.	I can't cope.	Anxiety, fear, over-reaction to threats.
Doomsday thinking Everything is dreadful.	Things are always awful. They'll never get any better.	Depression.

Neutralise the thought

When we allow our feelings to dictate how we live our life, we are like a puppet on a string, being jerked around by our emotions.[17] Being out of control like this feels dangerous, which tells us that strong feelings are dangerous.[18] As a result, we begin to fear them and try to control them. However, Action and Commitment Therapy (ACT) believes that we cannot control our thinking by the usual methods of avoidance, distraction, challenging the thought (looking for evidence that it isn't true, for example) or by thinking positively to counter it. When we try to control our thinking in these ways, first, we discover that we can't do it; second, we criticise ourselves for not being able to do it; and, third, we then obsess about not being able to do it – and the thought becomes more, rather than less, intrusive.[19] ACT says that this only gives negative thoughts extra attention that they don't deserve.

BOX 8.2 NAMING DOOMSDAY THINKING

I was working with a gifted 6-year-old who was refusing to go to school on the grounds that it was 'Always awful'. On a scale of 1 to 10, she assured me that every day was a zero. I expressed surprise at this because on some days she had library, and some days computer and some days music. If the days were all different, how could their rating be the same? To explain this, together we went through the list in Box 8.1 to see if she recognised any thinking pattern that she used a lot, and we agreed that she was a doomsday thinker.

I sent her off for two weeks to rate each school day. She returned after that period to report that, in fact, none of the days were zeros; instead, she had rated them as 4s, 5s and 6s. 'So I am a doomsday thinker... But,' she declared, 'I don't think I'll ever be able to stop it'. Being gifted, she immediately realised and confessed, 'You know, I just doomsday thought about my doomsday thinking'.

Therefore, instead of telling ourselves positive thoughts that we can't believe,[20] fighting our thoughts, or trying to correct them, we only need to stop believing them as strongly as we do. Instead of regarding them as a threat, we can rob them of their power over us by treating the words and images in our heads as mere stories. As Jeffers says, 'You don't have to hang out with enemies, even if they are within yourself'.[21]

The following strategies help us to distance ourselves from our thoughts. We need to do these with a sense of humour, without blaming ourselves for thinking them in the first place (because it's just the way the human mind works). And, when teaching these strategies to children, we need to make sure that it does not seem to them that we are making fun of or trying to minimise their feelings.[22]

- Regard your thoughts as being like music playing in the background or like cars driving past your house. You can pay attention to them if they are interesting, but let them slide on past if they are not helpful.[23]

- Set the thought to music (Jingle Bells, Happy birthday, or the Muppet song, for example) and sing it to yourself.

- Repeat the thought in a humorous voice (e.g. Homer Simpson's or Yoda's).

- Preface the thought with, 'I'm thinking that... (I'm stupid)'. Or, 'I'm noticing that...' Or 'I'm having the thought that... (I'm useless)'. Adding this preface reminds us that we can't believe everything we think: we would not believe ourselves if we declared, 'I'm thinking that... I'm a banana'.

- When you detect an unhelpful thought, tell yourself, 'Meh, that's the *I'm stupid* story again'. Maybe followed by 'BOR-ing... Heard it before... Whatever... Tell me when you've got something new'.

- Visual learners might enjoy seeing the thought on a computer screen in their mind's eye, and adjusting the font and the colours of the text. They can change the font size and spacing, put one word per line on the screen and bounce the words up and down... and so on.[24]

- You could visualise the thought written on a leaf, floating down the stream, or in space floating away into distant infinity.[25]

- Think of your ongoing commentary as *Radio Tripe F*: Fears, flaws and failures, with regular bulletins on everything you need to fear, updates on all your fears, and around-the-clock reminders of your failures.[26] Once you notice this commentary going on in your head, you can remind yourself, 'Aha, here's Radio Triple F again'.

- When you find yourself believing the doom and gloom of your mind's chatterbox, just remind yourself that you got hooked again (like a fish being reeled in on the angler's line): 'Oops, hooked again'.[27]

Changing our thinking in these ways is like learning a new language. We don't forget our first language, but the more we practise the second one, the more fluent we become in it.[28]

ACT is also aware that our species has feelings *about* our feelings and that the intensity of our emotions can sometimes scare us. Children can experience this when they are in meltdown mode and then, as if a switch flicks, they become hysterical, because their feelings are scaring them; adults can feel it when we are grieving.

To help with this second layer of feeling, Harris likens our mind to the sky, with our thoughts and feelings being the storm clouds that appear now and again.[29] He reminds us that, once these clouds (our thoughts and feelings) pass, the sky (our mind) is the same as it always was. I suspect that there are some exceptions when our mind is forever changed (such as when a parent loses a child). But for all everyday feelings, we can reassure ourselves that they have a limited life span and will go away by themselves if we give them time and if we don't give them airplay that they don't deserve.

EXPLAIN GROWING UP

This strategy is useful when children aged four and over are having an excessive number or intensity of meltdowns; I also use it to teach children toileting control (see my booklet on *Guiding children's early independence skills*).

Step 1. Explain to the children that growing up occurs in two places: on the outside, and on the inside (where their thoughts and feelings are).

Step 2. Next, let them know that you can see from looking at them, that they are growing up on the outside in just the right way for a person their age. If they are four years old, say, you can ask them to show you some skills and then comment that they can run fast, stand on one leg, have strong muscles, are *this* tall... and so on, none of which was true when they were three.

Step 3. Next, point out that their feelings are often overwhelming them or getting them into trouble. This tells you that their insides may have forgotten to grow up. They don't have to be worried about this: it happens to a lot of children. But it's hard to be two ages at once.

Step 4. Next, explain that, now that they are having a birthday soon (or the holidays are coming, or some other event is due), this is the right time to start *thinking* about whether they would like to teach their insides to grow up so that they can be the boss of their feelings. At this step, express faith that you know they can do it, because they are a Growing Up Expert (as demonstrated by their outsides). You know that they will be able to teach their feelings to grow up too – when they are ready.

Step 5. Do not give them suggestions or try to talk them into growing up. It has to be their decision. Instead, caution them to take a long time to think about it, because it is a big step. But, let them know that in the meantime, when their feelings do overwhelm them, you will help them (using mainly *time in* or *time away* – see below).

Of course, if they do manage to take command of their feelings, remember to congratulate them, be excited for them, and ask them how they did it – but *do not praise* (for the reasons that I gave in chapter 4).

Some children do not want to grow up because they believe that adults have no fun. They might not see you enjoying life, might hear only complaints about your work or other commitments, or think that because toys are fun and you have no toys, this must mean that you have no fun. So to explain the benefits of being grown up, you could talk with them about what you enjoy about being older – such as having more choices than you did as a child, and enjoying adult toys such as the household gadgets and your car – and also to be playful in your interactions with them so that they see you enjoying life.

TEACH ACCOUNTABILITY

Guidance believes that we are each responsible for ourselves and accountable for our actions. So that we do not lose sight of this fact, it is vital that we tell ourselves and others the truth about our choices. Instead, we often deny responsibility for ourselves by claiming that we 'have' to do something – as if there were some threat of being shot at dawn for failing to do it. Rosenberg says that we deny responsibility when we blame our actions on:[30]

- Vague, impersonal forces: 'I tidied up because I had to'.
- Our condition, personality or history: 'I can't help it. I've always been like that.'
- The actions of others: 'He started it'.
- The dictates of authority: 'I was only following orders'.
- Group pressure: 'Everyone else does it'.
- Policies, rules and regulations: 'He was sent to time out because that's school policy. My hands were tied'.
- Gender, age or social roles: 'I have to do the cooking because I'm the female'.
- Uncontrollable impulses: 'I couldn't help myself'.

Similarly, when we tell children that they 'have' to brush their teeth (for example), this is a falsehood. They *have* to do no such thing: there simply will be outcomes if they do not, outcomes which may be worse than the inconvenience of brushing their teeth.

Blaming outside forces disguises our choices and implies that we are helpless and not responsible for our own behaviour. Therefore, we have to challenge children when they deny being accountable for their actions, as in:

- I couldn't help it.
- He made me do it.
- It's not my fault.
- She got me angry.
- He started it.
- It's all your fault.
- I'd behave better if you weren't such a cow.

Therefore, without confronting or accusing children of mistaken thinking, we will translate these denials of accountability into statements that highlight children's agency. As the examples in Box 8.3 detail, we can do this by:[31]

- reflecting back the statement, without the non-accountability part
- raising counterexamples
- using the word 'and' to link feelings with accountability.

BOX 8.3 TRANSLATING DENIALS OF ACCOUNTABILITY

Denial of accountability	Translation
Reflection without the non-accountability element	
He teased me so I hit him.	You hit him.
You didn't give me my medication, so I couldn't concentrate.	You couldn't concentrate.
Supplying counterexamples	
I couldn't help it.	And yet yesterday when you were as angry as you are now, you were able to go off quietly to your room until you felt better.
Linking feelings and accountability	
He made me angry so I hit him.	It's okay to be angry and it's not okay to hit people.
She wouldn't let me play, so I told on her to the teacher.	You were sad and you told on her.

TEACH COPING SKILLS

When children are going through difficult life events, it is important to remind ourselves that pain does not equal trauma. And 'coping' does not mean that we feel no stress. (That would simply be a lack of awareness, in which case there would be something seriously wrong with our brain.) Instead, to cope means that we can use strategies to minimise the impact of the stress on our life. There are three potential strategies.[32]

- *Problem-focused action.* As its title implies, this involves solving the problem that is provoking stress.
- *Emotion-focused* strategies involve adjusting our thinking to change our emotional reactions.
- *Behavioural adjustment* involves changing our behaviour so that we can adjust better to circumstances that we cannot change.

The most useful strategy depends on the nature of the stressor. In general, we can encourage children to use problem-focused strategies when they have some control over a stressor, whereas they are best to use emotional or behavioural adjustments for issues that they cannot change.[33] If the stress is acute and uncontrollable, it can be wise just to disengage from it, but this doesn't help when problems are persistent.[34] The least effective strategies are emotional venting, engaging in wishful thinking, worrying, blaming themselves or attempting to ignore a problem and hope it will go away.[35]

Even so, aside from these ineffective coping measures, as long as children have positive options, it does not seem to matter precisely which one they use to cope.[36] Taking appropriate action both gives them experience of being in command of their lives and recruits support from others.[37] In turn, this social support itself will help reduce their stress levels.

And make sure that children get lots of free time to play so that they can wind down from stress. As I mentioned in chapter 3, people who have fun are happier, more productive, emotionally healthier and more resilient.[38]

MELTDOWNS

You might have been thinking as you were reading chapter 7 and the methods recommended so far in this chapter that the approaches sound all very well, but... And you would be right. They are all very well, but... all the methods that I've recommended so far involve talking. Yet there are times when talk doesn't do the work we need it to do. When children are in meltdown, they are beyond reason: and you cannot reason with people while they are being unreasonable. Or, put another way, when a person is drowning, that is *not* the time to give swimming lessons.[39]

By 'drowning' I'm thinking here of those times when children are drowning in emotion. When they are in meltdown mode, they will have to get calm again before being able to listen to our talk.

I have come across the following five common meltdowns.

Protesting: thrashing about, screaming, crying, spitting, self-harm (e.g. head banging). An older child might stomp about the house slamming doors; a younger child might be down on the floor, flailing arms and legs or, when upright, this is the stomping-flapping meltdown that is hilarious to watch but less of a joy to manage if you are the child's parent.

Whining or whingeing. This second pattern is the passive version of the protesting tantrum, involving sulking, whining, nagging and complaining. Although the decibels and duration differ between this and the protesting meltdown, the dynamic is the same: the children are disappointed about something and cannot get past that feeling to get on with what needs to be done. This form of meltdown appears at around three years of age, made possible by the children's advancing language skills and improved focus and attention span. At this age, they can go on and on and on about a grievance and, unlike the early two-year-old, *will not* be distracted.

Helplessness is the frustrated meltdown when children have failed at something and are giving up, perhaps throwing items around the room, declaring that they, the task or their teachers are 'stupid' or that they will never be able to do it.

Social meltdowns (aggression) include behaviours such as name calling, hitting others, biting (beyond the age of 18 months), bossing others, refusing to share or take turns, bullying and exclusion (including 'You can't come to my birthday party'). Aggression can take the following two forms.

- *Reactive* aggression, when children hit out 'hot-bloodedly' in reaction to a companion's behaviour that they perceive to be unjust. In that case, they are out of control of their emotions.

- *Proactive* aggression, when children 'cold-bloodedly' hurt others simply because they can. In that event, they are out of control of their impulses.

Uncooperativeness: not being able to overcome their distaste for a (reasonable) directive and therefore refusing to follow it, declaring in all conscience that they 'don't feel like it'. (This is where mother's speech comes to fore. This speech is best delivered looking like you've just sucked lemons and goes, 'Don't you realise that sometimes you have to do things whether you like it or not'.)

When children are displaying these or any other 'cues and clues' that their emotions are overwhelming them, it is important to remember that, because our species is born without the ability to manage our emotions, it is inevitable that children will occasionally 'lose it'. (We still do sometimes, even as adults.) If we punished children for getting out of control, we would be punishing them for *being* children – because children have lapses of control. Instead, therefore, we need to give them support, using one (or both) of the only two methods that our species uses to calm down.

TIME IN

When we are upset, our first option is to find a good friend to talk it over with: that is, we get close to someone for support. Similarly, when babies get distressed, we instinctively bring them in close to us and soothe them. But often our first impulse with older children is to send them away to sort themselves out alone. This is cruel.

In contrast, guidance uses *time in* at all ages. When children are young you can just cuddle them while they are distressed, soothing them and letting them cry – for as long as it takes for them to feel better. For children aged under four, this is perhaps your only option, because they typically cannot calm down alone.

Time in can take many forms. You might give children a hug, sit beside them on a sofa, hold their hand as you walk together, have them accompany you as you go about your chores, or sit on the floor of their bedroom while they cry on their bed... whatever. With older children who might not want you physically close right now, it might just involve emotional closeness: 'You look like you're having a tough time. Anything I can do?' or, 'Some days it's not easy being you, is it?'.

When children have hurt someone, soothe the target first and then use *time in* to calm perpetrators on the grounds that their actions indicate that they were out of control of themselves at the time.

Throughout *time in*, while the children are resolving their feelings, say very little. Do not explain yourself or the trigger for the meltdown (because they already know all this). As Rosenberg advises: Be a surfer and ride the wave of emotion,[40] going with its energy, rather than trying to hold it back or telling children to settle down. Above all, remember that *children need our compassion the most when they appear to 'deserve' it the least* – that is, being out of control is scary and, the younger you are, the scarier it is. Therefore, the children need your help to soothe themselves.

Using a 'broken record technique', every now and then, repeat empathic comments such as, 'I understand that you're upset/sad/angry. I'll be here for you until you feel better... I'm sorry you're feeling so awful. I'm here for you'. Do not try to hurry them into recovering, instead saying the likes of, 'Take your time. I'm here'. Express your faith that they can help themselves feel better (giving the 'I-believe-in-you' speech), and express pleasure for them or congratulate them (but do not praise) when they are beginning to feel better. Meanwhile, give them every physical comfort you can. With their consent, keep them cool by stripping off their outer clothing, or cool them down with a damp face cloth.

You can be flexible with how you use *time in*, interrupting it to care for another child, handing the child over to your partner when you need to be elsewhere or have had enough, allowing toilet stops, and so on. You know your children: trust your instincts, and experiment with what works for you.

The essence of this approach is that you are providing an emotional safety net for those times when the children cannot provide their own and for when their feelings are distressing them. Being out of control is unpleasant at any age but is even more scary when we are very young. In that case, we have to help children to recover.

With lots of practice, children will be able to soothe themselves, which will prevent their victims from being hurt again in future. Another benefit of *time in* is that it works with infants who cannot yet understand your words. They hear your soothing tone, but they also gather that you mean business. Say by way of an example that a six-month-old is repeatedly banging his head on his high chair tray. In that case, you will lift him out, soothe him, and return him to the high chair once he is calm... and do it again if he resumes head banging. The infant needs no language to understand that he must stop hurting himself.

Dealing with an escalation

When you use *time in*, sometimes a passive meltdown (whining or uncooperativeness) turns into a full-on active protest. This is not a sign that the method does not work, but simply tells you that the children's feelings were almost at boiling point. Their distress confirms that you were right to notice that their feelings were getting too much for them to handle alone. During this escalation or during any active meltdown (protesting or social), children typically go through four stages of emotional reaction:[41]

- anger
- sadness
- bargaining (a false calm)
- calm

– but not necessarily in a neat order. They might go back and forth between the stages again and again before finally calming down. All the while, you will reflect each feeling ('I'm sorry you're feeling angry/

sad/upset. I'll be here for you until you feel better... I can see you're starting to feel calm, but let's sit here a little while longer till you feel completely better' and so on.

Box 8.4 Tips for responding to children's meltdowns

- When children are *protesting*, listen and reflect their feelings, using a 'broken record' technique of repeating consoling statements, without debating the reasons for the child's protests: 'I understand that you're angry... I'm sorry you're feeling so upset... I'll be here for you until you feel better'.

- When children are regularly whining or *whingeing*, ask them if they can find their 'happy voice' or if they can ask again happily. If they cannot, they need soothing. Use *time in* if they are willing, or perhaps *time away* followed by *time in*.

- For *helplessness*, empathise with the children's frustration. Ask what they need so that they feel better, which will probably be a form of time away.

- For *social* meltdowns (aggression), in the presence of the aggressor, empathise with and soothe the victim, apologise on behalf of the aggressor and, once the victim is satisfied, turn to the aggressor and say, 'I wouldn't let them hurt you and I cannot let you hurt them'. Insist that the child remain in your company but separate from peers until she or he 'feels better and you know that the other children will be safe'.

- When children are *not cooperating* with a reasonable request, ask what their objection is. On occasion, allow them to have a 'slack attack' and not perform tasks that they object to. If their uncooperativeness is habitual, or the behaviour is compulsory (such as when they are refusing to wear a seat belt in a car), announce calmly, 'I'll wait'. There's no need to explain why they have to wear a seatbelt: they already know that. Instead, they just need time to get in touch with their own reasons for doing it and to overcome their reluctance.

Duration

Parents often ask me how long this takes. You must last until children have calmed down. To end earlier would put them at risk of getting into trouble again as soon as you release them. (If children act thoughtlessly soon after the procedure, this just means that you mis-read them and they were not as calm as you thought. Just bring them close to you again for some more *time in*.)

The first time can take up to an hour; but, within a week of repeated daily practice on any occasion when they have one of the five types of meltdown, the children manage it within a few minutes. They will have learned how to control themselves. All you will have to do from then on is read their behaviour for signs that they are getting distressed and ask, 'You look like you're getting upset. Do you need some help?'.

Given that the process can take a long time at first, there will be occasions when you simply cannot do it. You might need to get to work, you might be too angry yourself to want to do it, or one of your other children might need you. In these cases, don't use this approach, perhaps explaining, 'I can see you're upset, and I would like to help you, but I can't just now. I am sorry'. Use *time away* instead (– see the next section) or just manage the crisis the best you can.

Escape

If the children escape or run away during this process, do not chase them, because you will look ridiculous and it is dangerous. Instead, wait until they come back within your orbit and draw them in close to you again then. This works even if they are already calm.

Remember that escape is the last gasp of the dance of coercion and defiance (– see Figure 6.2) and that, therefore, children are less likely to run when they are not being controlled. Why *wouldn't* they choose to stay with you while you support them to feel better? They only run away in an effort to avoid being blamed, shamed and humiliated.

Protective force

If the children are thrashing about violently and might injure themselves or you, it can be necessary as a very last resort to use some force in the form of a restrictive hold. (You cannot do this if pregnant, and tends to be impossible past the age of four because the children will be too strong for you. And, after that age, they usually can manage their feelings alone.)

The hold involves sitting young children on one of your thighs and crossing your other leg over their lap, moving your bottom calf out of the way of their flailing legs. (If you forget to do this the first time, bruises are a fine teacher and you will remember next time.) If absolutely necessary to avoid being bitten or punched, you can hold their wrists and cross their arms over their chest. Progressively, you will release your hold so that it reverts to a normal cuddle as soon as the children can agree not to hurt you or themselves.

This is an application of protective force, aimed at preventing children from injuring themselves or hurting others while their emotions are running high. If you use it as a form of coercion, it doesn't work because children resist, rebel and retaliate against it.

Precautions

On most occasions, *time in* will just be a natural hug or cuddle, which carries no risk at all. However, if you plan to use the restrictive hold for children who are not your own, you will need permission from their parent. Second, be sure to get medical advice if you intend to hold children who have a heart condition or whose asthma could be exacerbated by emotional stress, for example.

Responding to meltdowns in public

If your children are protesting in the middle of an activity such as driving the car or shopping, on the understanding that you have a right not to perform tasks to the accompaniment of your children's screaming, stop and give them time to recover. Use *time in* and, once they can hear you, deliver an empathic assertive message, such as, 'I know that the shopping is taking a long time and I'm sorry that you're fed up with it... But I really need to finish it... What do you need so we can get it done and go home?'.

If a brief pause is not enough for the children to recover from a protesting meltdown, even if it means leaving a trolleyful of unbought goods at the supermarket checkout, go outside to your car or withdraw to a secluded area. Once outdoors, use *time in* to soothe them until they are back in command of themselves. This is the 'Change the child' option. Once they are calm again, return to what you were doing.

If the children simply cannot get back in charge of themselves, take them home. This suggestion applies whether you are shopping or visiting friends. It is the 'Change the demands' option. This is not a case of the children 'winning': you are simply choosing not to force yourself (or them) to function under these conditions.

You will not have to do this often. If the shopping has to be left until another day and there is no attractive food in the house in the meantime, the children will have to eat what's available. Of course so too will the adults, although this small sacrifice may ensure years of pleasant shopping in future – and you *could* order take-aways after the children have gone to bed!

If you are in someone else's home, are on the phone, or have visitors at your house, interrupt what you are doing and excuse yourself to deal with your children's behaviour. If it looks like it will take a while for the children to settle down, take yourself home, end your phone call, or invite your visitors to leave.

In public, onlookers are less likely to offer unsolicited advice when they see you responding effectively and compassionately to your children. But if someone does offer gratuitous advice, let it wash over you. You do not have to take seriously the opinions of people you have never met, and you have no obligation to respond to onlookers at the same time as trying to calm your child. Give yourself a break.

When your relatives give you advice, you are free to take it or ignore it. However, when you depart from that advice or advance a contrary opinion – particularly when your ideas differ from your parents' or parents'-in-law – they might become defensive and feel that you are accusing them of raising you incorrectly. However, their generation has a right to be loyal to their values and they cannot use ideas they have never heard of, so you will need to honour their standpoint, without necessarily following their advice.

TIME AWAY

When you have had a bad day and are furious and fed up, you might calm yourself down by doing some exercise or, doing the opposite by having a rest; by turning on the TV or watching You tube to distract yourself; or by listening to some loud music so you cannot hear yourself complaining. In other words, you will have chosen something physical, visual or auditory to soothe yourself, depending on your favoured learning style. (You will note that I've left alcohol out of my list of potential solutions!)

Whichever method you use to calm down, I guarantee that the one that you've never tried is to sit yourself on a chair in the laundry facing the wall.

This is the difference between *time out* and *time away*. *Time out* is a punishment which says to children that it is naughty to get upset. In contrast, *time away* recognises that people sometimes get over-whelmed by their feelings. They cannot, of course, inflict their feelings on others, so they will have to find some solitude and to do something that soothes them. You might, therefore, invite them to head to their room and play on their computer (unless having to turn that off was what triggered the original upset), play with their dolls or train, read a book, build with their construction toy, or whatever is their favourite thing – until they feel better.

Children aged under four cannot usually calm down without your help but if *time in* is failing you for some reason, or you cannot use it in the present circumstances, *time away* is a good option. At any age, you can follow *time away* with *time in* once the child is calm again.

The controlling style of parenting believes that allowing children to do something pleasant until they feel better just rewards 'bad' behaviour. Guidance, however, accepts that *time in* and *time away* are the only two methods known to our species for calming down when our feelings are overwhelming us: get some help from someone who cares about us, or do something relaxing.[42] The aim of these methods is to teach children to self-soothe, not to punish them for not knowing how.

MANAGING YOUR ANGER

Virginia Satir tells us that we have learned to fear anger because we were taught that anger causes fighting; that fighting is bad, and therefore that anger is bad.[43] We often try to suppress it or, especially in the case of females (who are taught that we are not allowed to be angry), mask it by converting it into sadness. Instead, anger merely signals that an underlying need is not being met.[44] We can think of it as a wake-up call, or in any of the following three ways.

- Our churning emotions are like a dashboard light warning us that our car's engine is overheating. We may wish that the light would go out, but the only way to achieve that is to fix the problem.
- Anger is like our phone ringing: it's our own feelings 'ringing our bell'. We have to pick up our receiver to discover what need of ours is at the other end.
- Anger is like an alarm clock, there to wake us up to what we need.[45]

Anger is the result of a three-step process. First, we need something that we are not receiving. This gives rise to a feeling – say, of hurt – that motivates us to act. Second, we fear that our needs will not be met. This heightens our arousal level. This is illustrated in Figure 8.1, in which anger is depicted as the part of the iceberg that is visible above water level, with the bulk of the feeling below the surface. Third, in this inflamed state of mind, we judge others to be in the wrong and demand that they *should* meet our needs. When they do not, we blame them for 'making' us angry.

FIGURE 8.1 THE ANGER ICEBERG

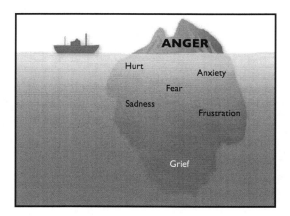

In other words, anger is stirred up by a diversion into demanding thinking that adds to the intensity and unpleasantness of our original feeling.[46]

Anger	=	a feeling that arises when a need is not met
	+	fear that the need will not be met
	+	demanding thinking.

At the end of this sequence of unhelpful thinking, we are likely to speak or behave in a way that will virtually guarantee that we will not get what we want – or that, if we do, it will not be given willingly.[47] Instead, rather than judging the child (for acting that way) or ourselves (for not knowing what to do about it), we can choose to connect empathically with both our own and the child's needs.[48] The steps for doing so are as follows.[49]

1. *Stop.* Take a few deep breaths. Take some time to connect with yourself.

2. *Identify the unmet need* that gives rise to your first feeling.

3. *Identify the judgmental thoughts* that are causing your anger. Listen out specifically for the words *should, shouldn't, ought, must* or *must not*.

4. *Reconnect with your intention or purpose*: decide what you want to achieve right now for yourself and for your relationship with the child.

5. *Express your feelings* and unfulfilled need. (Remember from chapter 7 that naming your feeling is optional and at times might even be unwise.)

6. *Request what the other person can do to meet your needs*, using language that avoids judgments and criticism.

These steps are based on the recognition that, like us, the child with whom we are angry is simply trying to meet a need. The conflict is not about our needs, but about the strategies we are using to meet them. Once we can identify the underlying need, we will be able to generate alternative strategies for meeting it. In this way, we have not achieved a compromise but a solution that suits both of us.

It is important to remember that when other people 'push your buttons', they didn't put the buttons there. Their actions activate your unconscious belief about how others should behave and should treat you. (Wouldn't it be handy if we could just write a list of our *shoulds* and hand them out to everyone we knew, so that they could just abide by them, without our having to tell them?) In other words, their actions didn't cause our feelings: these were lying dormant, waiting to be activated. As Katherine Sellery says, your reaction (or over-reaction) is a clue to your unconscious beliefs. Your reaction holds the secret to what is going on for you.[50]

It is vital to try to identify what you need, feel and are thinking; otherwise, your anger will prevent you from seeing what is going on for your children. For many of us, the issue may be that we are having difficulty seeing our children as separate individuals, with the result that we personalise what they do, when in reality it has nothing to do with us: it's about them.

CONSISTENCY

Life is inconsistent. *People* are inconsistent.[51] We cannot hide this fact from children by trying to be predictable and imposing order in the form of rules. Children are used to living with real people who have moods: they can navigate the 'complicated emotional terrain'[52] of daily life. As long as we are not explosive, children are perfectly capable of adjusting to our changing needs. Being able to do this is essential throughout their lives for their ability to adapt to change. But if rather than being human with them, we present a fake persona of the Authority Figure, they won't be able to find us behind all our rules – and will try various behaviours in order to uncover who we are and what we stand for. And when we are not honest with them, they cannot be honest with us.[53]

Therefore, guidance believes that consistency is both impossible and undesirable. It is also unnecessary. The example that I gave in chapter 1 is that when you want your child to learn to swim, you could take her to daily lessons for two weeks and she will learn to swim (at age level) within a fortnight. Or, you could give her lessons once a month. She will still learn to swim – but it will take longer. Similarly, the more often you can support children to get back in control of their feelings, the more quickly they will learn self-regulation. But if you simply can't help them during a particular meltdown, you don't have to worry, because they will lose the plot another time, and you can teach them how to calm down then.

Nevertheless, you will be steadfast in your convictions that everyone has rights and everyone must behave considerately and therefore that you will protect children and their targets from thoughtless behaviour. But how you respond on any given occasion can vary according to the circumstances at the time. This is the essence of wisdom.

Of course, the rest of the world will continue to try to control your children. Luckily, however, children will not believe that their worth depends on whether they receive rewards or punishments when you have never linked the two.

Change your mind

When you have refused your children something and they protest in disappointment, you can change your mind if, on reflection, you realise that doing so would not interfere with your rights. This is different from giving in when you don't want to, just to keep the peace, however.

Let's say that, in the supermarket your child has asked for an ice-cream and you have said 'No' because you were distracted at the time by the choice between the large or the small jar of olives. Your child is now in a puddle on the floor, screaming.

Of course, you will not change your mind if she has just polished off a packet of sweets, if she has a lactose intolerance, or if you can't afford an ice-cream. But if on reflection, you realise that she has not had any sweet treats for a while and that her request is fair, you might decide to change your mind.

You could do this with the following commentary: 'I see that you're very upset that I said you couldn't have an ice-cream. Now that I know that, I'm thinking about changing my mind... But I can't think with all this noise going on'. The child will cheer up pretty quickly. Once she is calm, you can go on to explain (with your precise language depending on her age): 'I'm happy for you to have an ice-cream. Of course, there are none here in the supermarket. We have to get one from the mall. What do you need right now to be able to finish the shopping before we go to the ice-cream shop?'. Once the child is calm enough to carry on with the shopping (again, depending on her age), you could end with, 'You know, next time you're disappointed in something I say, you don't have to get yourself so upset. You can just say, "Mum, are you sure?" and I will listen to you'.

Those from the controlling school think this will reward children for having meltdowns, and will teach them to have them again in an effort to get their own way. Guidance believes instead that no one enjoys feeling badly and that being flexible will teach your child many valuable lessons, including that:

- you will empathise with her, even when she is not communicating politely
- you will listen to her arguments or objections
- that is, you are reasonable, wise and fair
- she is allowed and is able to assert her own needs and opinions
- she can calm herself down
- she can postpone getting what she wants when she has hope that it will be supplied – that is, she can delay gratification.

All these lessons are far more important than learning that you are more stubborn than she is. (By the way, if you think you can be more stubborn than a three-year-old, good luck with that!)

PARENTING AS A TEAM

Participants at my seminars often ask what happens if one parent uses the controlling style, while the other uses guidance. My response is that the controlling parent's relationship with the children will suffer, but the *children* will not. They will be able to tell the difference between their two parents and will behave well for one and poorly for the other. So you will not have parenting problems... but you will have marital problems.

A common pattern is that when parents start out together, they often have similar ideas about how to parent. However, over time when faced with challenges, one parent gets more strict and, seeing this, the second parent becomes more permissive. In turn, the first parent sees that the other is being too lax and tries to tighten the reins;

in response to which the second tries to compensate by becoming even more permissive. Although the two started out on the same page, after a few months you could drive a truck between them.

Guidance principles really help here, because the two parents can often find common ground in that guidance is firm – it absolutely requires children to act thoughtfully (and therefore tends to suit those with more authoritarian views) – while, at the same time, it offers children support (and therefore tends to suit a more nurturing style).

One parent as the target

Sometimes, children behave well for one parent and really poorly for the other. This parent is usually the one who is with the children the most, getting them to eat their vegies, brush their teeth and go to bed, all of which are fertile ground for conflict. However, the unevenness of the children's behaviour can cause both parents to assume that one of them is incompetent. But the fact that the children behave well for other people means that they know how to do so, which tells you that *some*thing you are doing is working. Second – and most important – if they hold it together all day at school (say) and then let rip with you, this means that they know you are going to love them anyway. Instead of signalling your incompetence, this is an excellent sign that they trust you.

CONCLUSION

Guidance methods have many advantages. The first is that both parents can endorse them, because they are firm at the same time as being nurturing. Second, the approaches help to heal your relationship with your challenging children, whose behaviour to date might have left you disliking them and feeling inadequate yourself for not knowing how to stop the disruptions. Third, these methods *work*.

For their part, offering your children support instead of censure gives them the security of knowing that you will be there for them, even when they are at their worst. In the long term, having the skill to manage their own emotions allows children to trust themselves, giving them safety and self-esteem, while preventing their outbursts from troubling those around them. And it achieves all this without incurring the disadvantages of punishments.

SUMMARY OF PRINCIPLES

- You don't have to hang out with enemies, even if they are within yourself.
- We can't believe everything we think.
- Children need our compassion the most when they appear to 'deserve' it the least.
- You do not have to tolerate inconsiderate behaviour.
- You cannot reason with people while they are being unreasonable.
- When a person is drowning, that is not the time to give swimming lessons.
- Look for a solution, not a culprit.
- What other people think of us is none of our business.
- You don't have to take seriously the opinions of people you've never met.
- Consistency is unnecessary, but repeated practice helps.

Solving persistent problems 9

Difficulties turn into problems when our attempts to solve them have not worked. Everyone involved is stuck. At times like this, you might have even heard yourself saying that you have 'tried everything'. However, this usually means that you have tried everything you can think of to make it stop. In other words, you have tried every reward and punishment on the menu.

Not only do these methods not work, but our focus on the problem doesn't help. This is because we usually start by thinking about what is going wrong and trying to fix that. But sometimes, for example, the trigger happened in the past and we don't have a time machine to undo that, so we feel helpless. To get unstuck, we can begin with the awareness that problems don't happen all the time. This means that there are times when something is going right. Therefore, we can look for what is working and use that. This puts us in the role of the curious detective, who searches for clues to the solutions that are already working. This difference in focus is described in Box 9.1.

CHANGE LANGUAGE TO ACKNOWLEDGE POSSIBILITIES

Words and phrases such as *always, nobody, never,* or *all the time* cause us to feel stuck and to lose hope that things can change. They leave us despondent and imply criticism of either ourselves or someone else. Therefore, we will have to translate hopeless language about a problem into language that implies the possibility of change. As illustrated in Box 9.2, we do this by:

- converting our language from present to past tense
- translating words such as *always, never* etc. into partial statements
- highlighting the subjectivity of the statement.

BOX 9.1 PROBLEM SOLVING COMPARED WITH SOLUTION BUILDING[1]

Problem solving	Solution building
Attempts to understand what is going wrong and how to fix it.	Focuses on what is working and how to use it.
Examines instances of problems.	Examines exceptions to difficulties.
Asks 'why' people do things.	Asks 'how' people do things.
Focuses on the past.	Emphasises future possibilities.
Regards people as flawed.	Sees people as capable.
The parent is responsible for generating a solution.	The person experiencing the problem is the one to solve it..
The parent is certain.	The parent is curious.
The parent takes the credit for solving the problem.	The child takes credit for solving the problem.

SET GOALS

It is always easier to reach a destination if you know where you are going. Therefore, when trying to solve any chronic problem, it pays to have a destination or goal in mind. To achieve this, you could reflect on the following questions – or, if your children are old enough, you could ask them about their own behaviour:

- Once this problem is fixed, what will it look like?

- If, while you were sleeping tonight, a miracle happened and this problem were fixed, what would have changed? Who will be doing what differently?[2]

- Pretend that there are two movies of your life, one with the problem as it is now, and one without the problem: What does the second movie look like?[3]

- How would that make a difference to you?

INTERRUPT THE PATTERN

Remember that every behaviour is meeting a need. When a behaviour is troublesome, you cannot frustrate children's legitimate needs, but you *can* insist that the resulting behaviour is less disruptive to others by interrupting the sequence of events that leads up to the disturbing behaviour.[4]

BOX 9.2 CHANGING LANGUAGE

Complaint	Translation
Change of tense	
He's always in trouble.	So far, he's been in trouble a lot.
Things will never change.	Up to now, things haven't changed.
I just have a depressive type of personality. I can't change that.	So far, you haven't found a way to change your depressive thinking.
Partial statements	
Nothing ever goes right for me.	Right now it seems like nothing ever goes right for you.
She never behaves herself.	Sometimes it feels to you like she misbehaves all the time.
Highlighting subjectivity	
I can't do anything right.	You believe that you can't do anything right.
He'll never amount to anything.	Because of the difficulties he's having at the moment, it seems to you that he won't amount to anything.

The key to this strategy is awareness that a chain is only as strong as its weakest link. When a chain or series of actions leads time and again to the same outcome, you can disrupt the sequence or 'interrupt the pattern'. When you do so, the behaviour will change.

Box 9.3 gives examples of the following possibilities for pattern interruption:

- change the location of the behaviour
- change who is involved
- change the sequence of the steps involved
- interrupt the sequence in its initial stages ('derailing')
- introduce random starting or stopping
- increase the frequency of the behaviour (although you cannot do this for aggression).

BOX 9.3 EXAMPLES OF PATTERN INTERRUPTION

- *Change the location*: When children throw themselves down on the floor in a meltdown, as long as you can do so safely, you could move them onto the sofa, explaining that they will be more comfortable there.

- *Changing who is involved*: When children become distressed at separating from their parent to attend child care or school, it can help to have someone else take them.

- *Changing the sequence*: Let's say that a common sequence in your household is that once the children's favourite TV program starts, they fight over which chair to sit in. In that case, as long as they are not violent with each other, you could invite them to have their fight now, before the program starts, so that they do not miss out once it begins.

- *Derailing*: Before children start to refuse to tidy up their room, you could say, 'I bet you don't feel like tidying up'. Another example is when children fuss about their meal once they're at the dinner table. Instead you could invite them to fuss now, before their dinner is served.

- *Introducing random starting*: If children often get into disputes once they get home from school, after a few minutes, you could say: 'You've been home for ten minutes now and haven't had a go at each other yet. How about you say something mean now so that you don't have to bother later'.

- *Increasing the frequency*: When children become distressed at separating from their parent, you could let them know that it's okay to cry when they are sad and that they can keep crying until they don't feel sad anymore.

LOOK FOR EXCEPTIONS

When a problem has been occurring for a long time, it is easy to convince yourself that it is 'always' happening. But *nothing* ever happens 100 percent of the time. There will inevitably be times when the children either do not produce the troublesome behaviour, or it is less severe than usual. These instances are known as *exceptions*.

This method helps you examine what is different about those times when an exception happens, compared with when the challenging behaviour occurs. That information will help you to do more of what leads to the exceptions.

Step 1. Identify exceptions. The first step is to identify these exceptions. You might hear yourself thinking, 'She's hardly ever ready on time to leave for school... She doesn't have many friends...' or a child might declare, 'He usually starts it'. The words *hardly ever* or *many* or *usually* signal that the problem isn't always happening. You can reflect on the exceptions by asking some questions of either yourself or an older child (as listed in Box 9.4).

BOX 9.4 QUESTIONS THAT IDENTIFY EXCEPTIONS[5]

- When is the problem absent or less noticeable?
- Where do the children get into least trouble?
- At school, what is their best class?
- What's different about that class compared to their other classes?
- In what ways is that teacher different from their other teachers? What else?
- What difference does that difference make to them?
- At what time in the past week have things been a little better than usual?
- Think about a time recently when (the problem) wasn't happening. What was going on at the time?
- On a scale of 1 to 10, have the child rate her current level of happiness (for example). Let's say that the child gives herself a rating of 3. Then you can invite her to 'Think about a time in the past month when you were above a 3.. What helped you at that time to get higher than 3?'

Step 2. Identify strengths. In order to identify how children get the exceptions to happen, you next will have to understand the strengths and resources they bring to bear on the problem. To identify their strengths, if the children are too young to reflect, you could ask the questions in Box 9.5 of yourself in an effort to understand what is working. Or, you can ask older children and adolescents about their strengths. In listening to their answers, you will look out for examples of the following skills:[6]

- *actions* that indicate courage, healthy risk taking (adventurousness)
- *effort* that demonstrates strength, growth, application, impulse control
- *commitments* that show loyalty, dedication, devotion, follow-through, persistence, diligence
- *attitudes* that reflect tolerance, acceptance, flexibility, enthusiasm, confidence, patience
- *social orientation*, including empathy, caring, cooperation, loyalty, independence, compromise, negotiation, listening, assertiveness, problem solving

- *thoughts* that are creative, imaginative, positive, realistic, sensitive, insightful
- *goals* that are healthy, sensible, realistic, strategic, or growth producing
- *decisions* based on wise judgment, morality, self-awareness, maturity, planfulness.

BOX 9.5 QUESTIONS THAT IDENTIFY STRENGTHS[7]

Once you have noticed instances when the problem was absent or less severe than usual, you can ask 'positive blaming' questions to help children to identify what they did to generate these exceptions.

- How did you do that?
- How did you get that to happen?
- What did you do to pull that off?
- What did you tell yourself that helped you do that?
- What steps did you take leading up to it?
- How did you manage to get your work done in that class?
- How do you resist the urge to muck around?
- Did you know you could do that?
- Is that something different for you?
- Can you tell me about other times you've tried something useful like that?

A second set of follow-up questions implies something about the children's identity:

- What does it tell us about what is important to you in life that you were willing to do that?
- What does this tell you about yourself and your ability to solve this problem?
- What did the problem have you thinking about yourself before? What do you think about yourself now?

Your decision to focus on aspects other than the problem is not merely to help everyone feel better, but to gather information about children's skills and personal attributes that can become part of the solution.

Step 3. Highlight strengths. You will then build these instances of children's successes into positive stories about them that contradict the story that they 'are' or have a problem. In addition to discussing this new information directly with them, you can make sure they overhear you telling a story to your partner or a friend about something admirable they have done (in celebration, not manipulation, of course). This 'keyhole listening' can make these stories especially newsworthy for the children, because information is more meaningful when we overhear something that we think we are not supposed to.

Looking for children's strengths is powerful, because it implies that you believe that they can make things happen and gives them hope about their future.[8]

> Raising children is not about correcting their weaknesses and fixing whatever is wrong with them. Rather, it is about identifying and nurturing their strengths.[9]

Step 4. Expand on exceptions. Once you can identify the exceptions, you then expand your children's awareness of these so that they feel capable of using the strategies more often. There will be four possible scenarios. First, when your children can identify their successful strategies, you can ask what it would take for them to use those again.

Second, if the children doubt their ability to repeat a success, you can invite them to observe what is different about those times when they do manage to create an exception,[10] or invite them to experiment with ways to get it to happen again.

Third, when children believe that the exceptions are just flukes, you will have to raise their awareness that these are not mere accidents but come about because of something they do. To encourage them to use their solutions, you could enquire about their heroes and then ask: 'What do you think (their hero's name) would do if faced with this problem? Would that be something you'd be willing to try?'[11] Alternatively, you could suggest that they pretend that their miracle/solution/goal has been achieved.[12] For example, you could invite children who are often aggressive to pretend that they feel friendly. You can then conspire with them that each day their teacher will have to guess whether they are only pretending to be friendly, or are 'for real'.

Finally, when children are convinced that they have no control over the problem, you can ask them to think about how come it is no worse than it is: what is keeping it from becoming even more serious?[13] Another possibility is to ask an outsider such as their teacher to invite the child to act as his or her consultant, asking, 'When I have another child in my class with a problem like this, what do you think I could do to help him or her?'.[14]

EXTERNALISE THE PROBLEM

When everyone has thought that the problem is due to something internal to the children and that therefore they cannot do anything about it (as heard when a 10-year-old proclaims, 'I can't help it. I've got ADD'), we can avoid locating blame *within* children by giving their behaviour a name and speaking about it as if it were external to them. This reverses the internalising logic of guilt, embarrassment and shame.[15]

This method rests on the knowledge that the words that surround us and which others use to describe us get mapped onto our psyches, or are internalised. Moreover, they are totalising: that is, they take over, with the result that no other view of the child can penetrate. They acquire the status of 'truth' and become irrefutable. Despite the fact that labels reflect only *some* of the characteristics of individuals, the descriptions come to dominate observers' and the children's own concept of their *whole* self and, furthermore, highlight their deficits rather than their competencies. Externalising the problem, then, puts the problem back where it belongs: outside of the child.[16] The method can be particularly useful when the problem seems to have a life of its own, or when children report feeling helpless to control it. The steps are as follows.

Step 1. In discussion with your children, give the problem a name. Use their language to label the problem, or have them select from a list of potential labels that you generate, such as:

- outbursts of anger might be labelled as *Temper, Trouble, Agitation* or *Rage*
- sadness might be labelled as *Misery*
- for those with attention difficulties, it could be that *Squirmies, Rushing* or *Guessing* make them unsuccessful.[17]

You can also just refer to the problem as *It*, or *The Depression*. Or, you can name destructive interaction patterns that are blocking solutions. I have already demonstrated this in chapter 6 by calling the cycle of child defiance and adult coercion a 'dance'. Other interaction patterns can be named using questions such as:[18]

- How much say does *Bullying* have in your friendships at school?
- How much has *Secrecy* ruled over you and prevented you from getting help?

Step 2. Investigate the problem's strategies and 'pattern of entry'.[19] Ask the children what strategies The Problem uses to get them off course, or into trouble (as relevant):

- When does Misery make an appearance?
- When is it most likely to strike and catch you off guard?
- Does it sneak up on you, or burst onto you?
- Does it boss you around?

Step 3. Gauge their motivation. Once you know how The Problem manipulates them, gauge their motivation for change by asking questions such as:

- How do you feel being bossed around by *Trouble?*
- Are you happy about that?
- Are you happy being in the passenger's seat in your life, or would you prefer to be the driver?[20]
- Do you want to do something about it?

Step 4. Examine the Allies. Sometimes, Problems have Allies that team up with them and cause further oppression, such as *Self-doubt* or *Self-criticism*.[21] In that case, you can ask if the Ally insults them and, if so, does it whisper at them or shout at them?

Step 5. Gauge their feelings about the problem. Once you know the tactics that The Problem and its Allies use, you can again gauge how motivated the child is to tame, conquer, subdue, overcome or overpower them. You can ask or comment:

- What have you *ever done* to deserve being spoken to like that?
- Do you think it's fair to be spoken to like that? How do you feel about it?.

Although I dislike the language, children usually find that it makes sense when I ask them who their enemy is. They can usually name someone in their class; let's call that person Jamie. Then I ask, 'If Jamie said that you were stupid, what would you say back?'. They can usually produce some counter-attack. The next step is to tell them to use that same counter-attack when they are saying it to themselves. Abuse is still abuse, even when it is self-abuse.

Step 6. Teach children to distance themselves from the thoughts that the Problem and its Allies have caused them to believe about themselves (– see the section on *Teach helpful thinking in* chapter 8).

GIVE UP COERCION

This method is suitable for children with persistent aggression and for any behavioural difficulty where you believe that you have 'tried everything' to get a behaviour to stop. The approach is built on recognition that the vast majority of chronic behavioural problems in children aged over four years are reactive – that is, the children are protesting at being denied autonomy. Therefore, this approach simply abandons trying to 'make' them change.

Step 1. Tell the child that you and everyone else who has been involved (and name each adult individually) have tried everything you can think of to make the behaviour stop. You realise that this is not working, so are giving up trying.

Step 2. Explain that, nevertheless, it still has to stop (because, with aggression, for example, 'I wouldn't let other children hurt you, so I cannot let you hurt them'). Explain therefore that someone will have to think of something to get it to stop. (Given that everyone you have just named has run out of ideas, the clear implication is that the child will have to be the one to solve it.)

Step 3. Separate the child from the targets of his or her behaviour, on the grounds that surrounding children and adults have a right not to be hurt or intimidated.

This isolation can take many forms. You could direct two siblings who are continually arguing with each other to sit on separate armchairs, with you on another. They cannot watch TV or play computer games to distract them but, otherwise, you can talk with them pleasantly (not about their behaviour), they can read, have snacks and drinks... whatever it takes to make them comfortable – but they are to stay there until 'Someone thinks of something to make the fighting stop'. You can commiserate with their boredom and allow them toilet stops as required, but afterwards they must return to their chair until someone thinks of something. Without saying so outright, the clear message is that the 'someone' won't be you.

This process can be flexible. If two parents are available, one can accompany each child in a separate room, or one can step in and take over from the other. Or if you are a solo parent, you can leave to perform essential duties such as cooking meals, as long as the children agree to stay where they are until you return.

Persist for as long as necessary, until the child thinks of a way to stop the behaviour. Indeed, Glasser suggests that you last longer than the children think you will.[22] When children's behavioural problems are severe, this step can last anywhere from a few hours to many days. With school-aged children, you could even institute the procedure all day each Saturday and Sunday of successive weekends, for example.

Step 4. Once children declare that they have thought of a way to stop the behaviour, you will have to apply the brakes, because when we make hasty resolutions, we abandon them just as quickly (as our New Year's resolutions prove). Therefore, congratulate them for coming up with an idea, but advise them that the difference between a goal and a dream is that a goal has a plan.[23] They will have to stay where they are until they have put a plan together. In negotiation with you, the plan will ultimately have two parts: how they will manage their emotions and impulses, and what supports you will provide to help them do this. (This is an instance of a reciprocal contract, as detailed in chapter 7.)

Step 5. Once you are satisfied that their plan is viable, allow them to return to their normal activities. If subsequently there is a serious breach in behaviour, this just means that you misread their resolve, or that the plan was unworkable after all. In that case, insist that they remain with you once more. During this second withdrawal period, you will have to re-negotiate a contract that is more workable.

If the children escape during the process, don't give chase but wait until they return to you and resume the procedure then.

One objection to this method is that the isolation is no different from punishment. I agree that, yes, it involves the use of force, but protective not coercive force. I think of it as a natural outcome of antisocial behaviour: in a social species such as ours, if you cannot be sociable, you cannot be social. As a leader, you cannot tolerate inconsiderate behaviour: you must protect others' rights not to be hurt or intimidated, and children with aggressive behaviour have to be protected from developing a negative reputation. But, in recognition that there truly is nothing you can do to control another person and that there will be a reason for the aggression even though you don't know what that is, you will be supportive, kindly, empathic and interested in the child as a person but, equally, firm in your resolve that you will protect perpetrators and their targets. To convince the children that you have no intention of using coercion, it can help to give the 'I'm-not-your-enemy' speech which can be any variant on, 'I need you to know that I'm not your enemy. I am here to help you become the kind of person you want to be'.

Conditions needed for change

Giving up using coercion rests on the belief that the person performing the behaviour has to be the one accountable for making it stop. However, when children have been aggressive for some time, everyone around them is distressed by their behaviour, but the aggressors themselves are commonly doing quite nicely. They value and like that they are dominant. Therefore, they don't have a problem. They are not motivated to change, because change requires:

- *discomfort*: this motivates action
- *information about alternatives*: this informs change
- *self-efficacy*: the belief that we can make those alternatives a reality: this empowers change
- *self-esteem*: the conviction that we deserve better sparks the courage to make changes.

Giving up using coercion ensures that you meet all these conditions. First, it ensures that the children producing the troublesome behaviour are sufficiently discomforted to want to change it. Second, from the many lectures they have received in the past, they already have information about alternatives to being aggressive. Third, the method promotes their self-efficacy through your clear implication that you believe they can behave better. Finally, the method promotes their self-esteem because your willingness to persist and be there for them conveys your conviction that they deserve your time and support.

COPE WITH SETBACKS

Occasionally, children's behaviour improves at first but then deteriorates again. Expect this, and don't let it scare either them or you into believing that the problem is back in full force. Instead, relapses simply tell us that some of what we are doing is working and some is not, and that we have forgotten to continue doing what works. Relapses are a reminder to resume using the strategies that we originally used which worked to overcome the problem.[24]

Instead of focusing on the setback, you can search within it for evidence of a success, however partial. For example, if children have lost their temper, you can ask them, 'On a scale of 1 to 10, how angry did you feel at the time?' (Let's say the child gives a rating of 9)... 'How angry do you feel now?' (Let's say the child says 7)... 'How did you get from 9 to 7?'. The fact that the children can go from 9 to 7 tells us that they can go from 7 to 5 and from 5 to 3, and so on. In other words, instead of noticing the outburst, you can highlight the solution that the children are already using, and invite them to use that more often and earlier (before they reach a rating of 9).

When we have externalised the problem, we can teach children to regard relapses as ways that the problem tests them to see if they can 'get back on track' or as providing extra information about the tricks and tactics the problem uses to take over their lives.[25]

HAVE FAITH IN YOUR CHILD

A psychologist by the name of Nancy Carlsson-Paige tells the story of worrying about her adolescent son. Week after week, month after month he spent his days holed up in his bedroom. He was never going to amount to anything. Then, in his early 20s he emerged, having written *Good Will Hunting*. Her son is Matt Damon.

I tell their story because it reminds us that, even when our children seem to be off the rails, we have to trust our children's drive to become all they can be. This amounts to having faith in them. And, by definition, faith means believing in something even when there is no evidence. Having faith won't *guarantee* that our children will turn out well, but there truly is no alternative. We just have to hold the line and keep believing in them. It helps to remind ourselves that most of our deepest fears (in this case, about how our children will turn out) are, at heart, the fear that we will not be able to handle whatever comes our way.[26] If, instead, we knew that we (and they) could cope with anything, there would be nothing to fear or to worry about.[27]

HAVE FUN

By the time your child's behaviour has become a serious problem, life has grown very earnest. You feel inadequate and, because you're human, you might dislike the children for causing you to feel that way. Meanwhile, they think you pick on them all the time. One thing is certain: no one is having any fun. Therefore, if nothing else has worked, it could be time to play with the problem. When a child is in the midst of a meltdown, you could perform an ethnic dance, have a meltdown yourself, sing at the top of your lungs, do a handstand... or whatever. There isn't a child worth his or her salt who can carry on with a meltdown while you're being ridiculous. And if it doesn't fix the behaviour, at least you have enjoyed yourself.

CONCLUSION

Guidance has three options when children's behaviour is a problem for us: communicate to solve it; help children to self-regulate (not only because we have rights not to endure their meltdowns but, more important, because these are distressing for them); and, third, look for solutions that are already in place. This saves us having to be the one to solve a problem when we don't have enough information to do so. People always know more about themselves than outsiders ever will. So the children can be the source of the solution. Whenever we are tempted to revert to punishment in an effort to put a stop to the problem, we will have to remind ourselves that if punishment were going to work, it would have by now. When something isn't working, we need to stop it and do something different.

SUMMARY OF PRINCIPLES

- Problems signal that people are stuck, not sick.

- We can choose to look for what is broken and try to fix it, or to look for what is working and to use that.
- Nothing happens all the time. Change is inevitable.
- Raising children is not about correcting their weaknesses, but nurturing their strengths.
- Have faith in your children.
- When something isn't working, do something different.

10 The power within

As I described in chapters 1 and 2, guidance accepts that the only power each of us truly has is power over ourselves. We are in command of how we interpret the events in our lives and of what we do to ensure that we grow. We have the power to create joy and satisfaction in our lives, the power to act, and the power to love.[1] This sort of power liberates us from depending on the rest of the world to take care of us.

TAKING RESPONSIBILITY FOR YOURSELF

In essence, this is a matter of taking responsibility for ourselves as adults, rather than remaining in a childlike state of expecting other people to meet our needs. Taking responsibility means the many things listed in Box 10.1.

Self-efficacy as a parent

The core problem of the controlling style is that it gives us faith in consequences. When these do not work, we come to see ourselves as being ineffective at disciplining our children – that is, we develop low self-efficacy. Then, when our children do not do as we tell them, we become angry (at them and at ourselves for not being able to secure their compliance). In turn, we become more controlling or coercive... in response to which the children behave more poorly. (Remember the 'dance' in chapter 6). This confirms our fears that we cannot control our children.[2] As a result, we are likely to get into power struggles with the children and to see ourselves as their victims. Believing that we *should* be dominant, we activate coercive discipline to re-impose our authority. This puts both us and the children at risk of escalating emotional arousal, coercion and, potentially, child abuse.[3] The paradox is that parents who believe that they have the least power impose the most controls on their children.

Guidance offers a solution to this trap. It sees parenting not as being about power over children but about our own personal power to meet our own and our children's needs. This stance will give you a high sense of self-efficacy. Now feeling empowered, you will be able to engage in problem solving when you are in conflict with your children.[4] This will defuse rather than escalate the conflict.[5]

Pursue your purpose

As I mentioned in chapter 3, a life purpose inspires us and the values that underpin it act as a compass that keeps our lives on track. Your life purpose will be found in the following domains.[6]

- *Family*: belonging, care of others, having someone to love, having a happy family life.
- *Work and career*: this can be any occupation that is personally rewarding for you or in which in which you can master a skill: paid employment, volunteering, or homemaking.
- *Personal growth and education*: this entails developing ourselves as a human being, learning new skills and confronting new challenges.
- *Contribution* to others, helping others, leaving a legacy.
- *Leisure, play and adventure*: recreation absorbs us in our senses and in the activity for its own sake, allowing us to express a playful part of ourselves and have adventures.
- *Physical self-care and health*: taking care of your body through exercise and diet, either to live healthily to an older age or to be around for others.
- *Self-kindness and compassion*: showing acceptance of ourselves, our feelings, memories and old wounds.
- *Creativity*: in any discipline, such as the arts or music, writing, cooking, homemaking or gardening, for example.
- *Spirituality*: being inspired by the beauty and mysteries of life.

When you keep sight of your purpose as both a person and a parent, you will find it easier to act in ways that uphold your values and that contribute to achieving your goals for your family.

Box 10.1 Taking responsibility[7]

Taking responsibility means:

- Not blaming someone else for anything you are being, doing, having or feeling. You choose which thoughts you invite into your head about the events and other people in your life.

- Not blaming yourself. You have always done the best you could, given what you knew at the time. You are still learning.

- Being aware of when and where you do not take responsibility, so that you can begin to do for yourself what you have been expecting other people to do for you.

- Challenging the pessimistic 'chatterbox' inside your head that warns of doom and gloom. It is making you a victim.

- Being aware of the payoffs for staying stuck and for avoiding taking responsibility for meeting your own needs.

- Figuring out what you want in life and acting to attain it.

- Being aware of the many choices you have in any situation.

- Accepting that there are no wrong choices: only different pathways that provide opportunities for you to learn different lessons and that, whatever the outcome, you will be able to handle it.

Get a life

We often think of a 'good mother' as one who caters to her children's every need, for whom her children always come first. However, as we saw in chapter 2, being submissive leads to mutual resentment. Parents whose children supply their reason to exist end up dominating, over-protective, self-righteous and guilt-inducing.[8] This pattern, says Jeffers, comes from the parents' neediness, not from the children's. As well as being told they should be grateful (when they should not have to be grateful for something they didn't ask for, and being cared for is a child's birthright), the children get caught in the glare of their parents' headlights, as it were: frozen in fear that they will not measure up or not satisfy their parents' ambitions for them.

When parents sacrifice themselves for their children, they have one main aspect to their lives. As a result, their life looks like this:

```
┌─────────────────────────┐
│                         │
│       Parenting         │
│                         │
└─────────────────────────┘
```

Then, if their children manage to overcome their feelings of being beholden to their parents and to develop some independence, the self-sacrificing mother is miserable, because her life looks now like this:

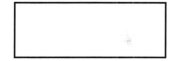

Instead, your life needs to have multiple aspects spanning love, work, education and fun.[9] In that way, you can achieve balance and satisfaction. And the loss of one aspect (such as a job, a partner or a relationship), while being an occasion for mourning, will not leave you with nothing. This is shown in Figure 10.1. (Although I have labelled each box, what titles you put in your own boxes is up to you, as long as you can fill in all nine boxes in the grid.)

Jeffers reminds us that if only one of these aspects truly matters to us, we have to give 100 percent commitment to the others in the grid so that they come to have meaning for us.[10] This does not mean that

FIGURE 10.1 ASPECTS OF A FULL LIFE

Friends	Parenting	Partner relationship
Leisure Hobbies Fun Adventure	Personal growth	Health
Community	Work	Extended family

everything you do has to become a passion or last forever but that, while you are engaged in it, you act as if what you are doing really counts and can make a difference.

Balance your fillers and drainers

If during the day we progressively drained an electric kettle without refilling it, we would eventually expose its element and it would burn out. So it is with people. To avoid burnout or exhaustion, we need to top up our energies throughout the day.

What fills us versus what drains our energy differs for each person. It can help, therefore, to take an inventory of your own 'fillers' and 'drainers', and aim to spend more time doing the things that give you energy and vitality. Note, however, that sometimes the things that we think are relaxing are not. For example, browsing through fashion magazines with their photo-shopped models can lower our self-esteem and therefore drain rather than fill us with energy.

Give yourself time away

Make sure that you routinely give yourself time away from caring for others. Even the safety demonstrations on aircraft tell us that in an emergency, we must put on our own oxygen mask before helping our children. In the long term, observing that you are willing to take care of yourself relieves children of the responsibility of looking after you. During crises, it teaches them that you too have to exercise self-control at times, perhaps by giving yourself some *time away*. A word of advice, though (gleaned from personal experience): if you take yourself outside for respite from a child in meltdown, take the house keys with you – because you will end up looking very foolish when you have to ask your child to unlock the door to let you back in!

Be compassionate about your mistakes

More than any other role that we occupy, parenting holds up a mirror that exposes our humanness, with our children quick to expose us when our walk does not match our talk.[11]

We have a choice about how to respond when we discover ourselves to be less than perfect. We can judge, blame, berate and punish ourselves, or respond compassionately and learn from our missteps, not losing sight of our competencies and personal qualities that enable us to parent with compassion. We can remember that a mistake is simply a strategy for meeting a need that has not worked out as hoped. Therefore, we can reconnect with the need and adjust our strategy.

THE LEGACY OF A HURTFUL CHILDHOOD

To be able to use guidance, we have to be emotionally intact. We must have the capacity to act as leaders or executives in our families who are able to look after our own needs, rather than expecting our children to take care of us. But if our own childhood left us needy, this is difficult for us to do until we give ourselves empathy and listen to the truth of our lives.

Our history might be one of physical or sexual abuse. But it could also be hurtful parenting that amounts to emotional abuse.

Being unwelcome. It may be that we were not wanted and as a child, felt apologetic for being alive or were told that we should feel guilty for being born, for needing to be looked after, or for the trouble we were putting our parents to.

Abandonment. It might be that our parents blackmailed us with threats to 'end it all'. Or their exaggerated health crises caused us to fear that they would die and leave us abandoned. Or they might have threatened to walk out and abandon us to fend for ourselves. Perhaps we were sent to boarding school at a young age because we were an inconvenience to our parents.

Parent watching. This can occur when our parents were so emotionally needy that we (as children) felt we had to meet their needs and, in turn, lacked their support. It might be that one of our parents over-stated minor illnesses and we constantly (and unnecessarily) looked after them, watching out for their wellbeing, instead of the reverse.

Neglect. Perhaps our parents were simply so self-absorbed that they didn't notice when we were struggling or in need of support. Or maybe they were so stressed that we felt we could not burden them further by asking for what we needed.

Lack of individuation. It might have been that our parents suffocated us with love, making it difficult for us to forge our own independence because their life would have been empty without us. Or it could be that any effort on our part to assert our own independence resulted in punishment or verbal or emotional abuse.

Parents' ambitions. It might be that our parents were ambitious for us to be successful at everything we did in order to raise their own status among their peers, or to compensate them for their disappointment about their own lack of fulfilment in life. Or it could be that they dismissed our goals in life and demanded that we enter a profession or job that was not our passion.

Let me be clear, however, that these scenarios are very different from situations where parents have an illness, disability or an acquired injury, and genuinely do need some physical care but, meanwhile, remain in charge of meeting their own emotional needs. The extra work for children who are contributing to the physical care of a family member can be burdensome at times and can mean that they miss out on some of the carefree experiences of youth – but the benefits can be that these young people develop empathy for those in adversity, appreciate their own health and gain in confidence and competence.[12] These positive outcomes occur only when there are appropriate boundaries between themselves and their parents, however.

Layers of abuse

When as children we are made responsible for the emotional wellbeing of our parents, we learn that we cause our parents' anger, pain or dissatisfaction with their lives. In this climate, we will have been deprived of the unconditional love that every child needs to thrive, because we had to change our behaviours and feelings to meet our parents' needs. In an effort to please our parents, we will have tried to be all that they wanted, only to find that even that was not enough to satisfy them. That is the first layer of abuse.

The second layer is that all this had to go on in silence because we were not allowed to acknowledge the injustice and deception; if we did express our pain or anger, our parents would demand that we suppress those feelings too.[13] Or our parents might have told us that they were doing it for our own good, and therefore we were expected to feel grateful for being maltreated. Or, when we protested at being ridiculed, they accused us of having no sense of humour and of not being able to take a joke. (Being laughed at is quite different from being laughed with, and is never funny.) Emotional or physical abuse makes it impossible for children to even notice or to defend themselves against the unfairness of their treatment, or to become outraged at being humiliated, disrespected or losing dignity.[14]

A third layer of abuse is the shaming message that we are not good enough to be loved, not worthy of being nurtured. This shame bites deep into the psyche and, during disciplinary encounters, we come to believe not just that we have made a mistake, but that *we are a mistake*'.[15] This cumulative emotional mistreatment is *soul murder*.[16]

As a result of not being cared for as children and being subjected to hurtful parenting, we are left with a lifelong yearning for love. The result is that as adults we try to get other people to give us what we have been looking for since childhood. But our partners or our children cannot. The only thing that would work is to have a time machine and a parent who was available and willing to learn how to nurture. At least one of these isn't going to happen.

RECOVERING FROM A HURTFUL CHILDHOOD

When we were harmed either by our parents' direct actions or by their failure to protect us from foreseeable harm, our body will store the pain of our childhood's unmet needs. The body, Miller says, never lies.[17] Through physical illness or emotional symptoms such as depression, it will fight to alert our conscious minds to the truth.[18]

If this is our history, to free ourselves so that we can nurture our own children, it is vital to listen to our feelings about the hurtful parenting that we endured in childhood. We can break the pattern of the generations and avoid repeating coercive parenting only when we attain peace with the truth of our own histories.[19] To quote Alice Miller:[20]

> If I know and can feel what my parents did to me when I was totally defenceless... I no longer need to react to what happened to me and take it out on innocent people because now I *know* what happened. And if I want to live my life consciously, without exploiting others, then I must actively accept that knowledge.

Especially in the case of outright abuse, expecting ourselves to love people who persecuted us will only cause our true feelings to go underground. Instead, we need to denounce what was done. The route to recovery, then, is to own our childhood experiences, to recognise that in childhood we had no choice but to love and appease our parents. However, in adulthood if our parents wronged us, we can choose to believe our own truth. As an adult, we *can* acknowledge these injustices.

Acknowledge your feelings

Therefore, the first step is to acknowledge the suffering of the child we once were. We will only be embittered as long as we feel powerless – and we will only feel powerless until we take the truth seriously.[21] We need to respect, accept and honour how we feel, recognising also that we did nothing to deserve the hurtful treatment we received from the very adults who were supposed to be protecting us.

Miller assures us that when we decide in favour of adulthood, our confusion about what we are 'supposed' to feel versus what we actually do feel, will disappear.[22] Thus liberated, we no longer have to believe that we are not worth loving, that we have to prove ourselves worthy of love, or that we are to blame for being ill-treated.[23]

We can acknowledge this truth with the support of friends who are on our side, or with the help of a counsellor who is willing to accept whatever we feel, without judgment.

Make space for your feelings

Harris tells the story of pouring a cup of salt into a cup of water, versus pouring the salt into a lake.[24] When the container is small, the water will be undrinkable. The same is true of our emotions. If we constrict around them, they will form a hard ball that we cannot shift. Instead, Harris advises us to make space for the feeling, breathing deeply to make room for it – and then engage in the world around us. The feeling hasn't gone: we've just stopped fearing it. This will allow us to act in ways that fit with our values.

Box 10.2 KEY POINTS ABOUT FEELINGS[25]

- What you feel now is exactly what you should be feeling, given your history and whatever you are doing or not doing.

- Your thoughts and feelings are not the main problem. The problem is getting caught up in them and avoiding or struggling with them.

- Difficult or unpleasant feelings are a necessary part of life and of struggling to live your values.

- Feelings simply *are*: they do not need to be judged.

- Your thoughts and feelings do not control your actions.

- Feelings have a natural life span: they do not have to be fixed or controlled because they will go away by themselves.

- Feelings cannot harm you. If your feelings are clouds and your mind is the sky, once the clouds disperse, the sky is the same as it always was.

- Difficult feelings are your allies: they alert you to your unmet needs.

- Difficult emotions teach you what matters enough in your life to hurt for.

- Accepting that pain is inevitable gives you the freedom to do what matters, and dignifies the effort you put in to living your life.

Neutralise your memories

When our childhood has been hurtful, our mind will constantly dredge up painful memories of the past. But no matter how painful the memories or negative the thoughts, we can detach or unhook ourselves from what our mind tells us, so that we no longer have to believe our thoughts or take them so seriously.[26] We can do this by noticing, naming and neutralising the thoughts in the ways I described in chapter 8 (under the section *Teach helpful thinking*).

Nothing will ever take away our memories of a traumatic past, but we can allow those memories to have less impact over us today. Harris describes this in this way:[27]

> When these memories show up, it's like watching a terrifying horror movie late at night, all alone by yourself, in a rickety old house, with all the lights off. Now suppose you have exactly the same movie playing, but this time the TV's in the corner of the room, it's broad daylight, sunlight's streaming in through the windows, your house is full of friends and family, and you're all interacting together – talking, laughing, eating, having fun. The movie hasn't changed one bit – it's still playing on the TV in the corner of the room – but now it's having much less effect on you.

Our goal, then, is not to avoid our unpleasant feelings or to replace them with 'good' feelings, but to learn new ways of handling them that work for us. This will entail not believing that our feelings are the truth, refusing to think of them as threatening, and refusing to believe that we must act on them.[28] (See Box 10.2 and *Teach helpful thinking* in chapter 8.)

Befriend yourself

In order to reconcile with a hurtful childhood, we need to mourn for the child we once were and to express empathy for that little girl or boy, whose sufferings went unnoticed and who was abandoned to cope alone.[29]

When I was learning hypnosis, I encountered a giant of a therapist named Milton Erickson who would guide clients under hypnosis to think back to a distressing period during their childhood and imagine that, instead of being abandoned and alone, they had a friend alongside them to support them and to tell them then what they knew now. It might be that they would survive and thrive; it might simply be that they had a friend; it might be that it was not their fault.

If as a child you were alone during a traumatic time and cannot think of someone who could be your friend, instead be your own best friend. Breathe deeply and let yourself go back to a traumatic incident but, this time, instead of seeing yourself alone, let yourself as an adult speak to yourself as a child and be your own comforter. You can do this through traumas or simply at birthdays or any other events when you felt alone.

Shape your relationship with your parents

When our parents have hurt us in the ways I have just described, we may experience confusion because, on the one hand, we will be justifiably hurt and pained but, on the other hand, we will have been told by our society and our religions that we must love and honour our parents. However, this is ridiculous: emotions cannot be controlled by rules, any more than breathing can.[30] It is an insidious game of emotional blackmail to be duped into thinking that, because our parents gave birth to us, we must forgive their malevolence. We might *want* to love them, but obedience, guilt, fear of reprisals and a desperation for affection are not love. Compelling ourselves to honour parents who did not honour us is a denial of our own reality.[31]

To re-define our relationship with our parents, we have to liberate ourselves from a dependency where we crave care and affection from people who are not able to give it. As adults, we have the choice to stop trying to earn the love that our parents could not or did not give us as children.

We must also free ourselves from a compulsion to idealise our parents and from our illusions of the perfect childhood. We do not have to be grateful for the good times or for any care that we did receive, because to be cared for is a child's birthright.

Feeling anger or seeking revenge (in this case about childhood maltreatment) are righteous in the sense that it is right to feel distressed about our unmet needs. Nevertheless, once we have acknowledged the truth of our history, we can choose to channel our distress into determining how our needs can be met from now on.

This generates two options, each valid. The first is to keep ourselves safe by withdrawing from contact with our parents if the abuse is still alive in our memory or is still part of our interaction pattern with them today. If the relationship is still manipulative, the pressure to pretend otherwise, to be insincere and hypocritical, will be exhausting.

Once we stop trying to appease our parents and to earn their love, they might welcome the change but, says Miller, they are more likely to try to get us to revert to being the good, loyal son or daughter who was indulgent of them and tolerant towards their ill-treatment of us. We will only become angry and resentful about this reaction, however, if we are still secretly seeking their approval.[32]

Our second option is to understand what made our parents (or other mistreating adults) the way they were and, in adulthood, we might choose to forgive and love them. However, a desire to forgive and to reconcile with one's persecutor is the prerogative of victims, and cannot be preached or imposed.[33]

Forgiveness can take any of three forms.[34]

- *Retributive* forgiveness, which victims offer only to those perpetrators who admit their wrongdoing and who submit to punishment for it.

- *Reparative* forgiveness, where victims forgive perpetrators who attempt to make amends. Particularly if our parents have recognised what they have done, this opens up the possibility of a genuine relationship where both can express their feelings to each other without fear.[35]

- *Restorative* or altruistic forgiveness, when we forgive voluntarily as a gift, regardless of whether perpetrators have 'earned' this by their remorse.

Forgiveness does not expect us to deny, stifle or repress our feelings, and it does not excuse or condone the wrong that we have suffered. Instead it guides us to transform our anger into grief which, while still intense and painful, is more authentic and – potentially – more constructive.

To that end, Seligman details a five-step process for forgiveness, guided by the acronym REACH:[36]

R   *Recall* the hurt, as objectively as possible. Take slow, calming breaths and visualise or recount the events.

E   *Empathise* with your own grief at your unmet needs. Mourn. In this way, the expression, 'I feel... because I need' can replace the accusation, 'I feel angry because you...'.

A   *Altruistically forgive*, not because perpetrators 'deserve' forgiveness because of their remorse or attempts at making amends, but as a gift. This step recognises that we cannot hurt perpetrators by refusing to forgive them, but we can hurt ourselves by holding onto bitterness. Remaining embittered is like cutting ourselves and hoping that the other person bleeds.

C   *Commit* yourself publicly to forgive. Write in your diary (journal), write a forgiving letter to the perpetrator (but *do not send it*), or tell a trusted friend what you have done.

H   *Hold* onto forgiveness. Your forgiveness cannot and should not erase the memory of past trauma, but it will change the meaning of the trauma in your life now. You will not have to dwell vengefully on the past, but instead can neutralise the effects of those memories on you now (as already mentioned). Perhaps you can periodically re-read your documents to remind yourself that you have forgiven.

CONCLUSION

It is common for parents to raise children the same way they were brought up. This is how unresponsive parenting flows down the generations, with all of its negative outcomes. But I have met many parents who were subjected to controlling or abusive parenting as children but who made a conscious decision to create a new tradition for their families and to raise their children under guidance principles.

Whether we want to radically change or just refine our parenting style, we have to take charge of meeting our own needs. Our children are not instruments for satisfying our needs. To have something to give to our children – and to feel satisfaction about our own lives – it is important that we look after ourselves.

Accepting responsibility for ourselves is a lifelong learning process, especially when our own childhood has left us needy and craving approval and love. Nevertheless, as long as there is life, there are opportunities for healing. Indeed, post-traumatic growth is more common than post-traumatic stress.[37] Each of us has a tremendous capacity for healing, for developing a renewed appreciation of life and for acting on its possibilities. I firmly believe for each and every one of us, that, 'There is nothing wrong with you that what's right with you can't fix'.[38]

Your wellbeing is in your hands. And your children's wellbeing depends on your courage to take responsibility for your choices.

SUMMARY OF PRINCIPLES

- Our values inspire our lives.
- Everything we do counts and can make a difference.
- We need to include in each day something that replenishes our energies.
- We each deserve unconditional love. When children are made responsible for their parents' wellbeing, they are deprived of the unconditional love that every child needs to thrive.
- Real change happens in small steps.
- There is nothing wrong with you that what's right with you can't fix.

Resources

GUIDANCE FOR PARENTS

Biddulph, S. (1998). *The secret of happy children.* (3rd ed.)   Sydney: Harper Collins / Minneapolis, MN: Free Spirit Press.

Gordon, T. (2000). *Parent effectiveness training.* (2nd ed.) New York: Three Rivers Press.

Greene, R. (2010). *The explosive child.* New York: Harper.

Grille, R. (2005). *Parenting for a peaceful world.* Alexandria, NSW: Longueville Media.

Grolnick, W.S. 2003 *The psychology of parental control: How well-meant parenting backfires.* Mahwah, NJ: Lawrence Erlbaum.

Hart, S. & Hodson, V.K. (2006). *Respectful parents; respectful kids: 7 keys to turn family conflict into co-operation.* Encinitas, CA: Puddle Dancer Press.

Kohn, A. (1992). *No contest: The case against competition.* Boston, MA: Houghton Mifflin.

___(1996). *Beyond discipline: From compliance to community.* Alexandria, VA: Association for Supervision and Curriculum Development.

___(1999). *Punished by rewards: The trouble with gold stars, incentive plans, A's, praise and other bribes.* (2nd ed.) Boston, MA: Houghton Mifflin.

___(2005). *Unconditional parenting: Moving from rewards and punishments to love and reason.* New York: Atria Books.

___(2014). *The myth of the spoiled child: Challenging the conventional wisdom about children and parenting.* Cambridge, MA: Da Capo Press.

GUIDANCE FOR TEACHERS

Glasser, W. (1969). *Schools without failure.* New York: Harper and Row.

___(1998a). *The quality school: Managing students without coercion.* (rev. ed.) New York: Harper Perennial.

___(1998b). *The quality school teacher.* (rev. ed.) New York: Harper Collins.Gordon, T. (1974). *Teacher effectiveness training.* New York: Peter H. Wyden.

Gordon, T. (1974). *Teacher effectiveness training.* New York: Peter H. Wyden.

Greene, R.W. (2008). *Lost at school.* New York: Scribner.

Hart, S. & Hodson, V.K. (2004). *The compassionate classroom: Relationship based teaching and learning.* Encinitas, CA: Puddle Dancer Press.

Holt, J. (1982). *How children fail.* (rev. ed.) New York: Merloyd Lawrence.

Holt, J. (1983). *How children learn.* (rev. ed.) New York: Merloyd Lawrence.

Kohn, A. (2000). *What to look for in a classroom ... and other essays.* San Francisco, CA: Jossey-Bass.

___(2004). *What does it mean to be well educated?* Boston, MA: Beacon Press.

___(2011). *Feel-bad education: And other contrarian essays on children and schooling.* Boston, MA: Beacon.

Noddings, N. (2003). *Happiness and education.* Cambridge, UK: Cambridge University Press.

Porter, L. (2008). *Young children's behaviour: Practical approaches for caregivers and teachers.* (3rd ed.) Sydney: Elsevier/Baltimore, MD: Brookes.

___(2014). *A guidance approach to discipline: Practitioner workbook.* (2nd ed.) Brisbane: Small Poppies International.

___(2014). *A comprehensive guide to classroom management: Facilitating engagement and learning in schools.* Sydney: Allen & Unwin. Also published as *Behaviour in schools.* (3rd ed.) Berkshire, UK: Open University Press.

Sapon-Shevin, M. (1999). *Because we can change the world: A practical guide to building cooperative, inclusive classroom communities.* Boston, MA: Allyn and Bacon.

NEEDS

Ben-Shahar, T. (2007). *Happier.* Boston, MA: McGraw Hill.

Brown, B. (2010). *The gifts of imperfection.* Center City, MN: Hazelden.

Harris, R. (2007). *The happiness trap: Stop struggling, start living.* Wollombi, NSW: Exisle.

Harris, R. (2011). *The confidence gap.* Boston, MA: Trumpeter.

Kindlon, D. & Thompson, M. (2000). *Raising Cain: Protecting the emotional lives of boys.* New York: Ballantine.

McKay, M., Forsyth, J.P. & Eifert, G.H. (2010). *Your life on purpose: How to find what matters and create the life you want.* Oakland, CA: New Harbinger.

Pollack, W. (1998). *Real boys: Rescuing our sons from the myths of boyhood.* New York: Holt.

Robinson, K. & Aronica, L. (2009). *The element: How finding your passion changes everything.* New York; Penguin.

___(2013). *Finding your element: How to discover your talents and passions and transform your life.* New York: Viking.

Seligman, M.E.P. (2002). *Authentic happiness.* New York: Simon and Schuster.

___(2006). *Learned optimism.* New York: Vintage.

___(2011). *Flourish: A visionary new understanding of happiness and well-being.* New York: Free Press.

Seligman, M.E.P., Reivich, K., Jaycox, L. & Gillham, J. (1995). *The optimistic child.* Sydney: Random House.

Thompson, M., Grace, C.O'N. & Cohen, L.J. (2001). *Best friends; worst enemies: Understanding the social lives of children.* New York: Ballantine.

COMPASSIONATE COMMUNICATION

Bolton, R. (1987). *People skills.* Sydney: Simon and Schuster.

Faber, A. & Mazlish, E. (1999). *How to talk so kids will listen and listen so kids will talk.* New York: Avon.

Faber, A., Mazlish, E., Nyberg, L. & Templeton, R.A. (1995). *How to talk so kids can learn at home and in school.* New York: Fireside.

Rosenberg, M.B. (2003). *Nonviolent communication: A language of life.* (2nd ed.) Encinitas, CA: Puddle Dancer Press.

___(2005). *The surprising purpose of anger: Beyond anger management: Finding the gift.* Encinitas, CA: Puddle Dancer Press.

SOLUTION-FOCUSED THEORY

Berg, I.K. & Steiner, S. (2003). *Children's solution work.* New York: Norton.

De Jong, P. & Berg, I.K. (2013). *Interviewing for solutions.* (4th ed.) Pacific Grove, CA: Brooks/Cole.

Durrant, M. (1995). *Creative strategies for school problems: Solutions for psychologists and teachers.* Epping, NSW: Eastwood Family Therapy Centre/ New York: Norton.

Freeman, J., Epston, D. & Lobovits, D. (1997). *Playful approaches to serious problems: Narrative therapy with children and their families.* New York: Norton.

Morgan, A. (Ed.) (1999). *Once upon a time... Narrative therapy with children and their families.* Adelaide, SA: Dulwich Centre Publications.

___(2000). *What is narrative therapy?: An easy-to-read introduction.* Adelaide, SA: Dulwich Centre Publications.

Murphy, J.J. (2008). *Solution-focused counseling in schools*. (2nd ed.) Alexandria, VA: American Counseling Association.

Murphy, J.J. & Duncan, B.L. (2007). *Brief intervention for school problems: Outcome-informed strategies*. (2nd ed.) New York: Guilford.

Porter, L. (2008). *Teacher-parent collaboration: From early childhood to adolescence*. Melbourne: ACER.

Selekman, M.D. (2010). *Collaborative brief therapy with children*. New York: Guilford.

Sklare, G.B. (2005). *Brief counseling that works: A solution-focused approach for school counselors and administrators*. (2nd ed.) Thousand Oaks, CA: Corwin Press.

Winslade, J. & Monk, G. (2007). *Narrative counseling in schools: Powerful and brief*. (2nd ed.) Thousand Oaks, CA: Corwin Press.

Websites

Alfie Kohn	www.alfiekohn.org
Bioresonance	www.lifeworkshealthclinic.com.au
Cate Crombie	www.metacommunicate.com

Center for Nonviolent Communication: www.cnvc.org

Louise Porter	www.louiseporter.com.au
Martin Seligman	www.authentichappiness.sas.upenn.edu
Positive Psychology Center	www.ppc.sas.upenn.edu
Ross Greene	www.livesinthebalance.org
Walsh Institute	www.walshinstitute.org

Solution-focused approaches

Brief Therapy Institute of Sydney: www.brieftherapysydney.com.au

Brief therapy practice, UK: www.brieftherapy.org.uk

Dulwich Centre, Adelaide, SA: www.dulwichcentre.com.au

Notes

Chapter 1 An introduction to guidance

1   Baumrind 1971a

2   Alberto & Troutman 2013: 18

3   Phelan 2003: 16

4   Boyson, in Holland 2004: 75. Boyson is a former school principal and one of the architects of Margaret Thatcher's Education policy in the UK.

5   Jacques Barzun, in Wager 1992. (At the time of writing this statement, Wager was a school principal.)

6   Watzlawick et al. 1974 : 33

7   Watzlawick et al. 1974 : 33

8   Bowles & Gintis 2011; Brownell et al. 2009; Liszkowski et al. 2006; Tomasello 2009; Vaish et al. 2009; Warneken & Tomasello 2006, 2007; Warneken et al. 2007

9   Olson & Spelke 2008; Tomasello 2009: 5

10   Bowles & Gintis 2011; Hublin 2009; Kohn 1992: 39; Stayton et al. 1971

11   Rakoczy et al. 2008, 2009; Tomasello 2009

12   Atwater & Morris 1988; Kochanska & Aksan 1995; Kochanska et al. 2005a, 2005b; Kuczynski & Kochanska 1990; Londerville & Main 1981; Stifter et al. 1999

13   Main & George 1985; Radke-Yarrow et al. 1973; Swick 2005; Young et al. 1999; Zhou et al. 2002

14   Holt 1983

15   Raskin & Rogers 2005

16   Soenens & Vansteenkiste 2010

17   Holt 1983: xii-xiii, emphasis added

18   Rosenberg 2003a: 22

19   Grayling 2013: 187

20   Grayling 2013: 171

21   Kohn 2014: 43

22   Buckingham 2000; Lee 2001

23   Kohn 2014: 7

24   Batson et al. 1978; Denham et al. 2002; Fabes et al. 1989

25   Kohn 2014: 136

26   Holt 1982: 237-8

27   McKay et al. 2010: 90

28   Gordon 2000

29   Satir 1976, in Kotzman 1989: 21

30   Grayling 2013: 104

31   van IJzendoorn 1997: 712-13

32   Bromberg & Johnson 2001; Metzner & Ryan 1995

33   Briggs & McVeity 2000

34   Kohn 2005; Kuczynski & Kochanska 1999

35   Grayling 2013: 140

36   Jeffers 2007: 26

37   See, e.g. Arthur et al. 2003; Emmer et al. 2009; Evertson et al. 2003

38   Green 2010: 255

39   Holt 1982: 294

40   Gordon 2000: 22

41   Goleman 1994

42   Rosenberg 2003a: 161-162

43   Murphy 2006; Winslade & Monk 2007: 11

44   e.g. Barber et al. 2005; Gershoff et al. 2010

45   Aguilar et al. 2000; Belsky et al. 1998; Campbell 1995; Shaw et al. 2000; Smith & Farrington 2004

46   See, for example Gartrell 1994, 2003, 2004; Gordon 1970, 1974, 1991; Kohn 1996, 2005; Rogers 1942, 1951, 1978; Rogers & Freiberg, 1994

47   Greene 2008

48   Greene 2008

49   Kohn 2014: 29

50   Brody et al. 2001; Gaylord-Harden 2008

51   Kochanska et al. 2001, 2003

52   Aguilar et al. 2000; Alink et al. 2008; Campbell & Ewing 1990; Campbell et al. 1996; Coldwell et al. 2006; Combs-Ronto et al. 2009; Côté et al. 2006; Crockenberg & Litman 1990; Denham et al. 2000; Donovan et al. 2000; Eccles et al. 1991; Fergusson et al. 2005; Hoffman 1960; Joussemet et al. 2008; Kochanska 1995; Kochanska et al. 2007; Lorber & Egeland 2011; Loukas 2009; Loukas et al. 2005; McFadyen-Ketchum et al. 1996; Miller-Lewis et al. 2006; NICHD Early Child Care Research Network 2004; O'Leary et al. 1999; Prinzie et al. 2006; Romano et al. 2005; Rubin et al. 2003; Scaramella et al. 2008; Shaw et al. 2003; Spieker et al. 1999; Stormshak et al. 2000; Tremblay 2004; Tremblay et al. 2004; Underwood et al. 2009; Veenstra et al. 2006; Williams et al. 2009

53   Aunola & Nurmi 2005; Baumrind 1967, 1971b; Crockenberg & Litman 1990; Denham et al. 2000; Donovan et al. 2000; Feldman & Klein 2003; Gilliom et al. 2002; Hoeve et al. 2009; Kochanska et al. 2005a; Lewis 1981; McLeod et al. 1994; Miller-Lewis et al. 2006; Parpal & Maccoby 1985; Rubin et al. 2003; C.L. Smith et al. 2004; Stayton et al. 1971; Stormshak et al. 2000; Weiss & Schwarz 1996; Zahn-Waxler et al. 1979

54   Brody et al. 2001; Hoeve et al. 2009; Miller et al. 2009; Prinzie et al. 2006; Pulkkinen & Hämäläinen 1995; Trinkner et al. 2012

55   Stattin & Kerr 2000; Trinkner et al. 2012; Williams & Steinberg 2011

56   Crockenberg & Litman 1990; Donovan et al. 2000; Gilliom et al. 2002; Stormshak et al. 2000

57   Assor et al. 2004; Bear et al. 2003; Covaleskie 1992; Dubanoski et al. 1983; McCaslin & Good 1992; Palmer & Hollin 2001; Wien 2004

58   Eisenberg et al. 1983; Lewis 1981; van IJzendoorn 1997: 714

59   Davidov & Grusec 2006; Hastings et al. 2000; Radke Yarrow et al. 1973; Strayer & Roberts 2004b; Zahn-Waxler et al. 1979

60   McCord 1991

61   Kochanska 1997; Sears et al. 1957, in Spera 2005

62   Hoffman & Saltzstein 1967; Kuczynski 1983, 1984

63   Batson et al. 1978; Fabes et al. 1989

64   Talwar & Lee 2011

65   Kins et al. 2012

66   Baumrind 1991; Duchesne & Ratelle 2010; Frodi et al. 1985; Moorman & Pomerantz 2008; Roth et al. 2009

67   Dornbusch et al. 1987; Eccles et al. 1991; Ginsberg & Bronstein 1993; Gonzalez-DeHass et al. 2005; Gottfried et al. 1994; Grolnick & Ryan 1989; Koestner et al. 1984; Maccoby & Martin 1983; Parker et al. 1999; Parker et al. 1999; Paulson et al. 1998; Steinberg et al. 1989, 1992, 1994

68   Dornbusch et al. 1987; Duchesne & Ratelle 2010; Eccles et al. 1991; Gonzalez-DeHass et al. 2005; Grolnick & Ryan 1989; Leung & Kwan 1998; Paulson et al. 1998; Purdue et al. 2009; Steinberg et al. 1989, 1992, 1994; Strage & Brandt 1999

69   Duchesne & Ratelle 2010; Roth et al. 2009

70   Emmer & Aussiker 1990; Grolnick 2003; Grolnick et al. 2002

71   Ginsberg & Bronstein 1993; Gottfried et al. 1994

72   Dornbusch et al. 1987; Duchesne & Ratelle 2010; Eccles et al. 1991; Gonzalez-DeHass et al. 2005; Grolnick & Ryan 1989; Leung & Kwan 1998; Paulson et al. 1998; Steinberg et al. 1989, 1992, 1994

73   Neumeister et al. 2009; Rice et al. 1996

74   DiPrima et al. 2011

75   Cotler & Palmer 1971

76   Aunola & Nurmi 2004; Chen et al. 1997; Deslandes et al. 1997; Emmer & Aussiker 1990; Ginsberg & Bronstein 1993; Grolnick 2003; Grolnick & Ryan 1989; Grolnick et al. 2002; Gottfried et al. 1994; Hennessey & Amabile 1998; Hong & Ho 2005; Koestner et al. 1984; Lamborn et al. 1991; Leung & Kwan 1998; Leung et al. 1998; Mattanah 200; Ryan & Stiller 1991; Singh et al. 1995; Steinberg et al. 1992; Taylor et al. 1995; Weiss & Schwarz 1996

77   Dearing 2004; Gaylord-Harden 2008; Gregory & Rimm-Kaufman 2008; Hamre & Pianta 2001

78   Burchinal & Cryer 2003; Gest et al. 2004; Raviv et al. 2004; Steelman et al. 2002

79   Dearing et al. 2006

80   Anderson et al. 2003; Jodl et al. 2001

81   Bean et al. 2003; Bernier et al. 2010; Grolnick 2003

82   Caron 2006; Dekovic et al. 2003; Garber et al. 1997; McClun & Merrell 1998; McDowell et al. 2003; Steinberg et al. 1989, 1992, 1994; Wentzel 1994

83   Dekovic et al. 2003; McClun & Merrell 1998; Soenens et al. 2007; Steinberg et al. 1989, 1992; Wentzel 1994

84 Baumrind 1967, 1971b; Ispa et al. 2004; Loukas 2009; Mukhopadhyay & Kumar 1999; Snyder et al. 2003; Strayer & Roberts 2004a

85 Weiss & Schwarz 1996; Williams et al. 2009

86 Hart et al. 1998; Propper & Moore 2006

87 Criss et al. 2009; Dearing 2004; Garber et al. 1997; Kaufmann et al. 2000; Propper & Moore 2006; Wyman et al. 1999

88 Cole et al. 2009; Denham et al. 1997; Eisenberg et al. 1999, 2005; Fabes et al. 2001; Garner & Spears 2000; Grolnick et al. 1996; Kochanska et al. 2005a; Lagacé-Séguin & Coplan 2005; Morris et al. 2007; Rubin et al. 2003; Shipman et al. 2007

89 Aguilar et al. 2000; Calkins & Johnson 1998; Dekovic et al. 2003; Eisenberg et al. 2005; Fabes et al. 2001; Feldman & Klein 2003; Gilliom et al. 2002; Gray & Steinberg 1999; Grolnick et al. 1996; Kochanska et al. 2000, 2005a; McClun & Merrell 1998; Merritt et al. 2012; Rubin et al. 2003; Spinrad et al. 2004; Steinberg et al. 1989, 1992; Wentzel 1994

90 Roth et al. 2009

91 Berlin & Cassidy 2003; Denham et al. 1997; Roth et al 2009

92 Campbell & Ewing 1990; Kochanska et al. 2007; Loukas et al. 2005; van IJzendoorn 1997

93 van IJzendoorn 1997

94 Aunola & Nurmi 2005; Baumrind 1991

95 Dekovic et al. 2003; Eisenberg et al. 2005; Fabes et al. 2001; Feldman & Klein 2003; Gray & Steinberg 1999; Grolnick et al. 1996; Kochanska et al. 2005a; McClun & Merrell 1998; Rubin et al. 2003; Steinberg et al. 1989, 1992; Wentzel 1994

96 Assor & Tal 2012; Baumrind 1991; Buri et al. 1988; Eccles et al. 1991; Garber et al. 1997; Kernis et al. 2000

97 Brown 2012: 227; Buri et al. 1988; Garber et al. 1997; Maccoby & Martin 1983; Rudy et al. 2008

98 Ackerman et al. 2002; Aguilar et al. 2000; Booth et al. 1994; Buyse et al. 2008; Campbell 1995; Campbell et al. 1991a, 1991b; Casas et al. 2006; Dearing et al. 2006; Deater-Deckard & Dodge 1997; Denham et al. 2002; Diener et al. 2003; Dodge et al. 1994; Hart et al. 1992a; MacKinnon-Lewis et al. 1999; McDowell et al. 2003; McFadyen-Ketchum et al. 1996; NICHD Early Child Care Research Network 2005; O'Connor 2002; Parke et al. 2004; Petterson & Albers 2001; Qi & Kaiser 2003; Rah & Parke 2008; Sturge-Apple et al. 2006; Vaillancourt et al. 2007

99 Szewczyk-Sokolowski 2005; Wray-Lake & Flanagan 2012

100 Hart et al. 1992a; Herrera & Dunn 1997

101 Herrera & Dunn 1997

102 Baumrind 1991; Denham et al. 1997; Hart et al. 1992a; Michalik et al. 2007

103 Donohue et al. 2003

104 Duong et al. 2009

105 Bates et al. 2003; Baumrind 1967, 1971b, 1991; Criss et al. 2003; Fletcher & Shaw 2000; Hart et al. 1992b; Ispa et al. 2004; NICHD Early Child Care Research Network 2001, 2003a, 2003b 2004; Russell et al. 1998; Rutherford & Mussen 1968; Ryan & Stiller 1991; Steelman et al. 2002

106 Barker et al. 2010

107 Roth et al. 2011

108 Harter et al. 1997

109 Unnever & Cornell 2004

110 Coplan et al. 2004; Ladd & Kochenderfer-Ladd 1998; Rubin et al. 2002

111 Brody et al. 2001; Criss et al. 2003

112 Farrell & White 1998

113 Donohue et al. 2003

114 Baumrind 1991; Donovan et al. 2000; Ispa et al. 2004

115 Berlin & Cassidy 2003

116 Baumrind 1991; Criss et al. 2003

117 Assor et al. 2004; Baumrind 1991; Kochanska et al. 2003; Roth et al. 2009

118 McCord 1991

119 van IJzendoorn 1997

120 Baumrind 1991; Eccles et al. 1991; Kins et al. 2012

121 Kochanska 2002a, 2002b; Kochanska & Aksan 2004; Kochanska et al. 1999, 2005a; Kuczynski 1984; Laible & Thompson 2002

122 Stattin & Kerr 2000

123 Kohn 2014: 34

124 Kohn 2005

125 Kohn 2014: 52

126 Robert Oxton Bolton

127 Ablard & Parker 1997; Kim et al. 2013

128 Kohn 2014: 113

129 Kohn 2011: 10

130 Kohn 2104: 92

131 Adapted from Adams et al. 1995: 5-22

CHAPTER 2 LEADERSHIP STYLES

1   Kohn 2014: 39

2   Kohn 2014: 7

3   Bryson 2004: 34

4   Bryson 2004: 38

5   Bryson 2004: 22 & 32

6   Bryson 2004: 40

7   Bryson 2004: 56

8   Berry 1988: 32-40; Gordon 2000: 27

9   Jeffers 2007: 160

10   Jeffers 2007: 163

11   Bryson 2004: 50

12   Dobson 1992; Greven 1992

13   Pinderhughes et al. 2000

14   Hart & Hodson 2006: 23

15   Kohn 1999

16   Kohn 2005

17   Kohn 1999

18   You might be familiar with the grammatical term, oxymoron, which means an inbuilt contradiction in terms. Some of my favourite example are smart bombs, Microsoft works, or airline food. In my era as a school student, I learned as an onlooker that one of the great oxymorons in life was the Sisters of Mercy.

19   Johnston 1972; Lerman & Vorndran 2002

20   Talwar & Lee 2011

21   Lerman & Vorndran 2002; Martin & Pear 2011: 153; McDonnell 1993

22   Greene 2008: 8

23   Greene 2008: 57

24   Skiba & Peterson 1999; Wheeler & Richey 2005

25   Kohn 2005: 63

26   Clark 2004; Durrant & Ensom 2012: 1374; Kazdin & Benjet 2003

27   Kohn 2005

28   Chapman & Zahn-Waxler 1982

29   Elliot & Thrash 2004

30   Smith 2006: 115; Straus & Paschall 2009: 459; Turner & Muller 2004: 762

31   Straus & Paschall 2009: 475; Turner & Muller 2004: 722

32   Deater-Deckard & Dodge 1997; Giles-Sims et al. 1995; Larzelere 2000; Straus & Paschall 2009; Straus & Stewart 1999

33   Talwar & Lee 2011: 1753

34   At the time of writing, the countries where corporal punishment is illegal are: Albania, Austria, Bulgaria, Republic of Congo, Costa Rica, Croatia, Curaçao (part of the Netherlands), Cyprus, Denmark and the Faroe Islands, Finland, Germany, Greece, Hungary, Iceland, Israel, Kenya. Latvia, Liechtenstein, Luxembourg, The Netherlands, New Zealand, Norway, Pitcairn Islands, Poland, Portugal, Republic of Moldova, Romania, Republic of South Sudan, Spain, Svalbad (Norway), Sweden, Togo, Tunisia, Ukraine, Uruguay and Venezuela (Source: www.endcorporalpunishment.org Retrieved 14/07/2013

35   Dixon et al. 2005b; Frias-Armenta 2002; Mapp 2006; Nix et al. 1999; Youssef et al. 1998a

36   Durrant & Ensom 2012; Smith 2006

37   Fairchild & Erwin 1997; Youssef et al. 1998b

38   Dixon et al. 2005b; Fine et al. 2004; Frias-Armenta 2002; Gershoff et al. 2010; Gunnoe & Mariner 1997; Hyman 1995; Larzelere 1986; Mapp 2006; Nix et al. 1999; Ohene et al. 2006; Pagani et al. 2004; Sheehan & Watson 2008; Smith 2006; Youssef et al. 1998a

39   Clark 2004; Holden 2002; MacMillan et al. 1999; Rodriguez 2003; Rohner et al. 1991; Smith 2006; Turner & Muller 2004

40   Gershoff et al. 2010; Gregory 1995: 461

41   Deater-Deckard et al. 1996; Gershoff et al. 2012; Grogan-Kaylor 2005; Mulvaney & Mebert 2007; Slade & Wissow 2004: 1327; Smith 2006; Taylor et al. 2010

42   Afifi et al. 2006; Aucoin et al. 2006; Colder et al. 1997; Côté et al. 2006; Eamon 2001; Gershoff 2002; Kuczynski & Kochanska 1999; Larzelere 2000; McCord

1997; Nelson et al. 2012; Olson et al. 1990; Palmer & Hollin 2001; Power & Chapieski 1986; Simons et al. 2002; Stormshak et al. 2000; Straus et al. 1997; Weiss et al. 1992

43   Palmer & Hollin 2001

44   Straus & Paschall 2009: 476

45   Smith 2006

46   Larzelere 1986: 33

47   Sapon-Shevin 1996: 196

48   Montgomery 1982: 48

49   Jakubowski 1977

50   Kotzman 1989: 121

51   Kotzman 1989: 127

52   Kotzman 1989: 127

53   Adapted from Kotzman 1989: 121-124

54   Jakubowski & Lange 1978: 42-43; Kotzman 1989: 116-117

55   Banks 2005: 17

56   Banks 2005: 17

CHAPTER 3 HUMAN NEEDS

1   Baumeister & Leary 1995

2   Ackerman et al. 2002, 2004; Aguilar et al. 2000; Belsky et al. 1998; Campbell 1995; Campbell & Ewing 1990; Campbell et al. 1991a, 1991b, 2000; Coldwell et al. 2006; Coolahan et al. 2002; Côté et al. 2006; Dearing et al. 2006; Duncan & Brooks-Gunn 2000; Evans & English 2002; Evans et al. 1999; Fergusson et al. 2004, 2005; Fujiura & Yamaki 2000; Gest et al. 2004; Hill et al. 2006; Kaiser et al. 2000; Macmillan et al. 2004; Mallick & Singh 2011; McGroder 2000; Meyers 1999; Miller-Lewis et al. 2006; NICHD Early Child Care Research Network 2005; O'Leary et al. 1999; Palagini & Rosenlicht 2011; Petterson & Albers 2001; Qi & Kaiser 2003; Raviv et al. 2004; Romano et al. 2005; Rubin et al. 2003; Schaffer 1998; Shaw et al. 1999, 2003; Smith & Farrington 2004; Spence et al. 2002; Sturge-Apple et al. 2006; Thompson et al. 2003; Tremblay 2004; Votruba-Drzal 2006

3   Sapon-Shevin 1999: 13

4   Anan & Barnett 1999; Bakermans-Kranenburg et al. 2004; Bohlin et al. 2000; DeMulder et al. 2000; Diener et al. 2003; Hamilton 2000; Kerns et al. 1998; Kochanska et al. 2001; Koren-Karie et al. 2002; Lewis et al. 2000; Moss et al. 2004, 2005; NICHD Early Child Care Research Network 2001, 2006; Pauli-Pott et al. 2007; Posada et al. 1999; Raval et al. 2001; Seifer et al. 2004; Stams et al. 2002; Verschueren & Marcoen 1999; Warren et al. 1997; Waters et al. 2000a, 2000b; Weinfield et al. 2000

5   Anda et al. 2006: 182; Morris et al. 2007; Pears et al. 2010; Schwartz et al. 1997; Teisl & Cicchetti 2008

6   Anda et al. 2006; Bolger & Patterson 2001; Bonner et al. 1992; Bromberg & Johnson 2001; Bugental & Happaney 2004; Bugental et al. 2003; Burack et al. 2006; Carrey et al. 1995; Feiring et al. 2002; Fergusson & Lynskey 1997; Flores et al. 2005; George & Main 1979; Glaser 2000; Goodwin et al. 2004; Haynes-Seman

& Baumgarten 1998; Hoffman-Plotkin & Twentyman 1984; Kim & Cicchetti 2004, 2006; Klimes-Dougan & Kistner 1990; Koenig et al. 2000, 2004; Lavoie et al. 2002; Luthar et al. 2000; Maughan & Cicchetti 2002; McGowan et al. 2009; Mullen et al. 1996; Nagel 2012: 4; Pears et al. 2010; Pollak et al. 2005; Rothbaum et al. 1997; Sheu et al. 2010; Shields et al. 2001; Shipman et al. 2007; Shonk & Cicchetti 2001; Solomon & Serres 1999; Teicher 2002; Thompson & Wyatt 1999; Tomoda et al. 2009; Trickett 1998; Vigil et al. 2005; Webster 2001; Zahn-Waxler & Radke-Yarrow 1990

7   Kernis 2003

8   Gecas 1982; Kernis 2003

9   Brown 2012

10   Baumeister et al. 2003

11   Baumeister et al. 2003; Birkeland et al. 2012; Diener & Diener 1995; Heatherton & Vohs 2000; Mruk 2006; Murray et al. 2002; Murrell et al. 1991; Trzesniewski et al. 2006

12   Pauletti et al. 2012

13   Pauletti et al. 2012

14   Brown 2012

15   Carrey et al. 1995; Fergusson & Lynskey 1997; Kim & Cicchetti 2004, 2006; Maughan & Cicchetti 2002; Mullen et al. 1996; Solomon & Serres 1999; Webster 2001

16   Baumeister et al. 1996; Frankel & Myatt 1996; Graham et al. 2006; López et al. 2006; Nansel et al. 2001; Salmivalli et al. 2005; Scholte et al. 2007

17   Tafarodi et al. 2001

18   Assor & Tal 2012; Crocker 2002; Kernis 2003

19   Covington & Müeller 2001

20   Assor & Tal 2012; Baumeister et al. 1993; Kernis 2003

21   Kohn 2014: 134

22   Kohn 2014: 134

23   Baumeister et al. 2003

24   Kohn 2014: 84

25   Baumeister et al. 1993; Hess 1994; Parker & Adkins 1995; Parker & Mills 1996

26   Gilman & Ashby 2003

27   Baumeister et al. 2003; Rudolph et al. 2005

28   Harter & Whitesell 2003: 1045

29   Rice et al. 1996; Harter & Whitesell 2003; Neumeister 2004b

30   Holt 1982: 287

31   Cole et al. 2001; Crocker & Wolfe 2001

32   Crocker & Wolfe 2001

33   Kernis 2003

34   Mruk 2006

35   Kernis 2003

36   Kohn 2014: 135

37   Kernis 2003: 9

38   Kernis 2003

39   Harter & Whitesell 2003: 1045

40   Mruk 2006

41   Baumeister et al. 1993, 2003; Rogers 1961, in Kernis 2003

42   LoCicero & Ashby 2000; Neumeister 2004a; Parker 1996; Parker & Adkins 1995; Salmivalli et al. 1999; Siegle & Schuler 2000; Wood & Care 2002

43   Gilman & Ashby 2003

44   Aguilar et al. 2000; Belsky et al. 1998; Campbell 1995; Shaw et al. 2000; Smith & Farrington 2004

45   Sommer & Baumeister 2002

46   Baumeister & Leary 1995

47   Brown 2012

48   Boulard et al. 2012; Buhs & Ladd 2001; De Wit et al. 2011; Dodge et al. 2003; Flook et al. 2005; Gazelle & Ladd 2003; Hay et al. 2004; Johnson et al. 2000; Keiley et al. 2000; Ladd 2006; Ladd & Burgess 2001; Laird et al. 2001; Letcher et al. 2009; Overbeek et al. 2010; Spinrad et al. 2004; Stormshak et al. 1999; Sturaro et al. 2011; Wentzel & Caldwell 1997; Werner & Crick 2004

49   Sletta et al. 1996

50   Grolnick 2003; Osterman 2000; Ryan & Deci 2000

51   Soenens et al. 2012

52   Stefanou et al. 2004

53   Seligman 1975

54   Baumeister et al. 2003; Chirkov et al. 2003; Deci & Ryan 2000; Deci et al. 1991, 1999; Gilman & Anderman 2006; Jang et al. 2009, 2010 ; Ryan & Deci 2000

55   Barber et al. 2005; Conger et al. 1997; Grolnick & Ryan 1989; Pomerantz & Wang 2009; Qin et al. 2009; Soenens & Vansteenkiste 2010; Soenens et al. 2010, 2012

56   Bean et al. 2003; Conger et al. 1997; Kakihara & Tilton-Weaver 2009; Loukas et al. 2005; Rudy et al. 2008; Shek 2007; Soenens et al. 2005a, 2005b

57   Mruk 2006

58   Seligman 2011

59   Csikszentmihályi 1990

60   Harris 2012: 16

61   Harris 2011: 17

62   Harris 2011: 142-143

63   Ben-Shahar 2007

64   McKay et al. 2010

65   Ben-Shahar 2007

66   Harris 2011: 138-140

67   Csikszentmihályi 1990

68   Csikszentmihályi 1990

69   McKay et al. 2010; Robinson & Aronica 2009

70   Harris 2011: 17

71   Robinson & Aronica 2013

72   Noddings 2003: 17

73   Seligman 2002

74   Csikszentmihályi 1990; Seligman 2002

75   Robinson & Aronica 2009, 2013

76   Peterson 2006; Seligman 2002

77   Seligman 2002, 2011

78   Seligman 2002: 43

79   Brown 2012; Seligman 2011

80   Rosenberg 2003a

CHAPTER 4 MEETING CHILDREN'S EMOTIONAL NEEDS

1   Bong & Skaalvik 2003

2   Bandura 1993: 138

3   Bong & Skaalvik 2003

4   Weiner 2000

5   Robertson 2000; Seligman et al. 1995

6   Ryan & Brown 2003

7   Roth et al. 2009

8   Thompson et al. 2002

9   Roth et al. 2009

10   Glasser 1998

11   Bruner 1960, in Noddings 2003: 111; Fields & Boesser 2002; Noddings 2003: 112 & 251

12   Miller 2006

13   Hart & Hodson 2006: 135

14   Frith 2004

15   Swick 2005

16   Main & George 1985

17   Denham et al. 1997

18   Young et al. 1999

19   Deci 1971

20   Deci 1972

21   Birch et al. 1984; Deci & Ryan 1987; Deci et al. 1991, 1999, 2001; Farson 1963, in Grolnick 2003; Kamins & Dweck 1999; Lepper & Greene 1975; Morgan 1983; Mueller & Dweck 1998; Rubinstein 1977; Ryan & Deci 1996, 2000; Vansteenkiste et al. 2008

22   Holt 1982: 79

23   Butler & Nisan 1986; Deci 1972

24   Freedman et al. 1992; Lepper et al. 1982; McCord 1991

25   Birch et al. 1995

26   Butler & Nisan 1986

27   Dweck 2006: 33

28   Dweck 2006: 36

29   Blackwell et al. 2007
30   Dweck 2006: 13
31   Dweck 2006: 174-175
32   Gagné 2003; Perkins et al. 1993; Ritchhart 2001
33   Dweck 2006: 193
34   Curry & Johnson 1990: 153
35   Dweck 2006: 180
36   Dweck 2006: 181
37   Dweck 2006: 231
38   Dweck 2006: 185
39   Frenzel et al. 2007
40   Dweck 2006: 207
41   Ryan & Patrick 2001: 455
42   Crockenberg et al. 1976; Deutsch 1979
43   Nelson et al. 1969; Ryan & Patrick 2001: 455; Warring et al. 1985
44   Kohn 1992: 30
45   Barnett & Bryan 1974; Lanzetta & Englis 1989
46   Ames 1981; Ames & Felker 1979
47   Johnson & Johnson 1974; Robinson 1975: 151
48   Harris 2011: 98
49   Covington & Müeller 2001; Dweck & Leggett 1988; Feldhusen et al. 2000; Neumeister 2004a, 2004b; Neumeister & Finch 2006; Sylva 1994
50   LoCicero & Ashby 2000; Parker 1996; Parker & Adkins 1995; Siegle & Schuler 2000; Wood & Care 2002
51   Neumeister 2004a
52   Jones & Jones 2013: 217

CHAPTER 5 LISTENING TO CHILDREN

1   Cate Crombie, pers. comm. 15/06/2013
2   Peterson 2006: 58
3   Rosenberg 2005: 11
4   Berlin & Cassidy 2003; Roth et al 2009
5   Denham et al. 1997
6   Fields & Boesser 2002
7   Harris 1983; Kostelnik et al. 2006
8   Goleman 1994
9   Harris 2011: 50
10   Ellis 1962; Gonzalez et al. 2004
11   Harris 2009
12   Rosenberg 2003a
13   Bernard 1988: 39; Montgomery 1982: 42-44

14   Porter & McKenzie 2000: 136

15   Kotzman 1989: 35

16   Rosenberg 2003b: 8

17   Kohn 2005: 127

18   Bolton 1987: 34-39; Kotzman 1989: 60-66

19   Rosenberg 2003a: 92

20   Hart & Hodson 2006: 107

21   Hart & Hodson 2006

22   Kotzman 1989: 35

23   Rosenberg 2003b

24   Rosenberg 2003b: 13

25   Gordon 1974, 2000

26   Cate Crombie, downloaded from www.metacommunicate.com

27   Kotzman 1989: 33

28   Kohn 2005

29   Kotzman 1989: 80-81

30   Kotzman 1989: 89-90

31   Biddulph 1998

32   Rosenberg 2003b: 8

33   Bolton 1987: 21

34   Bolton 1987: 22

35   Bolton 1987

36   This quote is usually attributed to Calvin Coolidge, although its exact source is unknown

37   Katherine Sellery, pers. comm.

CHAPTER 6 ORIGINS OF DISRUPTIVE BEHAVIORS

1   Bryson 2004: 74 & 79

2   Grayling 2013: 140

3   Krishnamurti 1988: 184

4   Porter 1999

5   Gordon 2000

6   Denham et al. 2000; NICHD Early Child Care Research Network 2004; Paterson & Sanson 1999; Sanson et al. 2004; Shaw et al. 2001

7   Gordon 2000

8   Kohn 2005: 55

9   For a review, see Porter 2014

10   Blair 2010; McGowan et al. 2009; Hyman 2009; Liu et al. 1997; Sapolsky 2004; Weaver et al. 2004

11   Blair et al. 2008, 2011; Burke et al. 2011; Evans & Schamberg 2009; Evans et al. 2007

12   Holt 1982

13   Holt 1982: 116

14   Holt 1982: 252

15   Holt 1982: 77

16   Graue & Walsh 1998

17   Raines 1995

18   Dix et al. 1989

19   Kohn 2014: 149

20   Bock & Stauth 2008: 62

21   Collison & Hall 1989: 33

22   Tortora & Derrickson 2006: 820

23   Campbell-McBride 2010: 21

24   Hadjivassiliou et al. 2001: 385; Mäki & Collin 1997: 1756; Percy & Propst 2008; Perlmutter & Loberg 2013

25   Mackarness 1990: 103; Philpott & Kalita 2000

26   Karlsson et al. 2012

27   Foucard 1985

28   Lebenthal 1979

29   Lyon 2000: 135

30   Chauhan & Chauhan 2006: 174

31   Gesser & Koo 1996

32   Barr et al. 1990; Murray et al. 1992

33   Shi et al. 2003: 301

34   Bock & Stauth 2008: 29-30; Franklin & Foa 2008: 166; Hagerman & Kalkenstein 1987

35   Bransfield et al. 2008; Kuhn et al. 2012

36   Bock & Stauth 2008; Lyon 2000; Pitman & Porter 2014

37   Tabrizian 2003

38   Pauling 1995

39   Brown et al. 2000; Brown & Susser 2008; Susser & Lin 1992; E. Walker et al. 2004: 409; Xu et al. 2009

40   Lazarides 2010: 87-88; Lyon 2000: 85; Noaghiul & Hibbein 2003; Peet 2004; Perlmutter & Loberg 2013: 74

41   Bock & Stauth 2007; Chauhan & Chauhan 2006: 175; Davidson & Myers 2007; Lazarides 2010: 190

42   Lantz 2009: 44-45

43   Tabrizian 2003: 8 & 112; Walsh 2012

44   Dinkmeyer & McKay 1989; Dinkmeyer et al. 1980, 1997

45   Greene 2008

46   Bioresonance uses a computer known an a BiCom machine. This employs the same technology as noise-cancelling headphones to detect and inverse pathological signals that the body is generating as instructions between cells, and the electrical signatures of substances, pathogens and toxins that burden the body. At the same time, it aims to improve the body's ability to detoxify, so that it improves its capacity to heal itself. For more information, see www.bioresonance.net.au; or www.lifeworkshealthclinic.com.au

CHAPTER 7 EVERYDAY PRACTICES

1   Hart & Hodson 2006
2   Hart & Hodson 2006
3   Hart & Hodson 2006: 66
4   Hart & Hodson 2006: 66
5   Baillargeon et al. 2007; Côté et al. 2006; Deynoot-Schaub & Riksen-Walraven 2006; Gilliom et al. 2002; Rubin et al. 2003; Shaw et al. 2003; Tremblay 2004
6   Côté et al. 2006; Hay et al. 2004; Schaeffer et al. 2003; Shaw et al. 2003
7   Some of these strategies were suggested by Gordon 2000: 160-169
8   Rosenberg 2003a: 79
9   Rosenberg 2003a: 83
10   Hart & Hodson 2004, 2006; Rosenberg 2003a
11   Hart & Hodson 2006
12   Kohn 1996: 78
13   Hart & Hodson 2006: 58
14   Bryson 2004: 19; Canter 2010: 73
15   Curwin & Mendler 1989: 83
16   Bryson 2004: 20
17   Ames 1992: 266
18   Assor et al. 2002
19   Deci & Ryan 1987
20   Gordon 1997: 37
21   Bolton 1987
22   Bolton 1987: 173
23   Baumrind 1971b: 99
24   Greene 2008: 75
25   Gordon 2000: 246
26   Greene 2008: 169
27   adapted from Spirito et al. 2012: 245
28   Gordon 2000: 263; Greene 2008, 2010
29   Greene 2008: 125
30   Greene 2008: 157
31   Gordon 1997: 90
32   Gordon 1997: 91-92
33   Waldroop & Butler 2000: 78
34   Hartling, in Brown 2010: 46
35   Brown 2008: 14
36   Rosenberg 2003b: 14
37   Rosenberg 2003b: 14

CHAPTER 8 TEACHING SELF-REGULATION

1   Moffitt et al. 2011

2   Eisenberg et al. 2004
3   Kochanska et al. 2001
4   Gilliom et al. 2002
5   Murphy et al. 1999
6   Eisenberg et al. 2004; Kohn 2014: 149; Letzring et al. 2005; Polivy 1998
7   This example comes from Albert Ellis, founder of Rational emotive therapy
8   Glasser 1998
9   Harris 2011: 82
10   Harris 2011: 54
11   Harris 2009, 2011
12   Harris 2011: 80
13   Harris 2011: 60
14   Harris 2011: 64
15   Harris 2011: 93
16   adapted from Roush 1984, in Kaplan & Carter 1995: 396
17   Harris 2011: 165
18   Harris 2011: 165
19   Harris 2007
20   Wood et al. 2009
21   Jeffers 2007: 50
22   Harris 2007, 2011
23   Harris 2009
24   Harris 2011: 73
25   Harris 2011: 83
26   Harris 2011: 81
27   Harris 2011
28   Harris 2011: 53
29   Harris 2007
30   Rosenberg 2003a: 20
31   Bertolino & Schultheis 2002: 224-226
32   Compas 1987; Halpern 2004
33   Spirito et al. 1991
34   Halpern 2004
35   Halpern 2004; Hunter & Boyle 2004; Lewis & Frydenberg 2002
36   Rutter 1985, 1999
37   Rutter 1999
38   Seligman 2002
39   Faber et al. 1995
40   Rosenberg 2003b: 8
41   These stages were described to me by Adelaide family therapist, Malcolm Robinson
42   Goleman 1994
43   Satir 1988: 122

44   Klein & Gibson 2005: 2

45   Rosenberg 2003a: 144

46   Rosenberg 2005: 12

47   Hart & Hodson 2004: 86

48   Rosenberg 2005: 20

49   Hart & Hodson 2004: 86

50   Katherine Sellery, pers. comm. 22/10/2013

51   Gordon 2000: 22

52   Holt 1982: 95

53   Holt 1982: 284

CHAPTER 9 SOLVING PERSISTENT PROBLEMS

1   Adapted from Kelly et al. 2008: 87

2   de Shazer 1988

3   Murphy 2006

4   Molnar & Lindquist 1989

5   Murphy 2008: 104-106

6   De Jong & Berg 2002; Sklare 2005: 56

7   Carey & Russell 2003; Selekman 2010: 184

8   De Jong & Berg 2002

9   Peterson 2006: 26

10   de Shazer 1988

11   Murphy 2006

12   Durrant 1995

13   Molnar & de Shazer 1987

14   Murphy 2006

15   Winslade & Monk 2007: 47

16   Winslade & Monk 2007: 44

17   Huntley 1999

18   Winslade & Monk 2007: 45

19   Winslade & Monk 2007: 7

20   Winslade & Monk 2007: 12

21   Morgan 2000

22   Glasser 1977: 61

23   I learned this from Dr Phil McGraw

24   Kowalski 1990

25   Morgan 1999

26   Jeffers 2007: 7

27   Jeffers 2007: 8

CHAPTER 10 THE POWER WITHIN

1   Jeffers 2007: 26
2   Grusec & Mammone 1995
3   Bugental et al. 1997
4   Grusec & Mammone 1995
5   Gerris et al. 1997; Hastings & Grusec 1997
6   McKay et al. 2010: 34-42 & 56
7   Jeffers 2007: 43-56
8   Jeffers 2007: 126
9   Harris 2011
10   Jeffers 2007: 13-132
11   Hart & Hodson 2006: 34
12   Lobato 1983: 349; Martin & Kay 2004; Meyer 1993; Schulz 1993; Seligman & Darling 1997
13   Miller 1987: 7
14   Miller 2006: 28
15   Brown 2008: 14
16   This was the title of a book by Morton Schatzman (1973). *Soul murder: Persecution in the family.* New York: Random House.
17   Miller 2006
18   Miller 2006: 167
19   Miller 2006: 152
20   Miller 2006: 168
21   Miller 2006: 97
22   Miller 2006: 113
23   Miller 2006: 150
24   Harris 2011: 174
25   Harris 2007, 2009; McKay et al. 2010: 168
26   Harris 2011: 54
27   Harris 2009: 64
28   Harris 2009: 21
29   Miller 2006: 154
30   Miller 2006: 33
31   Miller 2006: 96
32   Jeffers 2007: 96
33   Mani 2005: 518; Robertson 2006: 317
34   Bennett 2003: 73
35   Miller 2006: 151
36   Seligman 2002: 79-81
37   Seligman 2011
38   Baruch Shalem, in Selekman 2006: 27

References

Ablard, K.E. & Parker, W.D. (1997). Parents' achievement goals and perfectionism in their academically talented children. *Journal of Youth and Adolescence, 26* (6), 651-667.

Ackerman, B.P., Brown, E.D., D'Eramo, K.S. & Izard, C.E. (2002). Maternal relationship instability and the school behavior of children from disadvantaged families. *Developmental Psychology, 38* (5), 694-704.

Ackerman, B.P., Brown, E.D. & Izard, C.E. (2004). The relations between persistent poverty and contextual risk and children's behavior in elementary school. *Developmental Psychology, 40* (3), 367-377.

Adams, L., Denslow, K.K. & Emmons, S. (1995). *Instructor guide for Dr Thomas Gordon's Parent effectiveness training.* Solana Beach, CA: Gordon Training International.

Afifi, T.O., Brownridge, D.A., Cox, B.J. & Sareen, J. (2006). Physical punishment, childhood abuse and psychiatric disorders. *Child Abuse and Neglect, 30* (10), 1093-1103.

Aguilar, B., Sroufe, A., Egeland, B. & Carlson, E. (2000). Distinguishing the early-onset/persistent and adolescent-onset antisocial behavior types: From birth to 16 years. *Development and Psychopathology, 12* (2), 109-132.

Alberto, P.A. & Troutman, A.C. (2013). *Applied behavior analysis for teachers.* (9th ed.) Boston, MA: Pearson.

Alink, L.R.A., Mesman, J., van Zeijl, J., Stolk, M.N., Juffer, F., Bakermans-Kranenburg, M.J., van IJzedoorn, M.H. & Koot, H.M. (2008). Maternal sensitivity moderates the relation between negative discipline and aggression in early childhood. *Social Development, 18* (1), 99-120.

Ames, C. (1981). Competitive versus cooperative reward structures: The influence of individual and group performance factors on achievement attributions and affect. *American Educational Research Journal, 18* (3), 273-287.

____ (1992). Classrooms: Goals, structures, and student motivation. *Journal of Educational Psychology, 84* (3), 261-271.

Ames, C. & Felker, D.W. (1979). An examination of children's attributions and achievement-related evaluations in comparative, cooperative, and individualistic reward structures. *Journal of Educational Psychology, 71* (4), 413-420.

Anan, R.M. & Barnett, D. (1999). Perceived social support mediates between prior attachment and subsequent adjustment: A study of urban African American children. *Developmental Psychology, 35* (5), 1210-1222.

Anda, R.F., Felitti, V.J., Bremner, J.D., Walker, J.D., Whitfield, C., Perry, B.D., Dube, S.R. & Giles, W.H. (2006). The enduring effects of abuse and related adverse experiences in childhood: A convergence of evidence from neurobiology and epidemiology. *European Archives of Psychiatry and Clinical Neuroscience, 256* (3), 174-186.

Anderson, J.C., Funk, J.B., Elliott, R. & Smith, P.H. (2003). Parental support and pressure and children's extracurricular activities: Relationships with amount of involvement and affective experience of participation. *Journal of Applied Developmental Psychology, 24* (2), 241-257.

Arthur, M., Gordon, C. & Butterfield, N. (2003). *Classroom management: Creating positive learning environments.* Melbourne: Thomson.

Assor, A., Kaplan, H. & Roth, G. (2002). Choice is good, but relevance is excellent: Autonomy-enhancing and suppressing teacher behaviours predicting students' engagement in schoolwork. *British Journal of Educational Psychology, 72* (2), 261-278.

Assor, A., Roth, G. & Deci, E.L. (2004). The emotional costs of parents' conditional regard: A self-determination theory analysis. *Journal of Personality, 72* (1), 47-88.

Assor, A. & Tal, K. (2012). When parents' affection depends on child's achievement: Parental conditional positive regard, self-aggrandizement, shame and coping in adolescents. *Journal of Adolescence, 35* (2), 249-260.

Atwater, J.B. & Morris, E.K. (1988). Teachers' instructions and children's compliance in preschool classrooms: A descriptive analysis. *Journal of Applied Behavior Analysis, 21* (2), 157-167.

Aucoin, K.J., Frick, P.J. & Bodin, S.D. (2006). Corporal punishment and child adjustment. *Journal of Applied Developmental Psychology, 27* (6), 527-541.

Aunola, K. & Nurmi, J.-E. (2004). Maternal affection moderates the impact of psychological control on a child's mathematical performance. *Developmental Psychology, 40* (6), 965-978.

___(2005). The role of parenting styles in children's problem behavior. *Child Development, 76* (6), 1144-1159.

Baillargeon, R.H., Normand, C.L., Séguin, J.R., Zoccolillo, M., Japel, C., Pérusse, D., Wu, H.-X., Boivin, M. & Tremblay, R.E. (2007). The evolution of problem and social competence behaviors during toddlerhood: A prospective population-based cohort survey. *Infant Mental Health Journal, 28* (1), 12-38.

Bakermans-Kranenburg, M.J., van IJzendoorn, M.H. & Kroonenberg, P.M. (2004). Differences in attachment security between African-American and white children: Ethnicity or socio-economic status?. *Infant Behavior and Development, 27* (3), 417-433.

Bandura, A. (1993). Perceived self-efficacy in cognitive development and functioning. *Educational Psychologist, 28* (2), 117-148.

Banks, R. (2005). Solution-focused group therapy. In T.S. Nelson (Ed.) *Education and training in solution-focused brief therapy.* New York: Haworth Press, pp. 17-21.

Barber, B.K., Stolz, H.E., Olsen, J.A., Collins, W.A. & Burchinal, M. (2005). Parental support, psychological control, and behavioral control: Assessing relevance across time, culture, and method. *Monographs of the Society for Research in Child Development, 70* (4), i-147.

Barker, E.D., Vitaro, F., Lacourse, E., Fontaine, N.M.G., Carbonneau, R. & Tremblay, R.E. (2010). Testing the developmental distinctiveness of male proactive and reactive aggression with a nested longitudinal experimental intervention. *Aggressive Behavior, 36* (2), 127-140.

Barnett, M.A. & Bryan, J.H. (1974). Effects of competition with outcome feedback on children's helping behavior. *Developmental Psychology, 10* (6), 838-842.

Barr, C.E., Mednick, S.A. & Munk-Jorgensen, P. (1990). Exposure to influenza epidemics during gestation and adult schizophrenia: A 40-year study. *Archives of General Psychiatry, 47* (9), 869-874.

Bates, L., Luster, T. & Vandenbelt, M. (2003). Factors related to social competence in elementary school among children of adolescent mothers. *Social Development, 12* (1), 107-124.

Batson, C.D., Coke, J.S., Janoski, M.L. & Hanson, M. (1978). Buying kindness: Effect of an extrinsic incentive for helping on perceived altruism. *Personality and Social Psychology Bulletin, 4* (1), 86-91.

Baumeister, R.F., Campbell, J.D., Krueger, J.I. & Vohs, K.D. (2003). Does high self-esteem cause better performance, interpersonal success, happiness, or healthier lifestyles?. *Psychological Science in the Public Interest, 4* (1), 1-44.

Baumeister, R.F., Heatherton, T.F. & Tice, D.M. (1993). When ego threats lead to self-regulation failure: Negative consequences of high self-esteem. *Journal of Personality and Social Psychology, 64* (1), 141-156.

Baumeister, R.F. & Leary, M.F. (1995). The need to belong: Desire for interpersonal attachments as a fundamental human motivation. *Psychological Bulletin, 117* (3), 497-529.

Baumeister, R.F., Smart, L. & Boden, J.M. (1996). Relation of threatened egotism to violence and aggression: The dark side of high self-esteem. *Psychological Review, 103* (1), 5-33.

Baumrind, D. (1967). Child care practices anteceding three patterns of preschool behavior. *Genetic Psychology Monographs, 75*, 43-88.

_____(1971a). Current patterns of parental authority. *Developmental Psychology Monographs, 4* (1), 1-98.

_____(1971b). Harmonious parents and their preschool children. *Developmental Psychology, 4* (1), 99-102.

_____(1991). Effective parenting during the early adolescent transition. In P.A. Cowan and M. Hetherington (Eds.) *Advances in family research series: Family transitions.* Hillsdale, NJ: Lawrence Erlbaum, pp. 111-163.

Bean, R.A., Bush, K.R., McKenry, P.C. & Wilson, S.M. (2003). The impact of parental support, behavioral control, and psychological control on the academic achievement and self-esteem of African American and European American adolescents. *Journal of Adolescent Research, 18* (5), 523-541.

Bear, G.G., Manning, M.A. & Izard, C.E. (2003). Responsible behavior: The importance of social cognition and emotion. *School Psychology Quarterly, 18* (2), 140-157.

Belsky, J., Hsieh, K.-H. & Crnic, K. (1998). Mothering, fathering, and infant negativity as antecedents of boys' externalizing problems and inhibition at age 3 years: Differential susceptibility to rearing experience? *Development and Psychopathology, 10* (2), 301-319.

Ben-Shahar, T. (2007). *Happier.* Boston, MA: McGraw Hill.

Bennett, C. (2003). Is amnesty a collective act of forgiveness? *Contemporary Political Review, 2* (1), 67-76.

Berlin, L.J. & Cassidy, J. (2003). Mothers' self-reported control of their preschool children's emotional expressiveness: A longitudinal study of associations with infant-mother attachment and children's emotion regulation. *Social Development, 12* (4), 477-495.

Bernard, M.E. (1988). *Staying rational in an irrational world: Albert Ellis and rational-emotive therapy.* Melbourne: McCulloch.

Bernier, A., Carlson, S.M. & Whipple, N. (2010). From external regulation to self-regulation: Early parenting precursors of young children's executive functioning. *Child Development, 81* (1), 326-339.

Berry, C.R. (1988). *When helping you is hurting me.* San Francisco, CA: Harper and Row.

Bertolino, B. & Schultheis, G. (2002). *The therapist's notebook for families: Solution-oriented exercises for working with parents, children, and adolescents.* New York: Haworth.

Biddulph, S. (1998). *The secret of happy children.* (3rd ed.) Sydney: Harper Collins/ Minneapolis, MN: Free Spirit Press.

Birch, L.L., Johnson, S.L. & Fisher, J.A. (1995). Children's eating: The development of food-acceptance patterns. *Young Children, 50* (2), 71-78.

Birch, L.L., Martin, D.W. & Rotter, J. (1984). Eating as the 'means' activity in a contingency: Effects on young children's food preference. *Child Development, 55* (2), 431-419.

Birkeland, M.S., Melkevik, O., Holsen, I. & Wold, B. (2012). Trajectories of global self-esteem development during adolescence. *Journal of Adolescence, 35* (1), 43-54.

Blackwell, L.S., Trzesniewski, K.H. & Dweck, C.S. (2007). Theories of intelligence predict achievement across an adolescent transition: A longitudinal study and an intervention. *Child Development, 78* (1), 246-263.

Blair, C. (2010). Stress and the development of self-regulation in context. *Child Development Perspectives, 4* (3), 181-188.

Blair, C., Granger, D.A., Kivlighan, K.T., Mills-Koonce, R., Willoughby, M., Greenberg, M.T., Hibel, L.C., Fortunato, C.K. & Family Life Project Investigators (2008). Maternal and child contributions to cortisol response to emotional arousal in young children from low-income, rural communities. *Developmental Psychology, 44* (4), 1095-1109.

Blair, C., Granger, D.A., Willoughby, M., Mills-Koonce, R., Cox, M., Greenberg, M.T., Kivlighan, K.T., Fortunato, C.K. & the Family Life Project Investigators (2011). Salivary cortisol mediates effects of poverty and parenting on executive functions in early childhood. *Child Development, 82* (6), 1970-1984.

Bock, K. & Stauth, C. (2008). *Healing the new childhood epidemics: Autism, ADHD, asthma, and allergies*. New York: Ballantine.

Bohlin, G., Hagekull, B. & Rydell, A.-M. (2000). Attachment and social functioning: A longitudinal study from infancy to middle childhood. *Social Development, 9* (1), 24-39.

Bolger, K.E. & Patterson, C.J. (2001). Developmental pathways from child maltreatment to peer rejection. *Child Development, 72* (2), 549-568.

Bolton, R. (1987). *People skills*. Sydney: Simon and Schuster.

Bong, M. & Skaalvik, E.M. (2003). Academic self-concept and self-efficacy: How different are they really?. *Educational Psychology Review, 15* (1), 1-40.

Bonner, B.L., Kaufman, K.L., Harbeck, C. & Brassard, M.R. (1992). Child maltreatment. In C.E. Walker and M.C. Roberts (Eds.) *Handbook of clinical child psychology*. (2nd ed.) New York: John Wiley and Sons, pp. 967-1008.

Booth, C.L., Rose-Krasnor, L., McKinnon, J. & Rubin, K.H. (1994). Predicting social adjustment in middle childhood: The role of preschool attachment security and maternal style. *Social Development, 3* (3), 189-204.

Boulard, A., Quertemont, E., Gauthier, J.-M. & Born, M. (2012). Social context in school: Its relation to adolescents' depressive mood. *Journal of Adolescence, 35* (1), 143-152.

Bowles, S. & Gintis, H. (2011). *A cooperative species: Human reciprocity and its evolution*. Princeton, NJ: Princeton University Press.

Bransfield, R.C., Wulfman, J.S., Harvey, W.T. & Usman, A.I. (2008). The association between tick-borne infections, Lyme borreliosis and autism spectrum disorders. *Medical Hypotheses, 70* (5), 967-974.

Brendgen, M., Dionne, G., Girard, A., Boivin, M., Vitaro, F. & Pérusse, D. (2005). Examining genetic and environmental effects on social aggression: A study of 6-year-old twins. *Child Development, 76* (4), 930-946.

Briggs, F. & McVeity, M. (2000). *Teaching children to protect themselves*. Sydney: Allen and Unwin.

Brody, G.H., Ge, X., Conger, R., Gibbons, F.X., Murry, V.McB., Gerrard, M. & Simons, R.L. (2001). The influence of neighborhood disadvantage, collective socialization, and parenting on African American children's affiliation with deviant peers. *Child Development, 72* (4), 1231-1246.

Bromberg, D.S. & Johnson, B.T. (2001). Sexual interest in children, child sexual abuse, and psychological sequelae for children. *Psychology in the Schools, 38* (4), 343-355.

Brown, A.S. & Susser, E.S. (2008). Prenatal nutritional deficiency and risk of adult schizophrenia. *Schizophrenia Bulletin, 34* (6), 1054-1063.

Brown, A.S., van Os, J., Driessens, C., Hoek, H.W. & Susser, E.S. (2000). Further evidence of relation between prenatal famine and major affective disorder. *American Journal of Psychiatry, 157* (2), 190-195.

Brown, B. (2008). *I thought it was just me (but it isn't)*. New York: Gotham.

____(2010). *The gifts of imperfection*. Center City, MN: Hazelden.

____(2012). *Daring greatly*. New York: Gotham.

Brownell, C.A., Svetlova, M. & Nichols. S. (2009). To share or not to share: When do toddlers respond to another's needs? *Infancy, 14* (1), 117-130.

Bryson, K. (2004). *Don't be nice, be real: Balancing passion for self with compassion for others*. Santa Rosa, CA: Elite Books.

Buckingham, D. (2000). *After the death of childhood: Growing up in the age of electronic media*. Cambridge, UK: Polity Press.

Bugental, D.B. & Happaney, K. (2004). Predicting infant maltreatment in low-income families: The interactive effects of maternal attributions and child status at birth. *Developmental Psychology, 40* (2), 234-243.

Bugental, D.B., Lyon, J.E., Krantz, J. & Cortez, V. (1997). Who's the boss?: Differential accessibility of dominance ideation in parent-child relationships. *Journal of Personality and Social Psychology, 72* (6), 1297-1309.

Bugental, D.B., Martorell, G.A. & Barraza, V. (2003). The hormonal costs of subtle forms of infant maltreatment. *Hormones and Behavior, 43* (1), 237-244.

Buhs, E.S. & Ladd, G.W. (2001). Peer rejection as an antecedent of young children's social adjustment: An examination of mediating processes. *Developmental Psychology, 37* (4), 550-560.

Burack, J.A., Flanagan, T., Peled, T., Sutton, H.M., Zygmuntowicz, C. & Manly, J.T. (2006). Social perspective-taking skills in maltreated children and adolescents. *Developmental Psychology, 42* (2), 207-217.

Burchinal, M.R. & Cryer, D. (2003). Diversity, child care quality, and developmental outcomes. *Early Childhood Research Quarterly, 18* (4), 401-426.

Buri, J.R., Louiselle, P.A., Misukanis, T.M. & Mueller, R.A. (1988). Effects of parental authoritarianism and authoritativeness on self-esteem. *Personality and Social Psychology Bulletin, 14* (2), 271-282.

Burke, N.J., Hellman, J.L., Scott, B.G.,, Weems, C.F. & Carrion, V.G. (2011). The impact of adverse childhood experiences on an urban pediatric population. *Child Abuse and Neglect, 35* (6), 408-413.

Butler, R. & Nisan, M. (1986). Effects of no feedback, task-related comments, and grades on intrinsic motivation and performance. *Journal of Educational Psychology, 78* (3), 210-216.

Buyse, E., Verschueren, K., Doumen, S., Van Damme, J. & Maes, F. (2008). Classroom problem behavior and teacher-child relationships in kindergarten: The moderating role of classroom climate. *Journal of School Psychology, 46* (4), 367-391.

Cabot, S. & Jasinska, M. (2011). *Infertility: The hidden causes.* Camden, NSW: WHAS.

Calkins, S.D. & Johnson, M.C. (1998). Toddler regulation of distress to frustrating events: Temperamental and maternal correlates. *Infant Behavior and Development, 21* (3), 379-395.

Campbell, S.B. (1995). Behavior problems in preschool children: A review of recent research. *Journal of Child Psychology and Psychiatry, 36* (1), 113-149.

Campbell, S.B. & Ewing, L.J. (1990). Follow-up of hard-to-manage preschoolers: Adjustment at age 9 and predictors of continuing symptoms. *Journal of Child Psychology and Psychiatry, 31* (6), 871-889.

Campbell, S.B., March, C.L., Pierce, E.W., Ewing, L.J. & Szumowski, E.K. (1991a). Hard-to-manage preschool boys: Family context and the stability of externalizing behavior. *Journal of Abnormal Child Psychology, 19* (3), 301-318.

Campbell, S.B., Pierce, E.W., March, C.L. & Ewing, L.J. (1991b). Noncompliant behavior, overactivity, and family stress as predictors of negative maternal control with preschool children. *Development and Psychopathology, 3* (2), 175-190.

Campbell, S.B., Pierce, E.W., Moore, G., Marakovitz, S. & Newby, K. (1996). Boys' externalizing problems at elementary school age: Pathways from early behavior problems, maternal control, and family stress. *Development and Psychopathology, 8* (4), 701-719.

Campbell-McBride, N. (2010). *Gut and psychology syndrome.* Cambridge, UK: Medinform.

Canter, L. (2010). *Assertive discipline: Positive behavior management for today's classroom.* (4th ed.) Bloomington, IN: Solution Tree Press.

Carey, M. & Russell, S. (2003). Re-authoring: Some answers to commonly asked questions. *The International Journal of Narrative Therapy and Community Work, 2003* (3), 60-71.

Caron, A., Weiss, B., Harris, V. & Catron, T. (2006). Parenting behavior and child psychopathology: Specificity, task dependency, and interactive relations. *Journal of Clinical Child and Adolescent Psychology, 35* (1), 34-45.

Carrey, N.J., Butter, H.J., Persinger, M.A. & Bialik, R.J. (1995). Physiological and cognitive correlates of child abuse. *Journal of the American Academy of Child and Adolescent Psychiatry, 34* (8), 1067-1075.

Casas, J.F., Weigel, S.M., Crick, N.R., Ostrov, J.M., Woods, K.E., Yeh, E.A.J. & Huddleston-Casas, C.A. (2006). Early parenting and children's relational and physical aggression in the preschool and home contexts. *Journal of Applied Developmental Psychology, 27* (3), 209-227.

Chapman, M. & Zahn-Waxler, C. (1982). Young children's compliance and noncompliance to parental discipline in a natural setting. *International Journal of Behavioral Development, 5* (1), 81-94.

Chauhan, A. & Chauhan, V. (2006). Oxidative stress in autism. *Pathophysiology, 13* (3), 171-181.

Chen, X., Dong, Q. & Zhou, H. (1997). Authoritative and authoritarian parenting practices and social and school performance in Chinese children. *International Journal of Behavioral Development, 21* (4), 855-873.

Chirkov, V. & Ryan, R.M. (2001). Parent and teacher autonomy-support in Russian and U.S. adolescents. *Journal of Cross-Cultural Psychology, 32* (5), 618-635.

Clark, J. (2004). Against the corporal punishment of children. *Cambridge Journal of Education, 34* (3), 363-371.

Colder, C.R., Lochman, J.E. & Wells, K.C. (1997). The moderating effects of children's fear and activity level on relations between parenting practices and childhood symptomatology. *Journal of Abnormal Child Psychology, 25* (3), 251-263.

Coldwell, J., Pike, A. & Dunn, J. (2006). Household chaos – links with parenting and child behaviour. *Journal of Child Psychology and Psychiatry, 47* (11), 1116-1122.

Cole, D.A., Maxwell, S.E., Martin, J.M., Peeke, L.G., Seroczynski, A.D., Tram, J.M., Hoffman, K.B., Ruiz, M.D., Jacquez, F. & Maschman, T. (2001). The development of multiple domains of child and adolescent self-concept: A cohort sequential longitudinal design. *Child Development, 72* (6), 1723-1746.

Cole, P.M., Dennis, T.A., Smith-Simon, K.E. & Cohen, L.H. (2009). Preschoolers' emotion regulation strategy understanding: Relations with emotion socialization and child self-regulation. *Social Development, 18* (2), 324-352.

Collison, D.R. & Hall, T. (1989). *Why do I feel so awful?* Melbourne: Angus and Robertson.

Combs-Ronto, L.A., Olson, S.L., Lunkenheimer, E.S. & Sameroff, A.J. (2009). Interactions between maternal parenting and children's early disruptive behavior: Bidirectional associations across the transition from preschool to school entry. *Journal of Abnormal Child Psychology, 37* (8), 1151-1163.

Compas, B.E. (1987). Coping with stress during childhood and adolescence. *Psychological Bulletin, 101* (3), 393-403.

Conger, K.J., Conger, R.D. & Scaramella, L.V. (1997). Parents, siblings, psychological control, and adolescent adjustment. *Journal of Adolescent Research, 12* (1), 113-138.

Coolahan, K., McWayne, C., Fantuzzo, J. & Grim, S. (2002). Validation of a multidimensional assessment of parenting styles for low-income African-American families with preschool children. *Early Childhood Research Quarterly, 17* (3), 356-373.

Coplan, R.J., Prakash, K., O'Neil, K. & Armer, M. (2004). Do you 'want' to play?: Distinguishing between conflicted shyness and social disinterest in early childhood. *Developmental Psychology, 40* (2), 244-258.

Côté, S.M., Vaillancourt, T., LeBlanc, J.C., Nagin, D.S. & Tremblay, R.E. (2006). The development of physical aggression from toddlerhood to pre-adolescence: A nation wide longitudinal study of Canadian children. *Journal of Abnormal Child Psychology, 34* (1), 68-82.

Cotler, S. & Palmer, R.J. (1971). Social reinforcement, individual difference factors, and the reading performance of elementary school children. *Journal of Personality and Social Psychology, 18* (1), 97-104.

Covaleskie, J.F. (1992). Discipline and morality: Beyond rules and consequences. *The Educational Forum, 56* (2), 173-183.

Covington, M.V. & Müeller, K.J. (2001). Intrinsic versus extrinsic motivation: An approach/avoidance reformulation. *Educational Psychology Review, 13* (2), 157-176.

Criss, M.M., Shaw, D.S. & Ingoldsby, E.M. (2003). Mother-son positive synchrony in middle childhood: Relation to antisocial behavior. *Social Development, 12* (3), 379-400.

Criss, M.M., Shaw, D.S., Moilanen, K.L., Hitchings, J.E. & Ingoldsby, E.M. (2009). Family, neighborhood, and peer characteristics as predictors of child adjustment: A longitudinal analysis of additive and mediation models. *Social Development, 18* (3), 511-535.

Crockenberg, S.B., Bryant, B.K. & Wilce, L.S. (1976). The effects of cooperatively and competitively structured learning environments on inter- and intrapersonal behavior. *Child Development, 47* (2), 386-396.

Crockenberg, S. & Litman, C. (1990). Autonomy as competence in 2-year-olds: Maternal correlates of child defiance, compliance, and self-assertion. *Developmental Psychology, 26* (6), 961-971.

Crocker, J. (2002). The costs of seeking self-esteem. *Journal of Social Issues, 58* (3), 597-615.

Crocker, J. & Wolfe, C.T. (2001). Contingencies of self-worth. *Psychological Review, 108* (3), 593-623.

Csikszentmihalyi, M. (1990). *Flow: The psychology of optimal experience.* New York: Harper Perennial.

Curry, N.E. & Johnson, C.N. (1990). *Beyond self-esteem: Developing a genuine sense of human value.* Washington, DC: National Association for the Education of Young Children.

Curwin, R.L. & Mendler, A.N. (1989). We repeat, let the buyer beware: A response to Canter. *Educational Leadership, 46* (6), 83.

Davidov, M. & Grusec, J.E. (2006). Untangling the links of parental responsiveness to distress and warmth to child outcomes. *Child Development, 77* (1), 44-58.

Davidson, P.W. & Myers, G.J. (2007). Environmental toxins. In M.L. Batshaw, L. Pellegrino & N.J. Roizen (Eds.) *Children with disabilities.* (6th ed.) Sydney: Elsevier, pp. 63-72.

De Jong, P. & Berg, I.K. (2002). *Interviewing for solutions.* (2nd ed.) Pacific Grove, CA: Brooks/Cole Thomson.

DeMulder, E.K., Denham, S., Schmidt, M. & Mitchell, J. (2000). Q-sort assessment of attachment security during the preschool years: Links from home to school. *Developmental Psychology, 36* (2), 274-282.

de Shazer, S. (1988). *Clues: Investigating solutions in brief therapy.* New York: Norton.

De Wit, D.J., Karioja, K., Rye, B.J. & Shain, M. (2011). Perceptions of declining classmate and teacher support following the transition to high school: Potential correlates of increasing student mental health difficulties. *Psychology in the Schools, 48* (6), 556-572.

Dearing, E. (2004). The developmental implications of restrictive and supportive parenting across neighborhoods and ethnicities: Exceptions are the rule. *Journal of Applied Developmental Psychology, 25* (5), 555-575.

Dearing, E., Kreider, H., Simpkins, S. & Weiss, H.B. (2006). Family involvement in school and low-income children's literacy: Associations between and within families. *Journal of Educational Psychology, 98* (4), 653-664.

Deater-Deckard, K. & Dodge, K.A. (1997). Externalizing behavior problems and discipline revisited: Nonlinear effects and variation by culture, context, and gender. *Psychological Inquiry, 8* (3), 161-175.

Deater-Deckard, K., Dodge, K.A., Bates, J.E. & Pettit, G.S. (1996). Physical discipline among African American and European American mothers: Links to children's externalizing behaviors. *Developmental Psychology, 32* (6), 1065-1072.

Deci, E.L. (1971). Effects of externally mediated rewards on intrinsic motivation. *Journal of Personality and Social Psychology, 18* (1), 105-115.

_____(1972). Intrinsic motivation, extrinsic reinforcement, and equity. *Journal of Personality and Social Psychology, 22* (1), 113-120.

Deci, E.L., Koestner, R. & Ryan, R.M. (1999). A meta-analytic review of experiments examining the effects of extrinsic rewards on intrinsic motivation. *Psychological Bulletin, 125* (6), 627-668.

_____(2001). Extrinsic rewards and intrinsic motivation in education: Reconsidered once again. *Review of Educational Research, 71* (1), 1-27.

Deci, E.L. & Ryan, R.M. (1987). The support of autonomy and the control of behavior. *Journal of Personality and Social Psychology, 53* (6), 1024-1037.

_____(2000). The 'what' and 'why' of goal pursuits: Human needs and the self-determination of behavior. *Psychological Inquiry, 11* (4), 227-268.

Deci, E.L., Vallerand, R.J., Pelletier, L.G. & Ryan, R.M. (1991). Motivation and education: The self-determination perspective. *Educational Psychologist, 26* (3 & 4), 325-346.

Dekovic, M., Janssens, J.M.A.M. & Van As, N.M.C. (2003). Family predictors of antisocial behavior in adolescence. *Family Process, 42* (2), 223-235.

Denham, S.A., Caverly, S., Schmidt, M., Blair, K., DeMulder, E., Caal, S., Hamada, H. & Mason, T. (2002). Preschool understanding of emotions: Contributions to classroom anger and aggression. *Journal of Child Psychology and Psychiatry, 43* (7), 901-916.

Denham, S.A., Mitchell-Copeland, J., Strandberg, K., Auerbach, S. & Blair, K. (1997). Parental contributions to preschoolers' emotional competence: Direct and indirect effects. *Motivation and Emotion, 21* (1), 65-86.

Denham, S.A., Workman, E., Cole, P.M., Weissbrod, C., Kendziora, K.T. & Zahn-Waxler, C. (2000). Prediction of externalizing behavior problems from early to middle childhood: The role of parental socialization and emotion expression. *Development and Psychopathology, 12* (1), 23-45.

Deslandes, R., Royer, E., Turcotte, D. & Bertrand, R. (1997). School achievement at secondary level: Influence of parenting style and parent involvement in schooling. *McGill Journal of Education, 32* (3), 191-207.

Deutsch, M. (1979). Education and distributive justice: Some reflections on grading systems. *American Psychologist, 34* (5), 391-401.

Deynoot-Schaub, M.G. & Riksen-Walraven, J.M. (2006). Peer interaction in child care centres at 15 and 23 months: Stability and links with children's socio-emotional adjustment. *Infant Behavior and Development, 29* (2), 276-288.

Diener, E. & Diener, M. (1995). Cross-cultural correlates of life satisfaction and self-esteem. *Journal of Personality and Social Psychology, 68* (4), 653-663.

Diener, M.L., Nievar, M.A. & Wright, C. (2003). Attachment security among mothers and their young children living in poverty: Associations with maternal, child, and contextual factors. *Merrill-Palmer Quarterly, 49* (2), 154-182.

Dinkmeyer, D. & McKay, G. (1989). *Systematic training for effective parenting.* (3rd ed.) Circle Pines, MN: American Guidance Service.

Dinkmeyer, D. Sr, McKay, G.D., Dinkmeyer, J.S., Dinkmeyer, D. Jr, McKay, J.L. (1997). *Parenting young children: Systematic training for effective parenting (STEP) of children under six.* Circle Pines, MN: American Guidance Service.

Dinkmeyer, D., McKay, G. & Dinkmeyer, D. (1980). *Systematic training for effective teaching.* Circle Pines, MN: American Guidance Service.

DiPrima, A.J., Ashby, J.S., Gnilka, P.B. & Noble, C.L. (2011). Family relationships and perfectionism in middle school students. *Psychology in the Schools, 48* (8), 815-827.

Dix, T., Ruble, D.N. & Zambarano, R.J. (1989). Mothers' implicit theories of discipline: Child effects, parent effects, and the attribution process. *Child Development, 60* (6), 1373-1391.

Dixon, L., Hamilton-Giachritsis, C. & Browne, K. (2005). Attributions and behaviours of parents abused as children: A mediational analysis of the intergenerational continuity of child maltreatment (Part II). *Journal of Child Psychology and Psychiatry, 46* (1), 58-68.

Dobson, J. (1992). *The new dare to discipline.* Wheaton, IL: Tyndale House.

Dodge, K.A., Lansford, J.E., Burks, V.S., Bates, J.E., Pettit, G.S., Fontaine, R. & Price, J.M. (2003). Peer rejection and social information-processing factors in the development of aggressive behavior problems in children. *Child Development, 74* (2), 374-393.

Dodge, K.A., Pettit, G.S. & Bates, J.E. (1994). Socialization mediators of the relation between socioeconomic status and child conduct problems. *Child Development, 65* (2), 649-665.

Donohue, K.M., Perry, K.E. & Weinstein, R.S. (2003). Teachers' classroom practices and children's rejection by their peers. *Journal of Applied Developmental Psychology, 24* (1), 91-118.

Donovan, W.L., Leavitt, L.A. & Walsh, R.O. (2000). Maternal illusory control predicts socialization strategies and toddler compliance. *Developmental Psychology, 36* (3), 402-411.

Dornbusch, S.M., Ritter, P.L., Liederman, P.H., Roberts, D.F. & Fraleigh, M.J. (1987). The relation of parenting style to adolescent school performance. *Child Development, 58* (5), 1244-1257.

Dubanoski, R.A., Inaba, M. & Gerkewicz, K. (1983). Corporal punishment in schools: Myths, problems and alternatives. *Child Abuse and Neglect, 7* (7), 271-278.

Duchesne, S. & Ratelle, C. (2010). Parental behaviors and adolescents' achievement goals at the beginning of middle school: Emotional problems as potential mediators. *Journal of Educational Psychology, 102* (2), 497-507.

Duncan, G.J. & Brooks-Gunn, J. (2000). Family poverty, welfare reform, and child development. *Child Development, 71* (1), 188-196.

Duong, M.T., Schwartz, D., Chang, L., Kelly, B.M. & Tom, S.R. (2009). Associations between maternal physical discipline and peer victimization among Hong Kong Chinese children: The moderating role of child aggression. *Journal of Abnormal Child Psychology, 37* (7), 957-966.

Durrant, J. & Ensom, R. (2012). Physical punishment of children: Lessons from 20 years of research. *Canadian Medical Association Journal, 184* (12), 1371-1377.

Durrant, M. (1995). *Creative strategies for school problems.* Epping, NSW: Eastwood Family Therapy Centre/New York: Norton.

Dweck, C.S. (2006). *Mindset: The new psychology of success.* New York: Ballantine.

Dweck, C.S. & Leggett, E.L. (1988). A social-cognitive approach to motivation and personality. *Psychological Review, 95* (2), 256-273.

Eamon, M.K. (2001). Antecedents and socioemotional consequences of physical punishment on children in two-parent families. *Child Abuse and Neglect, 6* (6), 787-802.

Eccles, J.S., Buchanan, C.M., Flanagan, C., Fuligni, A., Midgley, C. & Yee, D. (1991). Control versus autonomy during early adolescence. *Journal of Social Issues, 47* (4), 53-68.

Eisenberg, N., Champion, C. & Ma, Y. (2004). Emotion-related regulation: An emerging construct. *Merrill-Palmer Quarterly, 50* (3), 236-259.

Eisenberg, N., Fabes, R.A., Shepard, S.A., Guthrie, I.K., Murphy, B.C. & Reiser, M. (1999). Parental reactions to children's negative emotions: Longitudinal relations to quality of children's social functioning. *Child Development, 70* (2), 513-534.

Eisenberg, N., Lennon, R. & Roth, K. (1983). Prosocial development: A longitudinal study. *Developmental Psychology, 19* (6), 846-855.

Eisenberg, N., Sadovsky, A., Spinrad, T.L., Fabes, R.A., Losoya, S.H., Valiente, C., Reiser, M., Cumberland, A. & Shepard, S.A. (2005a). The relations of problem behavior status to children's negative emotionality, effortful control, and impulsivity: Concurrent relations and prediction of change. *Developmental Psychology, 41* (1), 193-211.

Elias, M.J., Tobias, S.E. & Friedlander, B.S. (1999). *Emotionally intelligent parenting.* Sydney: Doubleday.

Elliot, A.J. & Thrash, T.M. (2004). The intergenerational transmission of fear of failure. *Personality and Social Psychology Bulletin, 30* (8), 957-971.

Ellis, A. (1962). *Reason and emotion in psychotherapy.* Secaucus, NJ: Lyle Stuart. Emmer, E.T. & Evertson, C.M. (2009). *Classroom management for middle and high school teachers.* (8th ed.) Upper Saddle River, NJ: Pearson.

Emmer, E.T. & Aussiker, A. (1990). School and classroom discipline programs: How well do they work?. In O. Moles (Ed.) *Student discipline strategies: Research and practice.* Albany, NY: State University of New York Press, pp. 129-166.

Emmer, E.T. & Evertson, C.M. (2009). *Classroom management for middle and high school teachers.* (8th ed.) Upper Saddle River, NJ: Pearson.

Evans, G.W. & English, K. (2002). The environment of poverty: Multiple stressor exposure, psychophysiological stress, and socioemotional adjustment. *Child Development, 73* (4), 1238-1248.

Evans, G.W., Kim, P., Ting, A.H., Tesher, H.B. & Shannis, D. (2007). Cumulative risk, maternal responsiveness, and allostatic load among young adolescents. *Developmental Psychology, 43* (2), 341-351.

Evans, G.W., Maxwell, L.E. & Hart, B. (1999). Parental language and verbal responsiveness to children in crowded homes. *Developmental Psychology, 35* (4), 1020-1023.

Evans, G.W. & Schamberg, M.A. (2009). Childhood poverty, chronic stress, and adult working memory. *Proceedings of the National Academy of Sciences, 106* (16), 6545-6549.

Evertson, C.M., Emmer, E.T. & Worsham, M.E. (2003). *Classroom management for elementary teachers.* (6th ed.) Boston, MA: Pearson Allyn and Bacon.

Faber, A., Mazlish, E., Nyberg, L. & Templeton, R.A. (1995). *How to talk so kids can learn at home and in school.* New York: Fireside.

Fabes, R.A., Fultz, J., Eisenberg, N., May-Plumlee, T. & Christopher, F.S. (1989). Effects of rewards on children's prosocial motivation: A socialization study. *Developmental Psychology, 25* (4), 509-515.

Fabes, R.A., Leonard, S.A., Kupanoff, K. & Martin, C.L. (2001). Parental coping with children's negative emotions: Relations with children's emotional and social responding. *Child Development, 72* (3), 907-920.

Fairchild, L. & Erwin, W.M. (1977). Physical punishment by parent figures as a model of aggressive behavior in children. *Journal of Genetic Psychology, 130* (2), 279-284.

Farrell, A.D. & White, K.S. (1998). Parental influences and drug use among urban adolescents: Family structure and parent-adolescent relationship as protective factors. *Journal of Consulting and Clinical Psychology, 66* (2), 248-258.

Feiring, C., Taska, L. & Lewis, M. (2002). Adjustment following sexual abuse discovery: The role of shame and attributional style. *Developmental Psychology, 38* (1), 79-92.

Feldhusen, J.F., Dai, D.Y. & Clinkenbeard, P.R. (2000). Dimensions of competitive and cooperative learning among gifted learners. *Journal for the Education of the Gifted, 23,* (3), 328-342.

Feldman, R. & Klein, P.S. (2003). Toddlers' self-regulated compliance to mothers, caregivers, and fathers: Implications for theories of socialization. *Developmental Psychology, 39* (4), 680-692.

Fergusson, D.M., Horwood, L.J. & Ridder, E.M. (2005). Show me the child at seven: The consequences of conduct problems in childhood for psychosocial functioning in adulthood. *Journal of Child Psychology and Psychiatry, 46* (8), 837-849.

Fergusson, D.M. & Lynskey, M.T. (1997). Physical punishment/maltreatment during childhood and adjustment in young adulthood. *Child Abuse and Neglect, 21* (7), 617-630.

Fergusson, D., Swain-Campbell, N. & Horwood, J. (2004). How does childhood economic disadvantage lead to crime?. *Journal of Child Psychology and Psychiatry, 45* (5), 956-966.

Fields, M. & Boesser, C. (2002). *Constructive guidance and discipline.* (3rd ed.) Upper Saddle River, NJ: Merrill Prentice Hall.

Fine, S.E., Trentacosta, C.J., Izard, C.E., Mostow, A.J. & Campbell, J.L. (2004). Anger perception, caregivers' use of physical discipline, and aggression in children at risk. *Social Development, 13* (2), 213-228.

Fletcher, A.C. & Shaw, R.A. (2000). Sex differences in associations between parental behaviors and characteristics of adolescent social integration. *Social Development, 9* (2), 133-148.

Flook, L., Repetti, R.L. & Ullman, J.B. (2005). Classroom social experiences as predictors of academic performance. *Developmental Psychology, 41* (2), 319-327.

Flores, E., Cicchetti, D. & Rogosch, F.A. (2005). Predictors of resilience in maltreated and nonmaltreated Latino children. *Developmental Psychology, 41* (2), 338-351.

Foucard, T. (1985). Development of food allergies with special reference to cow's milk allergy. *Pediatrics, 75* (1), 177-181.

Frankel, F. & Myatt, R. (1996). Self-esteem, social competence and psychopathology in boys without friends. *Personality and Individual Differences, 20* (3), 401-407.

Franklin, M.E. & Foa, E.B. (2008). Obsessive-compulsive disorder. In D.H. Barlow (Ed.) *Clinical handbook of psychological disorders: A step-by-step treatment manual.* (4th ed.) New York: Guilford, pp. 164-215.

Freedman, J.L., Cunningham, J.A. & Krismer, K. (1992). Inferred values and the reverse-incentive effect in induced compliance. *Journal of Personality and Social Psychology, 62* (3), 357-368.

Frenzel, A.C., Pekrun, R. & Goetz, T. (2007). Perceived learning environment and students' emotional experiences: A multilevel analysis of mathematics classrooms. *Learning and Instruction, 17* (5), 478-493.

Frias-Armenta, M. (2002). Long-term effects of child punishment on Mexican women: A structural model. *Child Abuse and Neglect, 26* (4), 371-386.

Frith, U. (2004). Emanuel Miller lecture: Confusions and controversies about Asperger syndrome. *Journal of Child Psychology and Psychiatry, 45* (4), 672-686.

Frodi, A., Bridges, L. & Grolnick, W. (1985). Correlates of mastery-related behavior: A short-term longitudinal study of infants in their second year. *Child Development, 56* (5), 1291-1298.

Fujiura, G.T. & Yamaki, K. (2000). Trends in demography of childhood poverty and disability. *Exceptional Children, 66* (2), 187-199.

Gagné, F. (2003). Transforming gifts into talents: The DMGT as a developmental theory. In N. Colangelo & G.A. Davis (Eds.) *Handbook of gifted education.* (3rd ed.) Boston, MA: Allyn and Bacon, pp. 60-74.

Garber, J., Robinson, N.S. & Valentiner, D. (1997). The relation between parenting and adolescent depression: Self-worth as a mediator. *Journal of Adolescent Research, 12* (1), 12-33.

Garner, P.W. & Spears, F.M. (2000). Emotion regulation in low-income preschoolers. *Social Development, 9* (2), 246-264.

Gartrell, D. (1994). *A guidance approach to discipline.* New York: Delmar.

_____(2003). *A guidance approach for the encouraging classroom.* (3rd ed.) New York: Delmar.

_____(2004). *The power of guidance: Teaching social-emotional skills in early childhood classrooms.* New York: Thomson.

Gaylord-Harden, N.K. (2008). The influence of student perceptions of parenting and coping on achievement and classroom behavior among African American children. *Psychology in the Schools, 45* (8), 763-777.

Gazelle, H. & Ladd, G.W. (2003). Anxious solitude and peer exclusion: A diathesis-stress model of internalizing trajectories in childhood. *Child Development, 74* (1), 257-278.

Gecas, V. (1982). The self-concept. *Annual Review of Sociology, 8,* 1-33.

George, C. & Main, M. (1979). Social interactions of young abused children: Approach, avoidance, and aggression. *Child Development, 50* (2), 306-318.

Gerris, J.R.M., Dekovic, M. & Janssens, J.M.A.M. (1997). The relationship between social class and childrearing behaviors: Parents' perspective taking and value orientations. *Journal of Marriage and the Family, 59* (4), 834-847.

Gershoff, E.T. (2002). Corporal punishment by parents and associated child behaviors and experiences: A meta-analytic and theoretical review. *Psychological Bulletin, 128* (4), 539-579.

Gershoff, E.T., Grogan-Kaylor, A., Lansford, J.E., Chang, L., Zelli, A. Deater-Deckard, K. & Dodge, K.A. (2010). Parent discipline practices in an international sample: Associations with child behaviors and moderation by perceived normativeness. *Child Development, 81* (2), 497-502.

Gershoff, E.T., Lansford, J.E., Sexton, H.R., Davis-Kean, P. & Sameroff, A.J. (2012). Longitudinal links between spanking and children's externalizing behaviors in a national sample of White, Black, Hispanic, and Asian American families. *Child Development, 83* (3), 838-843.

Gesser, R.M. & Koo, S.C. (1996). Oral inoculation with herpes simplex virus type 1 infects enteric neurons and mucosal nerve fibers within the gastrointestinal tract in mice. *Journal of Virology, 70* (6), 4097-4102.

Gest, S.D., Freeman, N.R., Domitrovich, C.E. & Welsh, J.A. (2004). Shared book reading and children's language comprehension skills: The moderating role of parental discipline practices. *Early Childhood Research Quarterly, 19* (2), 319-336.

Giles-Sims, J., Straus, M.A. & Sugarman, D.B. (1995). Child, maternal, and family characteristics associated with spanking. *Family Relations, 44* (2), 170-176.

Gilliom, M., Shaw, D.S., Beck, J.E., Schonberg, M.A. & Lukon, J.L. (2002). Anger regulation in disadvantaged preschool boys: Strategies, antecedents, and the development of self-control. *Developmental Psychology, 38* (2), 222-235.

Gilman, R. & Anderman, E.M. (2006). The relationship between relative levels of motivation and intrapersonal, interpersonal, and academic functioning among older adolescents. *Journal of School Psychology, 44* (5), 375-391.

Gilman, R. & Ashby, J.S. (2003). Multidimensional perfectionism in a sample of middle school students: An exploratory investigation. *Psychology in the Schools, 40* (6), 677-689.

Ginsberg, G.S. & Bronstein, P. (1993). Family factors related to children's intrinsic/extrinsic motivational orientation and academic performance. *Child Development, 64* (5), 1461-1474.

Glaser, D. (2000). Child abuse and neglect and the brain – A review. *Journal of Child Psychology and Psychiatry, 41* (1), 97-116.

Glasser, W. (1977). Ten steps to good discipline. *Today's Education, 66*, 61-63.

____(1998). *The quality school: Managing students without coercion.* (rev. ed.) New York: Harper Perennial.

Goleman, D. (1994). *Emotional intelligence.* New York: Bantam Books.

Gonzalez, J.E., Nelson, J.R., Gutkin, T.B., Saunders, A, Galloway, A. & Shwery, C.S. (2004). Rational emotive therapy with children and adolescents: A meta-analysis. *Journal of Emotional and Behavioral Disorders, 12* (4), 222-235.

Gonzalez-DeHass, A.R., Willems, P.P. & Holbein, M.F.D. (2005). Examining the relationship between parental involvement and student motivation. *Educational Psychology Review, 17* (2), 99-123.

Goodwin, R.D., Fergusson, D.M. & Horwood, L.J. (2004). Early anxious/withdrawn behaviours predict later internalising disorders. *Journal of Child Psychology and Psychiatry, 45* (4), 874-883.

Gordon, T. (1970). *Parent effectiveness training.* New York: Plume.\

____(1974). *Teacher effectiveness training.* New York: Peter H. Wyden.

____(1997). *Parent effectiveness training workbook: Revised Australian edition.* Solana Beach, CA: Gordon Training International.

____(2000). *Parent effectiveness training.* (2nd ed.) New York: Three Rivers Press.

Gottfried, A.E., Fleming, J.S. & Gottfried, A.W. (1994). Role of parental motivational practices in children's academic intrinsic motivation and achievement. *Journal of Educational Psychology, 86* (1), 104-113.

Graham, S., Bellmore, A.D. & Mize, J. (2006). Peer victimization, aggression, and their co-occurrence in middle school: Pathways to adjustment problems. *Journal of Abnormal Child Psychology, 34* (3), 363-378.

Graue, M.E. & Walsh, D.J. (1998). *Studying children in context: Theories, methods and ethics.* Thousand Oaks, CA: SAGE.

Gray, M.R. & Steinberg, L. (1999). Unpacking authoritative parenting: Reassessing a multidimensional construct. *Journal of Marriage and the Family, 61* (3), 574-587.

Grayling, A.C. (2013). *The God argument: The case against religion and for humanism.* London: Bloomsbury.

Greene, R.W. (2008). *Lost at school.* New York: Scribner.

____(2010). *The explosive child.* New York: Harper.

Gregory, A. & Rimm-Kaufman, S. (2008). Positive mother-child interactions in kindergarten: Predictors of school success in high school. *School Psychology Review, 37* (4), 499-515.

Gregory, J.F. (1995). The crime of punishment: Racial and gender disparities in the use of corporal punishment in U.S. public school. *Journal of Negro Education, 64* (4), 454-462.

Greven, P. (1990). *Spare the child: The religious roots of punishment and the psychological impact of physical abuse.* New York: Vintage.

Grogan-Kaylor, A. (2005). Corporal punishment and the growth trajectory of children's antisocial behavior. *Child Maltreatment, 10* (3), 283-292.

Grolnick, W.S. (2003). *The psychology of parental control: How well-meant parenting backfires.* Mahwah, NJ: Lawrence Erlbaum.

Grolnick, W.S., Bridges, L.J. & Connell, J.P. (1996). Emotion regulation in two-year-olds: Strategies and emotional expression in four contexts. *Child Development, 67* (3), 928-941.

Grolnick, W.S., Gurland, S.T., DeCourcey, W. & Jacob, K. (2002). Antecedents and consequences of mothers' autonomy support: An experimental investigation. *Developmental Psychology, 38* (1), 143-155.

Grolnick, W.S. & Ryan, R.M. (1989). Parent styles associated with children's self-regulation and competence in school. *Journal of Educational Psychology, 81* (2), 143-154.

Grusec, J.E. & Mammone, N. (1995). Features and sources of parents' attributions about themselves and their children. *Review of Personality and Social Psychology: Social Development,* (15), 49-73. N. Eisenberg (Ed.) Thousand Oaks, CA: SAGE.

Gunnoe, M.L. & Mariner, C.L. (1997). Toward a developmental-contextual model of the effects of parental spanking on children's aggression. *Archives of Pediatric and Adolescent Medicine, 151* (8), 768-775.

Hadjivassiliou, M., Grünewald, R.A., Lawden, M., Davies-Jones, G.A.B., Powell, T. & Smith, C.M.L. (2001). Headache and CNS white matter abnormalities associated with gluten sensitivity. *Neurology, 56* (3), 385-388.

Hagerman, R.J. & Falkenstein, A.R. (1987). Association between recurrent otitis media in infancy and later hyperactivity. *Clinical Pediatrics, 26* (5), 253-257.

Halpern, L.F. (2004). The relations of coping and family environment to preschoolers' problem behavior. *Journal of Applied Developmental Psychology, 25* (4), 399-421.

Hamilton, C.E. (2000). Continuity and discontinuity of attachment from infancy to adolescence. *Child Development, 71* (3), 690-694.

Hamre, P.K. & Pianta, R.C. (2001). Early teacher-child relationships and the trajectory of children's school outcomes through eighth grade. *Child Development, 72* (2), 625-638.

Harris, P.L. (1983). Children's understanding of the link between situation and emotion. *Journal of Experimental Child Psychology, 36* (3), 490-509.

Harris, R. (2007). *The happiness trap: Stop struggling, start living.* Wollombi, NSW: Exisle.

_____(2009). *ACT made simple: An easy-to-read primer on Acceptance and Commitment Therapy.* Oakland, CA: New Harbinger.

_____(2011). *The confidence gap.* Boston, MA: Trumpeter.

Hart, C.H., DeWolf, D.M. & Burts, D.C. (1992a). Linkages among preschoolers' playground behavior, outcome expectations, and parental disciplinary strategies. *Early Education and Development, 3* (4), 265-283.

Hart, C.H., DeWolf, D.M., Wozniak, P. & Burts, D.C. (1992b). Maternal and paternal disciplinary styles: Relations with preschoolers' playground behavioral orientations and peer status. *Child Development, 63* (4), 879-892.

Hart, S. & Hodson, V.K. (2004). *The compassionate classroom: Relationship based teaching and learning.* Encinitas, CA: Puddle Dancer Press.

_____(2006). *Respectful parents; respectful kids: 7 keys to turn family conflict into co-operation.* Encinitas, CA: Puddle Dancer Press.

Hart, C.H., Burts, D.C., Durland, M.A., Charlesworth, R., DeWolf, M. & Fleege, P.O. (1998). Stress behaviors and activity type participation of preschoolers in more and less developmentally appropriate classrooms: SES and sex differences. *Journal of Research in Childhood Education, 12* (2), 176-196.

Hart, C.H., DeWolf, D.M. & Burts, D.C. (1992a). Linkages among preschoolers' playground behavior, outcome expectations, and parental disciplinary strategies. *Early Education and Development, 3* (4), 265-283.

Hart, C.H., DeWolf, D.M., Wozniak, P. & Burts, D.C. (1992b). Maternal and paternal disciplinary styles: Relations with preschoolers' playground behavioral orientations and peer status. *Child Development, 63* (4), 879-892.

Harter, S. (1978). Pleasure derived from challenge and the effects of receiving grades on children's difficulty level choices. *Child Development, 49* (3), 788-799.

Harter, S., Waters, P. & Whitesell, N.R. (1997). Lack of voice as a manifestation of false self behavior among adolescents: The school setting as a stage upon which the drama of authenticity is enacted. *Educational Psychologist, 32* (3), 153-173.

Harter, S.. & Whitesell, N.R. (2003). Beyond the debate: Why some adolescents report stable self-worth over time and situation, whereas others report changes in self-worth. *Journal of Personality, 71* (6), 1027-1058.

Hastings, P. & Grusec, J.E. (1997). Conflict outcomes as a function of parental accuracy in perceiving child cognitions and affect. *Social Development, 6* (1), 76-90.

Hastings, P.D., Zahn-Waxler, C., Robinson, J., Usher, B. & Bridges, D. (2000). The development of concern for others in children with behavior problems. *Developmental Psychology, 36* (5), 531-546.

Hay, D.F., Payne, A. & Chadwick, A. (2004). Peer relations in childhood. *Journal of Child Psychology and Psychiatry, 45* (1), 84-108.

Haynes-Seman, C. & Baumgarten, D. (1998). The victimization of young children. In B.B.R. Rossman and M.S. Rosenberg (Eds.) *Multiple victimization of children: Conceptual, developmental, research, and treatment issues.* New York: Haworth Press, pp. 67-86.

Heatherton, T.F. & Vohs, K.D. (2000). Interpersonal evaluations following threats to self: Role of self-esteem. *Journal of Personality and Social Psychology, 78* (4), 725-736.

Hennessey, B.A. & Amabile, T.M. (1998). Reward, intrinsic motivation, and creativity. *American Psychologist, 53* (6), 674-675.

Herrera, C. & Dunn, J. (1997). Early experiences with family conflict: Implications for arguments with a close friend. *Developmental Psychology, 33* (5), 869-881.

Hess, L.L. (1994). Life, liberty and the pursuit of perfection. *Gifted Child Today, 17* (3), 28-31.

Hill, A.L., Degnan, K.A., Calkins, S.D. & Keane, S.P. (2006). Profiles of externalizing behavior problems for boys and girls across preschool: The roles of emotion regulation and inattention. *Developmental Psychology, 42* (5), 913-928.

Hoeve, M., Dubas, J.S., Eichelsheim, V.I., van der Laan, P.H., Smeenk, W. & Gerris, J.R.M. (2009). The relationship between parenting and delinquency: A meta-analysis. *Journal of Abnormal Child Psychology, 37* (6), 749-775.

Hoffman, M.L. (1990). Empathy and justice motivation. *Motivation and Emotion, 14* (2), 151-172.

Hoffman, M.L. & Saltzstein. H.D. (1967). Parent discipline and the child's moral development. *Journal of Personality and Social Psychology, 5* (1), 45-57.

Hoffman-Plotkin, D. & Twentyman, C.T. (1984). A multimodal assessment of behavioral and cognitive deficits in abused and neglected preschoolers. *Child Development, 55* (3), 794-802.

Holden, G.W. (2002). Perspectives on the effects of corporal punishment: Comment on Gershoff (2002). *Psychological Bulletin, 128* (4), 590-595.

Holland, P. (2004). *Picturing childhood: The myth of the child in popular imagery.* London: I.B. Tauris.

Holt, J. (1982). *How children fail.* (rev. ed.) New York: Merloyd Lawrence.

____(1983). *How children learn.* (rev. ed.) New York: Merloyd Lawrence.

Hong, S. & Ho, H.-Z. (2005). Direct and indirect longitudinal effects of parental involvement on student achievement: Second-order latent growth modeling across ethnic groups. *Journal of Educational Psychology, 97* (1), 32-42.

Hublin, J.-J. (2009). The prehistory of compassion. *Proceedings of the National Academy of Science, 106* (16), 6429-6430.

Hunter, S.C. & Boyle, J.M.E. (2004). Appraisal and coping strategy use in victims of school bullying. *British Journal of Educational Psychology, 74* (1), 83-107.

Huntley, J. (1999). A narrative approach to working with students who have 'learning difficulties'. In A. Morgan (Ed.) *Once upon a time... Narrative therapy with children and their families.* Adelaide, SA: Dulwich Centre Publications, pp. 35-49.

Hyman, I.A. (1995). Corporal punishment, psychological maltreatment, violence, and punitiveness in America: Research, advocacy, and public policy. *Applied and Preventive Psychology, 4* (2), 113-130.

Ispa, J.M., Fine, M.A., Halgunseth, L.C., Harper, S., Robinson, J., Boyce, L., Brooks-Gunn, J. & Brady-Smith, C. (2004). Maternal intrusiveness, maternal warmth, and mother-toddler relationship outcomes: Variations across low-income ethnic and acculturation groups. *Child Development, 75* (6), 1613-1631.

Jakubowski, P. (1977). Self-assertion training procedures for women. In E. Rowling and D. Carter (Eds.) *Psychotherapy for women.* Springfield, IL: Charles C. Thomas.

Jakubowski, P. & Lange, A. (1978). *The assertive option: Your rights and responsibilities.* Champaign, IL: Research Press.

Jang, H., Reeve, J. & Deci, E.L. (2010). Engaging students in learning activities: It is not autonomy support or structure, but autonomy support and structure. *Journal of Educational Psychology, 102* (3), 588-600.

Jang, H., Reeve, J., Ryan, R.M. & Kim, A. (2009). Can self-determination theory explain what underlies the productive, satisfying learning experiences of collectivistically oriented Korean students?. *Journal of Educational Psychology, 101* (3), 644-661.

Jeffers, S. (2007). *Feel the fear... and do it anyway.* New York: Ballantine.

Jodl, K.M., Michael, A., Malanchuk, O., Eccles, J.S. & Sameroff, A. (2001). Parents' roles in shaping early adolescents' occupational aspirations. *Child Development, 72* (4), 1247-1265.

Johnson, C., Ironsmith, M., Snow, C.W. & Poteat, G.M. (2000). Peer acceptance and social adjustment in preschool and kindergarten. *Early Childhood Education Journal, 27* (4), 207-212.

Johnson, D.W. & Johnson, R.T. (1974). Instructional goal structure: Cooperative, competitive, or individualistic. *American Educational Research Journal, 44* (2), 213-240.

Johnston, J.M. (1972). Punishment of human behavior. *American Psychologist, 27* (11), 1033-1054.

Jones, V.F. & Jones, L.S. (2013). *Comprehensive classroom management: Creating communities of support and solving problems.* (10th ed.) Boston, MA: Pearson.

Joussemet, M., Vitaro, F., Barker, E.D., Côté, S., Nagin, D.S., Zoccolillo, M. & Tremblay, R.E. (2008). Controlling parenting and physical aggression during elementary school. *Child Development, 79* (2), 411-425.

Kaiser, A.P., Hancock, T.B., Cai, X., Foster, E.M. & Hester, P.P. (2000). Parent-reported behavioral problems and language delays in boys and girls enrolled in Head Start classrooms. *Behavioral Disorders, 26* (1), 26-41.

Kakihara, F. & Tilton-Weaver, L. (2009). Adolescents' interpretations of parental control: Differentiated by domain and types of control. *Child Development, 80* (6), 1722-1738.

Kamins, M.L. & Dweck, C.S. (1999). Person versus process praise and criticism: Implications for contingent self-worth and coping. *Developmental Psychology, 35* (3), 835-847.

Kaplan, J.S. & Carter, J. (1995). *Beyond behavior modification: A cognitive-behavioral approach to behavior management in the school.* (3rd ed.) Austin, TX: Pro-Ed.

Karlsson, H., Blomström, A., Wicks, S., Yang, S., Yolken, R.H. & Dalman, C. (2012). Maternal antibodies to dietary antigens and risk of nonaffective psychosis in offspring. *American Journal of Psychiatry, 169* (6), 625-632.

Kaufmann, D., Gesten, E., Santa Lucia, R.C., Salcedo, O., Rendina-Gobioff, G. & Gadd, R. (2000). The relationship between parenting style and children's adjustment: The parents' perspective. *Journal of Child and Family Studies, 9* (2), 231-245.

Kazdin, A.E. & Benjet, C. (2003). Spanking children: Evidence and issues. *Current Directions in Psychological Science, 12* (3), 99-103.

Keiley, M.K., Bates, J.E., Dodge, K.E. & Pettit, G.S. (2000). A cross-domain growth analysis: Externalizing and internalizing behaviors during eight years of childhood. *Journal of Abnormal Child Psychology, 28* (2), 161-179.

Kelly, M.S., Kim, J.S. & Franklin, C. (2008). *Solution-focused brief therapy in schools: A 360-degree view of research and practice.* New York: Oxford University Press.

Kernis, M.H. (2003). Toward a conceptualization of optimal self-esteem. *Psychological Inquiry, 14* (1), 1-26.

Kernis, M.H., Brown, A.C. & Brody, G.H. (2000). Fragile self-esteem in children and its associations with perceived patterns of parent-child communication. *Journal of Personality, 68* (2), 225-252.

Kerns, K.A., Cole, A. & Andrews, P.B. (1998). Attachment security, parent peer management practices, and peer relationships in preschoolers. *Merrill-Palmer Quarterly, 44* (4), 504-522.

Kim, J. & Cicchetti, D. (2004). A longitudinal study of child maltreatment, mother-child relationship quality and maladjustment: The role of self-esteem and social competence. *Journal of Abnormal Child Psychology, 32* (4), 341-354.

____(2006). Longitudinal trajectories of self-system processes and depressive symptoms among maltreated and nonmaltreated children. *Child Development, 77* (3), 624-639.

Kim, S.Y., Wang, Y., Orozco-Lapray, D., Shen, Y. & Murtuza, M. (2013). Does 'tiger parenting' exist? Parenting profiles of Chinese Americans and adolescent developmental outcomes. *Asian American Journal of Psychology, 4* (1), 7-18.

Kins, E., Soenens, B. & Beyers, W. (2012). Parental psychological control and dysfunctional separation-individuation: A tale of two different dynamics. *Journal of Adolescence, 35* (5), 1099-1109.

Klein, S. & Gibson, N. (2005). *What's making you angry?: Ten steps to transforming anger so everyone wins.* La Crescenta, CA: Puddle Dancer Press.

Klimes-Dougan, B. & Kistner, J. (1990). Physically abused preschoolers' responses to peers' distress. *Developmental Psychology, 26* (4), 599-602.

Knight, B.A. (1995). The influence of locus of control on gifted and talented students. *Gifted Education International, 11* (1), 31-33.

Kochanska, G. (1995). Children's temperament, mothers' discipline, and security of attachment: Multiple pathways to emerging internalization. *Child Development, 66* (3), 597-615.

____(1997). Mutually responsive orientation between mothers and their young children: Implications for early socialization. *Child Development, 68* (1), 94-112.

____(2002a). Committed compliance, moral self, and internalization: A mediational model. *Developmental Psychology, 38* (3), 339-351.

____(2002b). Mutually responsive orientation between mothers and their young children: A context for the early development of conscience. *Current Directions in Psychological Science, 11* (6), 191-195.

Kochanska, G. & Aksan, N. (1995). Mother-child mutually positive affect, the quality of child compliance to requests and prohibitions, and maternal control as correlates of early internalization. *Child Development, 66* (1), 236-254.

____(2004). Conscience in childhood: Past, present and future. *Merrill-Palmer Quarterly, 50* (3), 299-310.

Kochanska, G., Aksan, N. & Nichols, K.E. (2003). Maternal power assertion in discipline and moral discourse contexts: Commonalities, differences, and implications for children's moral conduct and cognition. *Developmental Psychology, 39* (6), 949-963.

Kochanska, G., Aksan, N. & Carlson, J.J. (2005a). Temperament, relationships, and young children's receptive cooperation with their parents. *Developmental Psychology, 41* (4), 648-660.

Kochanska, G., Aksan, N. & Joy, M.E. (2007). Children's fearfulness as a moderator of parenting in early socialization: Two longitudinal studies. *Developmental Psychology, 43* (1), 222-237.

Kochanska, G., Coy, K.C. & Murray, K.T. (2001). The development of self-regulation in the first four years of life. *Child Development, 72* (4), 1091-1111.

Kochanska, G., Forman, D.R., Aksan, N. & Dunbar, S.B. (2005b). Pathways to conscience: Early mother-child mutually responsive orientation and children's moral emotion, conduct, and cognition. *Journal of Child Psychology and Psychiatry, 46* (1), 19-34.

Kochanska, G., Forman, D.R. & Coy, K.C. (1999). Implications of the mother-child relationship in infancy for socialization in the second year of life. *Infant Behavior and Development, 22* (2), 249-265.

Kochanska, G., Murray, K.T. & Harlan, E.T. (2000). Effortful control in early childhood: Continuity and change, antecedents, and implications for social development. *Developmental Psychology, 36* (2), 220-232.

Koenig, A.L., Cicchetti, D. & Rogosch, F.A. (2000). Child compliance/noncompliance and maternal contributors to internalization in maltreating and nonmaltreating dyads. *Child Development, 71* (4), 1018-1032.

____(2004). Moral development: The association between maltreatment and young children's prosocial behaviors and moral transgressions. *Social Development, 13* (1), 87-106.

Koestner, R., Ryan, R.M., Bernieri, F. & Holt, K. (1984). Setting limits on children's behavior: The differential effects of controlling vs. informational styles on intrinsic motivation and creativity. *Journal of Personality, 52* (3), 233-248.

Kohn, A. (1992). *No contest: The case against competition.* (rev. ed.) Boston, MA: Houghton Mifflin.

_____(1996). *Beyond discipline: From compliance to community.* Alexandria, VA: Association for Supervision and Curriculum Development.

_____(1999). *Punished by rewards: The trouble with gold stars, incentive plans, A's, praise and other bribes.* (2nd ed.) Boston, MA: Houghton Mifflin.

_____(2004). *What does it mean to be well educated?.* Boston, MA: Beacon Press.

_____(2005). *Unconditional parenting: Moving from rewards and punishments to love and reason.* New York: Atria Books.

_____(2011). *Feel-bad education: And other contrarian essays on children and schooling.* Boston, MA: Beacon.

_____(2014). *The myth of the spoiled child: Challenging the conventional wisdom about children and parenting.* Cambridge, MA: Da Capo Press.

Koren-Karie, N., Oppenheim, D., Smadar, D., Sher, E. & Etzion-Carasso, A. (2002). Mothers' insightfulness regarding their infants' internal experience: Relations with maternal sensitivity and infant attachment. *Developmental Psychology, 38* (4), 534-542.

Kostelnik, M.J., Whiren, A.P., Soderman, A.K. & Gregory, K. (2006). *Guiding children's social development: Theory to practice.* (5th ed.) New York: Thomson Delmar.

Kotzman, A. (1989). *Listen to me; listen to you.* Melbourne: Penguin Books.

Kowalski, K. (1990). The girl with the know-how: Finding solutions to a school problem. *Family Therapy Case Studies, 5* (1), 3-14.

Krishnamurti, J. (1988). *Freedom from the known.* Bramdean, UK: Krishnamurti Foundation Trust.

Kuczynski, L (1983). Reasoning, prohibitions, and motivations for compliance. *Developmental Psychology, 19* (1), 126-134.

_____(1984). Socialization goals and mother-child interaction: Strategies for long-term and short-term compliance. *Developmental Psychology, 20* (6), 1061-1073.

Kuczynski, L. & Kochanska, G. (1990). Development of children's noncompliance strategies from toddlerhood to age 5. *Developmental Psychology, 26* (3), 398-408.

_____(1999). Development of children's noncompliance strategies from toddlerhood to age 5. *Developmental Psychology, 26* (3), 398-408.

Kuhn, M., Grave, S., Bransfield, R. & Harris, S. (2012). Long term antibiotic therapy may be an effective treatment for children co-morbid with Lyme disease and autism spectrum disorder. *Medical Hypotheses, 78* (5), 606-615.

Ladd, G.W. (2006). Peer rejection, aggressive or withdrawn behavior, and psychological maladjustment from ages 5 to 12: An examination of four predictive models. *Child Development, 77* (4), 822-846.

Ladd, G.W. & Burgess, K.B. (2001). Do relational and protective factors moderate the linkages between childhood aggression and early psychological adjustment?. *Child Development, 72* (5), 1579-1601.

Ladd, G.W. & Kochenderfer-Ladd, B. (1998). Parenting behaviors and parent-child relationships: Correlates of peer victimization in kindergarten?. *Developmental Psychology, 34* (6), 1450-1458.

Lagacé-Séguin, D.G. & Coplan, R.J. (2005). Maternal emotional styles and child social adjustment: Assessment, correlates, outcomes and goodness of fit in early childhood. *Social Development, 14* (4), 613-636.

Laible, D.J. & Thompson, R. (2002). Mother-toddler conflict in the toddler years: Lessons in emotion, morality, and relationships. *Child Development, 73* (4), 1187-1203.

Laird, R.D., Jordan, K.Y., Dodge, K.A., Pettit, G.S. & Bates, J.E. (2001). Peer rejection in childhood, involvement with antisocial peers in early adolescence, and the development of externalizing behavior problems. *Development and Psychopathology, 13* (2), 337-354.

Lamborn, S.D., Mounts, N.S., Steinberg, L. & Dornbusch, S.M. (1991). Patterns of competence and adjustment among adolescents from authoritative, authoritarian, indulgent, and neglectful families. *Child Development, 62* (5), 1049-1065.

Lantz, S. (2009). *Chemical free kids.* Buddina, QLD: Joshua Books.

Lanzetta, J.T. & Englis, B.G. (1989). Expectations of cooperation and competition and their effects on observers' vicarious emotional responses. *Journal of Personality and Social Psychology, 56* (4), 543-554.

Larzelere, R.E. (1986). Moderate spanking: Model or deterrent of children's aggression in the family?. *Journal of Family Violence, 1* (1), 27-36.

____(2000). Child outcomes of nonabusive and customary physical punishment by parents: An updated literature review. *Clinical Child and Family Psychology Review, 3* (4), 199-221.

Lavoie, F., Hébert, M., Tremblay, R., Vitaro, F., Vézina, L. & McDuff, P. (2002). History of family dysfunction and perpetration of dating violence by adolescent boys: A longitudinal study. *Journal of Adolescent Health, 30* (5), 375-383.

Lazarides, L. (2010). *A textbook of modern naturopathy.* London: Health-Diets.net.

Lebenthal, E. (1979). Lactose malabsorption and milk consumption in infants and children. *American Journal of Diseases of Childhood, 131* (1), 21-23.

Lee, N. (2001). *Childhood and society: Growing up in an age of uncertainty.* Buckingham, UK: Open University Press.

Lepper, M.R. & Greene, D. (1975). Turning play into work: Effects of adult surveillance and extrinsic rewards on children's intrinsic motivation. *Journal of Personality and Social Psychology, 31* (3), 479-486.

Lepper, M.R., Sagotsky, G., Dafoe, J.L. & Greene, D. (1982). Consequences of superfluous social constraints: Effects on young children's social inferences and subsequent intrinsic interest. *Journal of Personality and Social Psychology, 42* (1), 51-65.

Lerman, D.C. & Vorndran, C.M. (2002). On the status of knowledge for using punishment: Implications for treating behavior disorders. *Journal of Applied Behavior Analysis, 35* (4), 431-464.

Letcher, P., Smart, D.. Sanson, A. & Toumbourou, J.W. (2009). Psychosocial precursors and correlates of differing internalizing trajectories form 3 to 15 years. *Social Development, 18* (3), 618-646.

Letzring, T.D., Block, J. & Funder, D.C. (2005). Ego-control and ego-resiliency: Generalization of self-report scales based on personality descriptions from acquaintances, clinicians, and the self. *Journal of Research in Personality, 39* (4), 395-422.

Leung, K., Lau, S. & Lam, W.-L. (1998). Parenting styles and academic achievement: A cross-cultural study. *Merrill-Palmer Quarterly, 44* (2), 157-172.

Lewis, C.C. (1981). The effects of parental firm control: A reinterpretation of findings. *Psychological Bulletin, 90* (3), 547-563.

Lewis, M., Feiring, C. & Rosenthal, S. (2000). Attachment over time. *Child Development, 71* (3), 707-720.

Lewis, R. & Frydenberg, E. (2002). Concomitants of failure to cope: What we should teach adolescents about coping. *British Journal of Educational Psychology, 72* (3), 419-431.

Liszkowski, U., Carpenter, M., Striano, T. & Tomasello, M. (2006). 12- and 18-month olds point to provide information for others. *Journal of Cognition and Development, 7* (2), 173-187.

Liu, D., Diorio, J., Tannenbaum, B., Caldji, C., Francis, D., Freedman, A., Sharma, S., Pearson, D.. Plotsky, P.M. & Meaney, M.J. (1997). Maternal care, hippocampal glucocorticoid receptors, and hypothalamic-pituitary-adrenal responses to stress. *Science, 277* (5332), 1659-1662.

Lobato, D. (1983). Siblings of handicapped children: A review. *Journal of Autism and Developmental Disorders, 13* (4), 347-364.

LoCicero, K.A. & Ashby, J.S. (2000). Multidimensional perfectionism in middle school age gifted students: A comparison to peers from the general cohort. *Roeper Review, 22* (3), 182-185.

Londerville, S. & Main, M. (1981). Security of attachment, compliance, and maternal training methods in the second year of life. *Developmental Psychology, 17* (3), 289-299.

López, E.E., Olaizola, J.H., Ferrer, B.M. & Ochoa, G.M. (2006). Aggressive and nonaggressive rejected students: An analysis of their differences. *Psychology in the Schools, 43* (3), 387-400.

Lorber, M.F. & Egeland, B. (2011). Parenting and infant difficulty: Testing a mutual exacerbation hypothesis to predict early onset conduct problems. *Child Development, 82* (6), 2006-2020.

Loukas, A. (2009). Examining temporal associations between perceived maternal psychological control and early adolescent internalizing problems. *Journal of Abnormal Child Psychology, 37* (8), 1113-1122.

Loukas, A., Paulos, S.K. & Robinson, S. (2005). Early adolescent social and overt aggression: Examining the roles of social anxiety and maternal psychological control. *Journal of Youth and Adolescence, 34* (4), 335-345.

Luthar, S.S., Cicchetti, D. & Becker, B. (2000). The construct of resilience: A critical evaluation and guidelines for future work. *Child Development, 71* (3), 543-562.

Lyon, M.R. (2000). *Healing the hyperactive brain: Through the new science of functional medicine.* Calgary, AB: Focused Publishing.

Maccoby, E.E. & Martin, J.A. (1983). Socialization in the context of the family: Parent-child interaction. In P.H. Mussen and E.M. Hetherington (Eds). *Handbook of child psychology vol. IV: Socialization, personality and social development.* (4th ed.) New York: Wiley, pp. 1-101.

Mackarness, R. (1990). *Not all in the mind.* London: Thorsons.

MacKinnon-Lewis, C., Rabiner, D. & Starnes, R. (1999). Predicting boys' social acceptance and aggression: The role of mother-child interactions and boys' beliefs about peers. *Developmental Psychology, 35* (3), 632-639.

MacMillan, H.E., Boyle, M.H., Wong, M.Y.-Y., Duku, E.K., Fleming, J.E. & Walsh, C.A. (1999). Slapping and spanking in childhood and its association with lifetime prevalence of psychiatric disorders in a general population sample. *Canadian Medical Association Journal, 161* (7), 805-809.

Macmillan, R., McMorris, B.J. & Kruttschnitt, C. (2004). Linked lives: Stability and change in maternal circumstances and trajectories of antisocial behavior in children. *Child Development, 75* (1), 205-230.

Main, M. & George, C. (1985). Responses of abused and disadvantaged toddlers to distress in agemates: A study in the day care setting. *Developmental Psychology, 21* (3), 407-412.

Mäki, M, & Collin, P. (1997). Coeliac disease. *The Lancet, 349* (9067), 1755-1759.

Mallick, B.N. & Singh, A. (2011). REM sleep loss increases brain excitability: Role of noradrenalin and its mechanism of action. *Sleep Medicine Reviews, 15* (3), 165-178.

Mani, R. (2005). Rebuilding an inclusive political community after war. *Security Dialogue, 36* (4), 511-526.

Mapp, S.C. (2006). The effects of sexual abuse as a child on the risk of mothers physically abusing their children: A path analysis using systems theory. *Child Abuse and Neglect, 30* (11), 1293-1310.

Martin, G. & Kay, T. (2004). On adolescence and having a parent with mental illness. In V. Cowling (Ed.) *Children of parents with mental illness: Personal and clinical perspectives.* Melbourne: ACER, pp. 57-71.

Martin, G. & Pear, J. (2011). *Behavior modification: What it is and how to do it.* (9th ed.) Boston, MA: Pearson.

Mattanah, J.F. (2001). Parental psychological autonomy and children's academic competence and behavioral adjustment in late childhood: More than just limit-setting and warmth. *Merrill-Palmer Quarterly, 47* (3), 355-376.

Maughan, A. & Cicchetti, D. (2002). Impact of child maltreatment and interadult violence on children's emotion regulation and socioemotional adjustment. *Child Development, 73* (5), 1525-1542.

McClun, L.A. & Merrell, K.A. (1998). Relationship of perceived parenting styles, locus of control orientation, and self-concept among junior high age students. *Psychology in the Schools, 35* (4), 381-390.

McCord, J. (1991). Questioning the value of punishment. *Social Problems, 38* (2), 167-179.

_____(1997). On discipline. *Psychological Inquiry, 8* (3), 215-217.

McDonnell, A.P. (1993). Ethical considerations in teaching compliance to individuals with mental retardation. *Education and Training in Mental Retardation, 28* (1), 3-12.

McDowell, D.J., Parke, R.D. & Wang, S.J. (2003). Differences between mothers' and fathers' advice-giving style and content: Relations with social competence and psychological functioning in middle childhood. *Merrill-Palmer Quarterly, 49* (1), 55-76.

McFadyen-Ketchum, S.A., Bates, J.E., Dodge, K.A. & Pettit, G.S. (1996). Patterns of change in early childhood aggressive-disruptive behavior: Gender differences in predictions from early coercive and affectionate mother-child interactions. *Child Development, 67* (5), 2417-2433.

McGowan, P.O., Sasaki, A., D'Alessio, A.C., Dymov, S., Labonté, B., Szyf, M., Turecki, G. & Meaney, M.J. (2009). Epigenetic regulation of the glucocorticoid receptor in human brain associates with childhood abuse. *Nature Neuroscience, 12* (3), 342-348.

McGrath, J., Brown, A. & St Clair, D. (2011). Prevention and schizophrenia: The role of dietary factors. *Schizophrenia Bulletin, 37* (2), 272-283.

McGroder, S.M. (2000). Parenting among low-income, African American single mothers with preschool-age children: Patterns, predictors, and developmental correlates. *Child Development, 71* (3), 752-771.

McKay, M., Forsyth, J.P. & Eifert, G.H. (2010). *Your life on purpose: How to find what matters and create the life you want.* Oakland, CA: New Harbinger.

McLeod, J.D., Kruttschnitt, C. & Dornfeld, M. (1994). Does parenting explain the effects of structural conditions on children's antisocial behavior?: A comparison of Blacks and Whites. *Social Forces, 73* (2), 575-604.

Merritt, E.G., Wanless, S.B., Rimm-Kauffman, S.E., Cameron, C. & Peugh, J.L. (2012). The contribution of teachers' emotional support to children's social behaviors and self-regulatory skills in first grade. *School Psychology Review, 41* (2), 141-159.

Metzner, J.L. & Ryan, G.D. (1995). Sexual abuse perpetration. In G.P. Sholevar (Ed.) *Conduct disorders in children and adolescents.* Washington, DC: American Psychiatric Press, pp. 119-142.

Meyer, D.J. (1993). Lessons learned: Cognitive coping strategies of overlooked family members. In A.P. Turnbull, J.M. Patterson, S.K. Behr, D.L. Murphy, J.G. Marquis and M.J. Blue-Banning (Eds.) *Cognitive coping, families and disability.* Baltimore, MD: Paul H. Brookes, pp. 81-93.

Meyers, S.A. (1999). Mothering in context: Ecological determinants of parent behavior. *Merrill-Palmer Quarterly, 45* (2), 332-357.

Michalik, N.M., Eisenbeerg, N., Spindrad, T.L., Ladd, B., Thompson, M. & Valiente, C. (2007). Longitudinal relations among parental emotional expressivity and sympathy and prosocial behavior in adolescence. *Social Development, 16* (2), 286-309.

Miller, A. (1987). *For your own good: The roots of violence in child-rearing.* London: Virago Press.

_____(2006). *The body never lies: The lingering effects of hurtful parenting.* New York: Norton.

Miller, S., Loeber, R. & Hipwell, A. (2009). Peer deviance, parenting and disruptive behavior among young girls. *Journal of Abnormal Child Psychology, 37* (2), 139-152.

Miller-Lewis, L.R., Baghurst, P.A., Sawyer, M.G., Prior, M.R., Clark, J.J., Arney, F.M. & Carbone, J.A. (2006). Early childhood externalizing behaviour problems: Child, parenting, and family-related predictors over time. *Journal of Abnormal Child Psychology, 34* (6), 891-906.

Milner, J.D., Stein, D.M., McCarter, R. & Moon, R.Y. (2004). Multivitamin supplementation is associated with increased risk for food allergy and asthma. *Pediatrics, 114* (1), 27-32.

Moffitt, T.E., Arseneault, L., Belsky, D., Dickson, N., Hancox, R.J., Harrington, H., Houts, R., Poulton, R., Roberts, B.W., Ross, S., Sears, M.R., Thomson, W.M. & Caspi, A. (2011). A gradient of self-control predicts health, wealth, and public safety. *Proceedings of the National Academy of Science, 108* (7), 2693-2698.

Molnar, A. & de Shazer, S. (1987). Solution-focused therapy: Toward the identification of therapeutic tasks. *Journal of Marital and Family Therapy, 13* (4), 349-358.

Molnar, A. & Lindquist, B. (1989). *Changing problem behavior in schools.* San Francisco, CA: Jossey-Bass.

Montgomery, B. (1982). *Coping with stress.* Melbourne: Pitman.

Moorman, E.A. & Pomerantz, E.M. (2008). The role of mothers' control in children's mastery orientation: A time frame analysis. *Journal of Family Psychology, 22* (5), 734-741.

Morgan, A. (Ed.) (1999). *Once upon a time... Narrative therapy with children and their families.* Adelaide, SA: Dulwich Centre Publications.

_____(2000). *What is narrative therapy?: An easy-to-read introduction.* Adelaide, SA: Dulwich Centre Publications.

Morgan, M. (1983). Decrements in intrinsic motivation among rewarded and observer subjects. *Child Development, 54* (3), 636-644.

Morris, A.S., Silk, J.S., Steinberg, L., Myers, S.S. & Robinson, L.R. (2007). The role of the family context in the development of emotion regulation. *Social Development, 16* (2), 361-388.

Moss, E., Cyr, C., Bureau, J.-F., Tarabulsy, G.M. & Dubois-Comtois, K. (2005). Stability of attachment during the preschool period. *Developmental Psychology, 41* (5), 773-783.

Moss, E., Cyr, C. & Dubois-Comtois, K. (2004). Attachment at early school age and developmental risk: Examining family contexts and behavior problems of controlling-caregiving, controlling-punitive, and behaviorally disorganized children. *Developmental Psychology, 40* (4), 519-532.

Mruk, C.J. (2006). *Self-esteem research, theory, and practice.* (3rd ed.) New York; Springer.

Mueller, C.M. & Dweck, C.S. (1998). Praise for intelligence can undermine children's motivation and performance. *Journal of Personality and Social Psychology, 75* (1), 33-52.

Mukhopadhyay, P. & Kumar, J. (1999). Academic pressure: Its impact on the mental health of children. *Social Science International, 15* (2), 39-45.

Mullen, P.E., Martin, J.L., Anderson, J.C., Romans, S.E. & Herbison, G.P. (1996). The long-term impact of the physical, emotional, and sexual abuse of children: A community study. *Child Abuse and Neglect, 20* (1), 7-21.

Mulvaney, M.K. & Mebert, C.J. (2007). Parental corporal punishment predicts behavior problems in early childhood. *Journal of Family Psychology, 21* (3), 389-397.

Murphy, B.C., Eisenberg, N., Fabes, R.A., Shepard, S. & Guthrie, I.K. (1999). Consistency and change in children's emotionality and regulation: A longitudinal study. *Merrill-Palmer Quarterly, 45* (3), 413-444.

Murphy, J.J. (2006). *Solution-focused counseling in middle and high schools.* Upper Saddle River, NJ: Pearson Merrill Prentice Hall.

_____(2008). *Solution-focused counseling in schools.* (2nd ed.) Alexandria, VA: American Counseling Association.

Murray, R.M., Jones, P., O'Callaghan, E., Takei, N. & Sham, P. (1992). Genes, viruses and neurodevelopmental schizophrenia. *Journal of Psychiatric Research, 26* (4), 225-235.

Murray, S.L., Rose, P., Bellavia, G.M., Holmes, J.G. & Kusche, A.G. (2002). When rejection stings: How self-esteem constrains relationship-enhancement processes. *Journal of Personality and Social Psychology, 83* (3), 556-572.

Murrell, S.A., Meeks, S. & Walker, J. (1991). Protective functions of health and self-esteem against depression in older adults facing illness or bereavement. *Psychology and Aging, 6* (3), 352-360.

Nagel, M.C. (2012). *In the beginning: The brain, early development and learning.* Melbourne: ACER.

Nansel, T.R., Overpeck, M., Pilla, R.S., Ruan, W.J., Simons-Morton, B. & Scheidt, P. (2001). Bullying behaviors among US youth: Prevalence and association with psychosocial adjustment. *Journal of the American Medical Association, 285* (16), 2094-2100.

NICHD Early Child Care Research Network (2001). Child-care and family predictors of preschool attachment and stability from infancy. *Developmental Psychology, 37* (6), 847-862.

_____(2003a). Social functioning in first grade: Associations with earlier home and child care predictors and with current classroom experiences. *Child Development, 74* (6), 1639-1662.

_____(2003b). Does amount of time spent in child care predict socioemotional adjustment during the transition to kindergarten?. *Child Development, 74* (4), 976-1005.

_____(2004). Affect dysregulation in the mother-child relationship in the toddler years: Antecedents and consequences. *Development and Psychopathology, 16* (1), 43-68.

_____(2005). Duration and developmental timing of poverty and children's cognitive and social development from birth through third grade. *Child Development, 76* (4), 795-810.

____(2006). Infant-mother attachment classification: Risk and protection in relation to changing maternal caregiving quality. *Developmental Psychology, 42* (1), 38-58.

Nelson, J.D., Gelfand, D.M. & Hartmann, D.P. (1969). Children's aggression following competition and exposure to an aggressive model. *Child Development, 40* (4), 1085-1097.

Nelson, D.A., Hart, C.H., Yang, C., Olson, J.A. & Jin, S. (2006). Aversive parenting in China: Associations with child physical and relational aggression. *Child Development, 77* (3), 554-572.

Neumeister, K.L.S. (2004a). Understanding the relation between perfectionism and achievement motivation in gifted college students. *Gifted Child Quarterly, 48* (3), 219-231.

____(2004b). Factors influencing the development of perfectionism in gifted college students. *Gifted Child Quarterly, 48* (4), 259-274.

Neumeister, K.L.S. & Finch, H. (2006). Perfectionism in high-ability students: Relational precursors and influences on achievement motivation. *Gifted Child Quarterly, 50* (3), 218-251.

Neumeister, K.L.S., Williams, K.K. & Cross, T.L. (2009). Gifted high-school students' perspectives on the development of perfectionism. *Roeper Review, 31* (4), 198-206.

Nix, R.L., Pinderhughes, E.E., Dodge, K.A., Bates, J.E., Pettit, G.S. & McFadyen-Ketchum, S.A. (1999). The relation between mothers' hostile attribution tendencies and children's externalizing behavior problems: The mediating role of mothers' harsh discipline. *Child Development, 70* (4), 896-909.

Noaghiul, S. & Hibbein, J.R. (2003). Cross-national comparisons of seafood consumption and rates of bipolar disorders. *The American Journal of Psychiatry, 160* (12), 2222-2227.

Noddings, N. (2003). *Happiness and education.* Cambridge, UK: Cambridge University Press.

O'Connor, T.G. (2002). Annotation: The 'effects' of parenting reconsidered: Findings, challenges, and applications. *Journal of Child Psychology and Psychiatry, 43* (5), 555-572.

O'Leary, S.G., Slep, A.M.S. & Reid, M.J. (1999). A longitudinal study of mothers' overreactive discipline and toddlers' externalizing behavior. *Journal of Abnormal Child Psychology, 27* (5), 331-341.

Ohene, S.-A., Ireland, M., McNeely, C. & Borowsky, I.W. (2006). Parental expectations, physical punishment, and violence among adolescents who score positive on a psychosocial screening test in primary care. *Pediatrics, 117* (2), 441-447.

Olson, S.L., Bates, J.E. & Bayles, K. (1990). Early antecedents of childhood impulsivity: The role of parent-child interaction, cognitive competence, and temperament. *Journal of Abnormal Child Psychology, 18* (3), 317-334.

Olson, K.R. & Spelke, E.S. (2008). Foundations of cooperation in young children. *Cognition, 108* (1), 222-231.

Osterman, K.F. (2000). Students' need for belonging in the school community. *Review of Educational Research, 70* (3), 323-367.

Overbeek, G., Zeevalkink, H., Vermulst, A. & Scholte, R.H.J. (2010). Peer victimization, self-esteem, and ego resilience types in adolescents: A prospective analysis of person-context interactions. *Social Development, 19* (2), 270-284.

Pagani, L.S., Tremblay, R.E., Nagin, D., Zoccolillo, M., Vitaro, F. & McDuff, P. (2004). Risk factor models for adolescent verbal and physical aggression towards mothers. *International Journal of Behavioral Development, 28* (6), 528-537.

Palagini, L. & Rosenlicht, N. (2011). Sleep, dreaming, and mental health: A review of historical and neurobiological perspectives. *Sleep Medicine Reviews, 15* (3), 179-186.

Palmer, E.J. & Hollin, C.R. (2001). Sociomoral reasoning, perceptions of parenting and self-reported delinquency in adolescents. *Applied Cognitive Psychology, 15* (1), 85-100.

Parke, R.D., Coltrane, S., Duffy, S., Buriel, R., Dennis, J., Powers, J., French, S. & Widaman, K.F. (2004). Economic stress, parenting, and child adjustment in Mexican American and European American families. *Child Development, 75* (6), 1632-1656.

Parker, F.L., Boak, A.Y., Griffin, K.W., Ripple, C. & Peay, L. (1999). Parent-child relationship, home learning environment, and school readiness. *School Psychology Review, 28* (3), 413-425.

Parker, W. (1996). Psychological adjustment in mathematically gifted students. *Gifted Child Quarterly, 40* (3), 154-161.

Parker, W. & Adkins, K.K. (1995). Perfectionism and the gifted. *Roeper Review, 17* (3), 173-176.

Parker, W. & Mills, C.J. (1996). The incidence of perfectionism in gifted students. *Gifted Child Quarterly, 40* (4), 194-199.

Parpal, M. & Maccoby, E.E. (1985). Maternal responsiveness and subsequent child compliance. *Child Development, 56* (5), 1326-1334.

Paterson, G. & Sanson, A. (1999). The association of behavioural adjustment to temperament, parenting and family characteristics among 5-year-old children. *Social Development, 8* (3), 293-309.

Pauletti, R.E., Menon, M., Menon, M. Tobin, D.D. & Perry, D.G. (2012). Narcissism and adjustment in preadolescence. *Child Development, 83* (3), 831-837.

Pauli-Pott, U., Haverkock, A., Pott, W. & Beckmann, D. (2007). Negative emotionality, attachment quality, and behavior problems in early childhood. *Infant Mental Health Journal, 28* (1), 39-53.

Pauling, L. (1995). Orthomolecular psychiatry: Varying the concentration of substances normally present in the human body to control mental disease. *Journal of Nutritional and Environmental Medicine, 5* (2), 187-199.

Paulson, S.E., Marchant, G.J. & Rothlisberg, B.A. (1998). Early adolescents' perceptions of patterns of parenting, teaching, and school atmosphere: Implications for achievement. *Journal of Early Adolescence, 18* (1), 5-26.

Pears, K.C., Fisher, P.A., Bruce, J., Kim, H.K. & Yoerger, K. (2010). Early elementary school adjustment of maltreated children in foster care: The roles of inhibitory control and caregiver involvement. *Child Development, 81* (5), 1550-1564.

Peet, M. (2004). International variations in the outcome of schizophrenia and the prevalence of depression in relation to national dietary practices: An ecological analysis. *British Journal of Psychiatry, 184* (5), 404-408.

Percy, M. & Propst, E. (2008). Celiac disease: Its many faces and relevance to developmental disabilities. *Journal of Developmental Disabilities, 14* (2), 105-110.

Perkins, D.N., Jay, E. & Tishman, S. (1993). Beyond abilities: A dispositional theory of thinking. *Merrill Palmer Quarterly, 39* (1), 1-21.

Perlmutter, D. & Loberg, K. (2013). *Grain brain.* New York: Little, Brown & Co.

Perry, L. (1999). Mitakuyu Oyasin – All of my relations: Exploring metaphors of connectedness. In A. Morgan (Ed.) *Once upon a time: Narrative therapy with children and their families.* Adelaide, SA: Dulwich Centre Publications, pp. 125-144.

Peterson, C. (2006). *A primer in positive psychology.* Oxford, UK: Oxford University Press.

Petterson, S.M. & Albers, A.B. (2001). Effects of poverty and maternal depression on early child development. *Child Development, 72* (6), 1794-1813.

Phelan, T.W. (2003). *1-2-3-magic: Effective discipline for children 2-12.* (3rd ed.) Glen Ellyn, IL: ParentMagic Inc.

Philpott, W.H. & Kalita, D.K. (2000). *Brain allergies: The psychonutrient and magnetic connections.* (2nd ed.) Chicago, IL: Keats Publishing.

Pinderhughes, E.E., Dodge, K.A., Bates, J.E., Pettit, G.S. & Zelli, A. (2000). Discipline responses: Influences of parents' socioeconomic status, ethnicity, beliefs about parenting, stress, and cognitive-emotional processes. *Journal of Family Psychology, 14* (3), 380-400.

Pitman, M. & Porter, L. (2014). *A theory of natural healing.* Brisbane: Life Works Health Clinic.

Polivy, J. (1998). The effects of behavioral inhibition: Integrating internal cues, cognition, behavior, and affect. *Psychological Inquiry, 9* (3), 181-204.

Pollak, S.D., Vardi, S., Bechner, A.M.P. & Curtin, J.J. (2005). Physically abused children's regulation of attention in response to hostility. *Child Development, 76* (5), 968-977.

Pomerantz, E.M. & Wang. Q. (2009). The role of parental control in children's development in Western and East Asian countries. *Current Directions in Psychological Science, 18* (5), 285-289.

Porter, L. (1999). *Behaviour management practices in child care centres.* Unpublished doctoral thesis. Adelaide: University of South Australia.

____(2014). *A comprehensive guide to classroom management: Facilitating engagement and learning in schools.* Sydney: Allen and Unwin.

Porter, L. & McKenzie, S. (2000). *Professional collaboration with parents of children with disabilities.* Sydney: Elsevier; London: Whurr.

Posada, G., Jacobs, A., Carbonell, O.A., Alzate, G., Bustamante, M.R. & Arenas, A. (1999). Maternal care and attachment security in ordinary and emergency contexts. *Developmental Psychology, 35* (6), 1379-1388.

Power, T.G. & Chapieski, M.L. (1986). Childrearing and impulse control in toddlers: A naturalistic investigation. *Developmental Psychology, 22* (2), 271-275.

Prinzie, P., Onghena, P. & Hellinckx, W. (2006). A cohort-sequential multivariate latent growth curve analysis of normative CBCL aggressive and delinquent problem behavior: Associations with harsh discipline and gender. *International Journal of Behavioral Development, 30* (5), 444-459.

Propper, C. & Moore, G.A. (2006). The influence of parenting on infant emotionality: A multi-level psychobiological perspective. *Developmental Review, 26* (4), 427-460.

Pulkkinen, L. & Hämäläinen, M. (1995). Low self-control as a precursor to crime and accidents in a Finnish longitudinal study. *Criminal Behaviour and Mental Health, 5* (4), 424-438.

Purdue, N.H., Manzeske, D.P. & Estell, D.B. (2009). Early predictors of school engagement: Exploring the role of peer relationships. *Psychology in the Schools, 46* (10), 1084-1097.

Qi, C.H. & Kaiser, A.P. (2003). Behavior problems of preschool children from low-income families. *Topics in Early Childhood Special Education, 23* (4), 188-216.

Qin, L., Pomerantz, E.M. & Wang, Q. (2009). Are gains in decision-making autonomy during early adolescence beneficial for emotional functioning?: The case of the United States and China. *Child Development, 80* (6), 1705-1721.

Radke-Yarrow, M., Scott, P.M. & Zahn-Waxler, C. (1973). Learning concern for others. *Developmental Psychology, 8* (2), 240-260.

Rah, Y. & Parke, R.D. (2008). Pathways between parent-child interactions and peer acceptance: The role of children's social information processing. *Social Development, 17* (2), 341-357.

Raines, S. (1995). *Never ever serve sugary snacks on rainy days: The official little instruction book for teachers of young children.* Beltsville, MD: Gryphon House.

Rakoczy, H., Brosche, N., Warneken, F. & Tomasello, M. (2009). Young children's understanding of the context-relativity of normative rules in conventional games. *British Journal of Developmental Psychology, 27* (2), 445-456.

Rakoczy, H., Warneken, F. & Tomasello, M. (2008). The sources of normatility: Young children's awareness of the normative structure of games. *Developmental Psychology, 44* (3), 875-881.

Raskin, N.J. & Rogers, C.R. (2005). Person-centered therapy. In R.J. Corsini and D. Wedding (Eds.) *Current psychotherapies.* (7th ed.) Belmont, CA: Thomson Brooks/Cole, pp. 130-165.

Raval, V., Goldberg, S., Atkinson, L., Benoit, D., Myhal, N., Poulton, L. & Zwiers, M. (2001). Maternal attachment, maternal responsiveness and infant attachment. *Infant Behavior and Development, 24* (3), 281-304.

Raviv, T., Kessenich, M. & Morrison, F.J. (2004). A mediational model of the association between socioeconomic status and three-year-old language abilities: The role of parenting factors. *Early Childhood Research Quarterly, 19* (4), 528-547.

Rice, K.G., Ashby, J.S. & Preusser, K.J. (1996). Perfectionism, relationships with parents, and self-esteem. *Individual Psychology, 52* (3), 246-260.

Richardson Andrews, R.C. (1990). Unification of the findings in schizophrenia by reference to the effects of gestational zinc deficiency. *Medical Hypotheses, 31* (2), 141-153.

Ritchhart, R. (2001). From IQ to IC: A dispositional view of intelligence. *Roeper Review, 23* (3), 143-150.

Robertson, G. (2006). *Crimes against humanity: The struggle for global justice.* (3rd ed.) Melbourne: Penguin.

Robertson, J.S. (2000). Is attribution training a worthwhile classroom intervention for K-12 students with learning difficulties?. *Educational Psychology Review, 12* (1), 111-134.

Robinson, K. & Aronica, L. (2009). *The element: How finding your passion changes everything.* New York: Penguin.

____(2013). *Finding your element: How to discover your talents and passions and transform your life.* New York: Viking.

Robinson, W.P. (1975). Boredom at school. *British Journal of Educational Psychology, 45* (2), 141-152.

Rodriguez, C.M. (2003). Parental discipline and abuse potential affects on child depression, anxiety and attributions. *Journal of Marriage and the Family, 65* (4), 809-817.

Rogers, C.R. (1942). *Counseling and psychotherapy: Newer concepts in practice.* Boston, MA: Houghton Mifflin.

____(1951). *Client-centred therapy.* London: Constable.

____(1978). *On personal power.* London: Constable.

Rogers, C.R. & Freiberg, H. (1994). *Freedom to learn.* (3rd ed.) New York: Merrill.

Rohner, R.P., Kean, K.J. & Cournoyer, D.E. (1991). Effects of corporal punishment, perceived caretaker warmth, and cultural beliefs on the psychological adjustment of children in St. Kitts, West Indies. *Journal of Marriage and the Family, 53* (3), 681-693.

Romano, E., Tremblay, R.E., Boulerice, B. & Swisher, R. (2005). Multilevel correlates of childhood physical aggression and prosocial behavior. *Journal of Abnormal Child Psychology, 33* (5), 565-578.

Rosenberg, M.B. (2003a). Nonviolent communication: A language of life. (2nd ed.) Encinitas, CA: Puddle Dancer Press.

____(2003b). *Getting past the pain between us: Healing and reconciliation without compromise.* Encinitas, CA: Puddle Dancer Press.

____(2005). *The surprising purpose of anger: Beyond anger management: Finding the gift.* Encinitas, CA: Puddle Dancer Press.

Roth, G., Assor, A., Niemiec, C.P., Ryan, R.M. & Deci, E.L. (2009). The emotional and academic consequences of parental conditional regard: Comparing conditional positive regard, conditional negative regard, and autonomy support as parenting practices. *Developmental Psychology, 45* (4), 1119-1142.

Roth, R.A., Kanat-Maymon, Y. & Bibi, U. (2011). Prevention of school bullying: The important role of autonomy-supportive teaching and internalization of pro-social values. *British Journal of Educational Psychology, 81* (4), 654-666.

Rubin, K.H., Burgess, K.B., Dwyer, K.M. & Hastings, P.D. (2003). Predicting preschoolers' externalizing behaviors from toddler temperament, conflict, and maternal negativity. *Developmental Psychology, 39* (1), 164-176.

Rubin, K.H., Burgess, K.B. & Hastings, P.D. (2002). Stability and social-behavioral consequences of toddlers' inhibited temperament and parenting behaviors. *Child Development, 73* (2), 483-495.

Rubinstein, R.P. (1977). Changes in self-esteem and anxiety in competitive and noncompetitive camps. *Journal of Social Psychology, 102* (1), 55-57.

Rudolph, K.D., Caldwell, M.S. & Conley, C.S. (2005). Need for approval and children's well-being. *Child Development, 76* (2), 309-323.

Rudy, D., Awong, T. & Lambert, M. (2008). Parental psychological control and authoritarianism in Chinese-Canadian and European-Canadian cultural groups: Their meanings and implications for university students' adjustment. *Journal of Comparative Family Studies, 39* (4), 471-490.

Russell, A., Pettit, G.S. & Mize, J. (1998). Horizontal qualities in parent-child relationships: Parallels with and possible consequences for children's peer relationships. *Developmental Review, 18* (3), 313-352.

Rutherford, E. & Mussen, P. (1968). Generosity in nursery school boys. *Child Development, 39* (3), 755-765.

Rutter, M. (1985). Resilience in the face of adversity: Protective factors and resistance to psychiatric disorder. *British Journal of Psychiatry, 147* (6), 598-611.

____(1999). Resilience concepts and findings: Implications for family therapy. *Journal of Family Therapy, 21* (2), 119-144.

Ryan, A.M. & Patrick, H. (2001). The classroom social environment and changes in adolescents' motivation and engagement during middle school. *American Educational Research Journal, 38* (2), 437-460.

Ryan, R.M. & Deci, E.L. (1996). When paradigms clash: Comments on Cameron and Pierce's claim that rewards do not undermine intrinsic motivation. *Review of Educational Research, 66* (1), 33-38.

____(2000). Self-determination theory and the facilitation of intrinsic motivation, social development, and well-being. *American Psychologist, 55* (1), 68-78.

Ryan, R.M. & Brown, K.W. (2003). Why we don't need self-esteem: On fundamental needs, contingent love, and mindfulness. *Psychological Inquiry 14* (1), 71-76.

Salmivalli, C., Kaukiainen, A., Kaistaniemi, L. & Lagerspetz, K.M.J. (1999). Self-evaluated self-esteem, peer-evaluated self-esteem, and defensive egotism as predictors of adolescents' participation in bullying situations. *Personality and Social Psychology Bulletin, 25* (10), 1268-1278.

Salmivalli, C., Ojanen, T., Haanpää, J. & Peets, H. (2005). 'I'm OK but you're not' and other peer-relational schemas: Explaining individual differences in children's social goals. *Developmental Psychology, 41* (2), 363-375.

Sanson, A., Oberklaid, F., Pedlow, R. & Prior, M. (1991). Risk indicators: Assessment of infancy predictors of pre-school behavioural maladjustment. *Journal of Child Psychology and Psychiatry, 32* (4), 609-626.

Sapolsky, R.M. (2004). Mothering style and methylation. *Nature Neuroscience, 7* (8) 791-792.

Sapon-Shevin, M. (1996). Beyond gifted education: Building a shared agenda for school reform. *Journal for the Education of the Gifted, 19* (2), 194-214.

____(1999). *Because we can change the world: A practical guide to building cooperative, inclusive classroom communities.* Boston, MA: Allyn and Bacon.

Satir, V. (1988). *The new people making.* Mountain View, CA: Science and Behavior Books.

Scaramella, L.V., Neppl, T.K., Ontai, L.L. & Conger, R.D. (2008). Consequences of socioeconomic disdvantage across three generations: Parenting behavior and child externalizing problems. *Journal of Family Psychology, 22* (5), 725-733.

Schaeffer, C.M., Petras, H., Ialongo, N., Poduska, J. & Kellam, S. (2003). Modeling growth in boys' aggressive behavior across elementary school: Links to later criminal involvement, conduct disorder, and antisocial personality disorder. *Developmental Psychology, 39* (6), 1020-1025.

Scholte, R.H.J., Engles, R.C.M.E., Overbeek, G., de Kemp, R.A.T. & Haselager, G.J.T. (2007). Stability in bullying and victimization and its association with social adjustment in childhood and adolescence. *Journal of Abnormal Child Psychology, 35* (2), 217-228.

Schulz, J.B. (1993). Heroes in disguise. In A.P. Turnbull, J.M. Patterson, S.K. Behr, D.L. Murphy, J.G. Marquis and M.J. Blue-Banning (Eds.) *Cognitive coping, families and disability.* Baltimore, MD: Paul H. Brookes, pp. 31-41.

Schwartz, D., Dodge, K.A., Pettit, G.S. & Bates, J.E. (1997). The early socialization of aggressive victims of bullying. *Child Development, 68* (4), 665-675.

Seifer, R., LaGasse, L.L., Lester, B., Bauer, C.R., Shankaran, S., Bada, H.S., Wright, L.L., Smeriglio, V.L. & Liu, J. (2004). Attachment status in children prenatally exposed to cocaine and other substances. *Child Development, 75* (3), 850-868.

Selekman, M.D. (2006). *Working with self-harming adolescents: A collaborative, strengths-based therapy approach.* New York: Norton.

____(2010). *Collaborative brief therapy with children.* New York: Guilford.

Seligman, M. & Darling, R.B. (1997). *Ordinary families; special children: A systems approach to childhood disability.* (2nd ed.) New York: Guilford.

Seligman, M.E.P. (1975). *Helplessness: On depression, development and death.* San Francisco, CA: W.H. Freeman.

____(2002). *Authentic happiness.* New York: Simon & Schuster.

____(2011). *Flourish: A visionary new understanding of happiness and well-being.* New York: Free Press.

Seligman, M.E.P., Reivich, K., Jaycox, L. & Gillham, J. (1995). *The optimistic child.* Sydney: Random House.

Shaw, D.S., Bell, R.Q. & Gilliom, M. (2000). A truly early starter model of antisocial behavior revisited. *Clinical Child and Family Psychology Review, 3* (3), 155-172.

Shaw, D.S., Gilliom, M., Ingoldsby, E.M. & Nagin, D.S. (2003). Trajectories leading to school-age conduct problems. *Developmental Psychology, 39* (2), 189-200.

Shaw, D.S., Owens, E.B., Giovannelli, J. & Winslow, E.B. (2001). Infant and toddler pathways leading to early externalizing disorders. *Journal of the American Academy of Child and Adolescent Psychiatry, 40* (1), 36-43.

Shaw, D.S., Winslow, E.B. & Flanagan, C. (1999). A prospective study of the effects of marital status and family relations on young children's adjustment among African American and European American families. *Child Development, 70* (3), 742-755.

Sheehan, M.J. & Watson, M.W. (2008). Reciprocal influences between maternal discipline techniques and aggression in children and adolescents. *Aggressive Behavior, 34* (3), 245-255.

Shek, D.T.L. (2007). A longitudinal study of perceived parental psychological control and psychological well-being in Chinese adolescents in Hong Kong. *Journal of Clinical Psychology, 63* (1), 1-22.

Sheu, Y.-S., Polcari, A., Anderson, C.M. & Teicher, M.H. (2010). Harsh corporal punishment is associated with increase T2 relaxation time in dopamine-rich regions. *NeuroImage, 51* (2), 412-419.

Shi, L., Sidwell, R.W., & Patterson, P.H. (2003). Maternal influenza infection causes marked behavioral and pharmacological changes in the offspring. *The Journal of Neuroscience, 23* (1), 297-302.

Shields, A., Ryan, R.M. & Cicchetti, D. (2001). Narrative representations of caregivers and emotion dysregulation as predictors of maltreated children's rejection by peers. *Developmental Psychology, 37* (3), 321-337.

Shipman, K.L., Schneider, R., Fitzgerald, M.M., Sims, C., Swisher, L. & Edwards, A. (2007). Maternal emotion socialization in maltreating and non-maltreating families: Implications for children's emotion regulation. *Social Development, 16* (2), 268-285.

Shonk, S.M. & Cicchetti, D. (2001). Maltreatment, competency deficits, and risk for academic and behavioral maladjustment. *Developmental Psychology, 37* (1), 3-17.

Siegle, D. & Schuler, P.A. (2000). Perfectionism differences in gifted middle school students. *Roeper Review, 23* (1), 39-44.

Simons, R.L., Lin, K.-H., Gordon, L.C., Brody, G.H., Murry, V. & Conger, R.D. (2002). Community differences in the association between parenting practices and child conduct problems. *Journal of Marriage and the Family, 64* (2), 331-345.

Singh, K., Bickley, P.G., Trivette, P., Keith, T.Z., Keith, P.B. & Anderson, E. (1995). The effects of four components of parental involvement on eighth-grade student achievement: Structural analysis of NELS-88 data. *School Psychology Review, 24* (2), 299-317.

Skiba, R.J. & Peterson, R.L. (1999). The dark side of zero tolerance: Can punishment lead to safe schools?. *Phi Delta Kappan, 80* (5), 372-376.

Sklare, G.B. (2005). *Brief counseling that works: A solution-focused approach for school counselors and administrators.* (2nd ed.) Thousand Oaks, CA: Corwin Press.

Slade, E.P. & Wissow, L.S. (2004). Spanking in early childhood and later behavior problems: A prospective study of infants and young toddlers. *Pediatrics, 113* (5), 1321-1330.

Sletta, O., Valås, H., Skaalvik, E. & Sebstad, F. (1996). Peer relations, loneliness, and self-perceptions in school-aged children. *British Journal of Educational Psychology, 66* (4), 431-445.

Smith, A.B. (2006). The state of research on the effects of physical punishment. *Social Policy Journal of New Zealand, 27*, 114-127.

Smith, C.A. & Farrington, D.P. (2004). Continuities in antisocial behavior and parenting across three generations. *Journal of Child Psychology and Psychiatry, 45* (2), 230-247.

Smith, C.L., Calkins, S.D., Keane, S.P., Anastopoulos, A.D. & Shelton, T.L. (2004). Predicting stability and change in toddler behavior problems: Contributions of maternal behavior and child gender. *Developmental Psychology, 40* (1), 29-42.

Snyder, J., Brooker, M., Patrick, M.R., Snyder, A., Schrepferman, L. & Stoolmiller, M. (2003). Observed peer victimization during early elementary school: Continuity, growth, and relation to risk for child antisocial and depressive behavior. *Child Development, 74* (6), 1881-1898.

Soenens, B. & Vansteenkiste, M. (2010). A theoretical upgrade of the concept of parental psychological control: Proposing new insights on the basis of self-determination theory. *Developmental Review, 30* (1), 74-99.

Soenens, B., Vansteenkiste, M., Luyten, P., Duriez, B. & Goossens, L. (2005a). Maladaptive perfectionistic self-representations: The meditational link between psychological control and adjustment. *Personality and Individual Differences, 38* (2), 487-498.

Soenens, B., Elliot, A.J., Goossens, L., Vansteenkiste, M., Luyten, P. & Duriez, B. (2005b). The intergenerational transmission of perfectionism: Parents' psychological control as an intervening variable. *Journal of Family Psychology, 19* (3), 358-366.

Soenens, B., Vansteenkiste, M., Lens, W., Luyckx, K., Goossens, L., Beyers, W. & Ryan, R.M. (2007). Conceptualizing parental autonomy support: Adolescent perceptions of promotion of independence versus promotion of volitional functioning. *Developmental Psychology, 43* (3), 633-646.

Soenens, B., Vansteenkiste, M. & Luyten, P. (2010). Toward a domain-specific approach to the study of parental psychological control: Distinguishing between dependency-oriented and achievement-oriented psychological control. *Journal of Personality, 78* (1), 217-256.

Soenens, B., Park, S.-Y., Vansteenkiste, M. & Mouratidis, A. (2012). Perceived parental psychological control and adolescent depressive experiences: A cross-cultural study with Belgian and South-Korean adolescents. *Journal of Adolescence, 35* (2), 261-272.

Solomon, C.R. & Serres, F. (1999). Effects of parental verbal aggression on children's self-esteem and school marks. *Child Abuse and Neglect, 23* (4), 339-351.

Sommer, K.L. & Baumeister, R.F. (2002). Self-evaluation, persistence, and performance following implicit rejection: The role of trait self-esteem. *Personality and Social Psychology Bulletin, 28* (7), 926-938.

Spence, S.H., Najman, J.M., Bor, W., O'Callaghan, M.J. & Williams, G.M. (2002). Maternal anxiety and depression, poverty and marital relationship factors during early childhood as predictors of anxiety and depressive symptoms in adolescence. *Journal of Child Psychology and Psychiatry, 43* (4), 457-469.

Spera, C. (2005). A review of the relationship among parenting practices, parenting styles, and adolescent school achievement. *Educational Psychology Review, 17* (2), 125-146.

Spieker, S.J., Larson, N.C., Lewis, S.M., Keller, T.E. & Gilchrist, L. (1999). Developmental trajectories of disruptive behavior problems in preschool children of adolescent mothers. *Child Development, 70* (2), 443-458.

Spinrad, T.L., Stifter, C.A., Donelan-McCall, N. & Turner, L. (2004). Mothers' regulation strategies in response to toddlers' affect: Links to later emotion self-regulation. *Social Development, 13* (1), 40-55.

Spirito, A., Stark, L.J., Grace, N. & Stamoulis, D. (1991). Common problems and coping strategies reported in childhood and early adolescence. *Journal of Youth and Adolescence, 20* (5), 531-544.

Spirito, A., Esposito-Smythers, C., Weismoore, J. & Miller, A. (2012). Adolescent suicidal behavior. In P.C. Kendall (Ed.) *Child and adolescent therapy: Cognitive-behavioral procedures.* (4th ed.) New York: Guilford, pp. 234-256.

Stams, G.J.M., Juffer, F. & van IJzendoorn, M.H. (2002). Maternal sensitivity, infant attachment, and temperament in early childhood predict adjustment in middle childhood: The case of adopted children and their biologically unrelated parents. *Developmental Psychology, 38* (5), 806-821.

Stattin, H. & Kerr, M. (2000). Parental monitoring: A reinterpretation. *Child Development, 71* (4), 1072-1085.

Stayton, C.J., Hogan, R. & Ainsworth, M.D.S. (1971). Infant obedience and maternal behavior: The origins of socialization reconsidered. *Child Development, 42* (4), 1057-1069.

Steelman, L.M., Assel, M.A., Swank, P.R., Smith, K.E. & Landry, S.H. (2002). Early maternal warm responsiveness as a predictor of child social skills: Direct and indirect paths of influence over time. *Journal of Applied Developmental Psychology, 23* (2), 135-156.

Stefanou, C.R., Perencevich, K.C., DiCintio, M. & Turner, J.C. (2004). Supporting autonomy in the classroom: Ways teachers encourage decision making and ownership. *Educational Psychologist, 39* (2), 97-110.

Steinberg, L., Elmen, J.D. & Mounts, N.S. (1989). Authoritative parenting, psychosocial maturity, and academic success among adolescents. *Child Development, 60* (6), 1424-1436.

Steinberg, L., Lamborn, S.D., Dornbusch, S.M. & Darling, N. (1992). Impact of parenting practices on adolescent achievement: Authoritative parenting, school involvement, and encouragement to succeed. *Child Development, 63* (5), 1266-1281.

Steinberg, L., Lamborn, S.D., Darling, N., Mounts, N.S. & Dornbusch, S.M. (1994). Over-time changes in adjustment and competence among adolescents from authoritative, authoritarian, indulgent, and neglectful families. *Child Development, 65* (3), 754-770.

Stifter, C.A., Spinrad, T.L., Braungart-Rieker, J.M. (1999). Toward a developmental model of child compliance: The role of emotion regulation in infancy. *Child Development, 70* (1), 21-32.

Stormshak, E.A., Bierman, K.L., Bruschi, C., Dodge, K.A., Coie, J.D. & The Conduct Problems Prevention Research Group (1999). The relation between behavior problems and peer preference in different classroom contexts. *Child Development, 70* (1), 169-182.

Stormshak, E.A., Bierman, K.L., McMahon, R.J., Lengua, L.J. & The Conduct Problems Prevention Research Group (2000). Parenting practices and child disruptive behavior problems in early elementary school. *Journal of Clinical Child Psychology, 28* (1), 17-29.

Strage, A. & Brandt, T.S. (1999). Authoritative parenting and college students' academic adjustment and success. *Journal of Educational Psychology, 91* (1), 146-156.

Straus, M.A. & Paschall, M.J. (2009). Corporal punishment by mothers and development of children's cognitive ability: A longitudinal study of two nationally representative age cohorts. *Journal of Aggression, Maltreatment and Trauma, 18* (5), 459-483.

Straus, M.A. & Stewart, J.H. (1999). Corporal punishment by American parents: National data on prevalence, chronicity, severity, and duration, in relation to child and family characteristics. *Clinical Child and Family Psychology Review, 2* (2), 55-70.

Straus, M.A., Sugarman, D.B. & Giles-Sims, J. (1997). Spanking by parents and subsequent antisocial behavior of children. *Archives of Pediatrics and Adolescent Medicine, 151* (8), 761-767.

Strayer, J. & Roberts, W. (2004a). Empathy and observed anger and aggression in five-year-olds. *Social Development, 13* (1), 1-13.

_____(2004b). Children's anger, emotional expressiveness, and empathy: Relations with parents' empathy, emotional expressiveness, and parenting practices. *Social Development, 13* (2), 229-254.

Sturaro, C., van Lier, P.A.C., Cuijpers, P. & Koot, H.M. (2011). The role of peer relationships in the development of early school-age externalizing problems. *Child Development, 82* (3), 758-765.

Sturge-Apple, M.L., Davies, P.T. & Cummings, E.M. (2006). Impact of hostility and withdrawal in interparental conflict on parental emotional unavailability and children's adjustment difficulties. *Child Development, 77* (6), 1623-1641.

Susser, E.S. & Lin, S.P. (1992). Schizophrenia after prenatal exposure to the Dutch hunger winter of 1944-1945. *Archives of General Psychiatry, 49* (12), 983-988.

Swick, K.J. (2005). Preventing violence through empathy development in families. *Early Childhood Education Journal, 33* (1), 53-59.

Sylva, K. (1994). School influences on children's development. *Journal of Child Psychology and Psychiatry and Related Disciplines, 35* (1), 135-170.

Szewczyk-Sokolowski, M., Bost, K.K. & Wainwright, A.B. (2005). Attachment, temperament, and preschool children's peer acceptance. *Social Development, 14* (3), 379-397.

Tabrizian, I. (2003). *Nutritional medicine: Fact and fiction.* (4th ed.) Perth, WA: Nutrition Review Service Publications.

Tafarodi, R.W., Tam, J. & Milne, A.B. (2001). Selective memory and persistence of paradoxical self-esteem. *Personality and Social Psychology Bulletin, 27* (9), 1179-1189.

Talwar, V. & Lee, K. (2011). A punitive environment fosters children's dishonesty: A natural experiment. *Child Development, 82* (6), 1751-1758.

Taylor, C.A. Manganello, J.A., Lee, S.J. & Rice, J.C. (2010). Mothers' spanking of 3-year-old children and subsequent risk of children's aggressive behavior. *Pediatrics, 125* (5), e1057-e1065.

Taylor, L.C., Hinton, I.D. & Wilson, M.N. (1995). Parental influences on academic performance in African-American students. *Journal of Child and Family Studies, 4* (3), 293-302.

Teicher, M.H. (2002). Scars that won't heal: The neurobiology of child abuse. *Scientific American, 286* (3), 68-75.

Teisl, M. & Cicchetti, D. (2008). Physical abuse, cognitive and emotional processes, and aggressive/disruptive behavior problems. *Social Development, 17* (1), 1-23.

Thompson, A., Hollis, C. & Richards, D. (2003). Authoritarian parenting attitudes as a risk for conduct problems: Results from a British national cohort study. *European Child and Adolescent Psychiatry, 12* (2), 84-91.

Thompson, M., Cohen, L.J. & Grace, C.O'N. (2002). *Mom, they're teasing me: Helping your child solve social problems.* New York: Ballantine.

Thompson, R.A. & Wyatt, J.M. (1999). Current research on child maltreatment: Implications for educators. *Educational Psychology Review, 11* (3), 173-201.

Tollefson, N. (2000). Classroom applications of cognitive theories of motivation. *Educational Psychology Review, 12* (1), 63-83.

Tomasello, M. (2009). *Why we cooperate.* Cambridge, MA: Boston Review.

Tomoda, A., Suzuki, H., Rabi, K., Sheu, Y.-S., Polcari, A. & Teicher, M.H. (2009). Reduced prefrontal cortical gray matter volume in young adults exposed to harsh corporal punishment. *NeuroImage, 47* (Suppl. 2), T66-T71.

Tortora, G.J. & Derrickson, B. (2006). *Principles of anatomy and physiology.* (11th ed.) New York: Wiley.

Tremblay, R.E. (2004). Decade of behavior distinguished lecture: Development of physical aggression during infancy. *Infant Mental Health Journal, 25* (5), 399-407.

Tremblay, R.E., Nagin, D.S., Séguin, J.R., Zoccolillo, M., Zelazo, P.D., Boivin, M., Pérusse, D. & Japel. C. (2004). Physical aggression during early childhood: Trajectories and predictors. *Pediatrics, 114* (1), e43-e50.

Trickett, P.K. (1998). Multiple maltreatment and the development of self and emotion regulation. In B.B.R. Rossman & M.S. Rosenberg (Eds.) *Multiple victimization of children: Conceptual, developmental, research and treatment issues.* New York: Haworth Press, pp. 171-187.

Trinkner, R., Cohn, E.S., Rebellon, C.J. & Van Grundy, K. (2012). Don't trust anyone over 30: Parental legitimacy as a mediatior between parenting style and changes in delinquent behavior over time. *Journal of Adolescence, 35* (1), 119-132.

Trzesniewski, K.H., Donnellan, M.B., Moffitt, T.E., Robins, R.W., Poulton, R. & Caspi, A. (2006). Low self-esteem during adolescence predicts poor health, criminal behavior, and limited economic prospects during adulthood. *Developmental Psychology, 42* (2), 381-390.

Turner, H.A. & Muller, P.A. (2004). Long-term effects of child corporal punishment on depressive symptoms in young adults. *Journal of Family Issues, 25* (6), 761-782.

Underwood, M.K., Beron, K.J. & Rosen, L.H. (2009). Continuity and change in social and physical aggression from middle childhood through early adolescence. *Aggressive Behavior, 35* (5), 357-375.

Unnever, J.D. & Cornell, D.G. (2004). Middle school victims of bullying: Who reports being bullied?. *Aggressive Behavior, 30* (5), 373-388.

Van IJzendoorn, M.H. (1997). Attachment, emergent morality, and aggression: Toward a developmental socioemotional model of antisocial behaviour. *International Journal of Behavioral Development, 21* (4), 703-727.

Vaillancourt, T., Miller, J.L., Fagbemi, J. Côté, S. & Tremblay, R.E. (2007). Trajectories and predictors of indirect aggression: Results from a nationally representative longitudinal study of Canadian children aged 2-10. *Aggressive Behavior, 33* (4), 314-326.

Vaish, A., Carpenter, M. & Tomasello, M. (2009). Sympathy through affective perspective taking and its relation to prosocial behavior in toddlers. *Developmental Psychology, 45* (2), 534-543.

Vansteenkiste, M., Timmermans, T., Lens, W., Soenens, B. & Ven den Broeck, A. (2008). Does extrinsic goal framing enhance extrinsic goal-oriented individuals' learning and performance? An experimental test of the match perspective versus self-determination theory. *Journal of Educational Psychology, 100* (2), 387-397.

Veenstra, R., Oldehinkel, A.J., De Winter, A.F., Lindenberg, S. & Ormel, J. (2006). Temperament, environment, and antisocial behavior in a population sample of preadolescent boys and girls. *International Journal of Behavioral Development, 30* (5), 422-432.

Verschueren, K. & Marcoen, A. (1999). Representation of self and socioemotional competence in kindergartners: Differential and combined effects of attachment to mother and to father. *Child Development, 70* (1), 183-201.

Vigil, J.M., Geary, D.C. & Byrd-Craven, J. (2005). A life history assessment of early childhood sexual abuse in women. *Developmental Psychology, 41* (3), 553-561.

Votruba-Drzal, E. (2006). Economic disparities in middle childhood development: Does income matter?. *Developmental Psychology, 42* (6), 1154-1167.

Wager, B.R. (1992). No more suspension: Creating a shared ethical culture. *Educational Leadership, 50* (4), 34-37.

Waldroop, J. & Butler, T. (2000). *The 12 bad habits that hold good people back.* New York: Currency.

Walker, E., Kestler, L., Bollini, A. & Hochman, K.M. (2004). Schizophrenia: Etiology and course. *Annual Review of Psychology, 55*, 401-430.

Walsh, W.J. (2012). *Nutrient power: Heal your biochemistry and heal your brain.* New York: Skyhorse.

Warneken, F. & Tomasello, M. (2006). Altruistic helping in human infants and young chimpanzees. *Science, 311* (5765), 1301-1303.

——(2007). Helping and cooperation at 14 months of age. *Infancy, 11* (3), 271-294.

Warneken, F., Hare, B., Melis, A.P., Hanus, D. & Tomasello, M. (2007). Spontaneous altruism by chimpanzees and young children. *PLoS Biology, 5* (7), 1414-1420.

Warren, S.L., Huston, L., Egeland, B. & Sroufe, L.A. (1997). Child and adolescent anxiety disorders and early attachment. *Journal of the American Academy of Child and Adolescent Psychiatry, 36* (5), 637-644.

Warring, D., Johnson, D.W., Maruyama, G. & Johnson, R. (1985). Impact of different types of cooperative learning on cross-ethnic and cross-sex relationships. *Journal of Educational Psychology, 77* (1), 53-59.

Waters, E., Hamilton, C.E. & Weinfield, N.S. (2000a). The stability of attachment security from infancy to adolescence and early adulthood: General introduction. *Child Development, 71* (3), 678-683.

Waters, E., Merrick, S., Treboux, D., Crowell, J. & Albersheim, L. (2000b). Attachment security in infancy and early adulthood: A twenty-year longitudinal study. *Child Development, 71* (3), 684-689.

Watzlawick, P., Weakland, J. & Fisch, R. (1974). *Change: Principles of problem formation and problem resolution.* New York: W.W. Norton.

Weaver, I.C.G., Cervoni, N., Champagne, F.A., D'Alessio, A.C., Sharma, S., Seckl, J.R., Dymov, S., Szyf, M. & Meaney, M.L. (2004). Epigenetic programming by maternal behavior. *Nature Neuroscience, 7* (8), 847-854.

Webster, R.E. (2001). Symptoms and long-term outcomes for children who have been sexually assaulted. *Psychology in the Schools, 38* (6), 533-547.

Weiner, B. (2000). Interpersonal and intrapersonal theories of motivation from an attributional perspective. *Educational Psychology Review, 22* (1), 1-14.

Weinfield, N.S., Sroufe, L.A. & Egeland, B. (2000). Attachment from infancy to early adulthood in a high-risk sample: Continuity, discontinuity, and their correlates. *Child Development, 71* (3), 695-702.

Weiss, B., Dodge, K.A., Bates, J.E. & Pettit, G.S. (1992). Some consequences of early harsh discipline: Child aggression and a maladaptive social information processing style. *Child Development, 63* (6), 1321-1335.

Weiss, L.H. & Schwarz, J.C. (1996). The relationship between parenting types and older adolescents' personality, academic achievement, adjustment, and substance use. *Child Development, 67* (5), 2101-2114.

Wentzel, K.R. (1994). Family functioning and academic achievement in middle school: A social-emotional perspective. *Journal of Early Adolescence, 14* (2), 268-291.

Wentzel, K.R. & Caldwell, J. (1997). Friendships, peer acceptance, and group membership: Relations to academic achievement in middle school. *Child Development, 68* (6), 1198-1209.

Werner, N.E. & Crick, N.R. (2004). Maladaptive peer relationships and the development of relational and physical aggression during middle childhood. *Social Development, 13* (4), 495-514.

Wheeler, J.J. & Richey, D.D. (2005). *Behavior management: Principles and practices of positive behavior support.* Upper Saddle River, NJ: Pearson Merrill Prentice Hall.

Wien, C.A. (2004). From policing to participation: Overturning the rules and creating amiable classrooms. *Young Children, 59* (1), 34-40.

Williams, L.R., Degnan, K.A., Perez-Edgar, K.E., Henderson, H.A., Rubin, K.H., Steinberg, L. & Fox, N.A. (2009). Impact of behavioral inhibition and parenting style on internalizing and externalizing problems from early childhood through adolescence. *Journal of Abnormal Child Psychology, 37* (8), 1063-1075.

Williams, L.R. & Steinberg, L. (2011). Reciprocal relations between parenting and adjustment in a sample of juvenile offenders. *Child Development, 82* (2), 633-645.

Winslade, J. & Monk, G. (2007). *Narrative counseling in schools: Powerful and brief.* (2nd ed.) Thousand Oaks, CA: Corwin Press.

Wood, J.V., Perunovic, W.Q.E. & Lee, J.W. (2009). Positive self-statements: Power for some, peril for others. *Psychological Science, 20* (7), 860-866.

Wood, K.J. & Care, E. (2002). The relationship between perfectionism and intelligence in a group of adolescents. *The Australasian Journal of Gifted Education, 11* (1), 22-29.

Wray-Lake, L. & Flanagan, C.A. (2012). Parenting practices and the development of adolescents' social trust. *Journal of Adolescence, 35* (3), 549-560.

Wyman, P.A., Cowen, E.L., Work, W.C., Hoyt-Meyers, L., Magnus, K.B. & Fagen, D.B. (1999). Caregiving and developmental factors differentiating young at-risk urban children showing resilient versus stress-affected outcomes: A replication and extension. *Child Development, 70* (3), 645-659.

Xu, M.-Q., Sun, W.-S., Liu, B.-X., Feng, G.-Y., Yu, L., Yang, L., He, G., Sham, P., Susser, E., St Clair, D. & He, L. (2009). Prenatal malnutrition and adult schizophrenia: Further evidence from the 1959-1961 Chinese famine. *Schizophrenia Bulletin, 35* (3), 568-576.

Young, S.K., Fox, N.A. & Zahn-Waxler, C. (1999). The relations between temperament and empathy in 2-year-olds. *Developmental Psychology, 35* (5), 1189-1197.

Youssef, R.M., Attia, M. S.-E.-D. & Kamel, M.I. (1998a). Children experiencing violence I: Parental use of corporal punishment. *Child Abuse and Neglect, 22* (10), 959-973.

_____(1998b). Children experiencing violence II: Prevalence and determinants of corporal punishment in schools. *Child Abuse and Neglect, 22* (10), 975-985.

Zahn-Waxler, C. & Radke-Yarrow, M. (1990). The origins of empathic concern. *Motivation and Emotion, 14* (2), 107-130.

Zahn-Waxler, C., Radke-Yarrow, M. & King, R.A. (1979). Child rearing and children's prosocial initiations toward victims of distress. *Child Development, 50* (2), 319-330.

Zhou, Q., Eisenberg, N., Losoya, S.H., Fabes, R.A., Reiser, M., Guthrie, I.K., Murphy, B.C., Cumberland, A.J. & Shepard, S.A. (2002). The relations of parental warmth and positive expressiveness to children's empathy-related responding and social functioning: A longitudinal study. *Child Development, 73* (3), 893-915.

Index

Printed in Great Britain
by Amazon